Metaphysics and Morality

Metaphysics and Morality

Essays in Honour of J. J. C. Smart

Edited by
Philip Pettit,
Richard Sylvan
and Jean Norman

Basil Blackwell

First published 1987

Basil Blackwell Ltd
108 Cowley Road, Oxford, OX4 1JF, UK

Basil Blackwell Inc.
432 Park Avenue South, Suite 1503
New York, NY 10016, USA

British Library Cataloguing in Publication Data

Metaphysics and morality : essays in honour
of J.J.C. Smart.
1. Philosophy
I. Smart, J.J.C.   II. Pettit, Philip
III. Sylvan, Richard   IV. Norman, Jean
199'.94   B5701
ISBN 0–631–15043–9

Library of Congress Cataloging in Publication Data

Metaphysics and morality.
"A bibliography of the works of J.J.C. Smart": p.
Includes index.
Contents: Smart and the secondary qualities /
D.M. Armstrong -- Laws, coincidences, and relations
between universals / L.J. Cohen -- The ontology of
scientific realism / Brian Ellis -- [etc.]
1. Philosophy.   2. Ethics.   3. Smart, J. J. C.
(John Jamieson Carswell), 1920–   I. Smart,
J. J. C. (John Jamieson Carswell), 1920–
II. *Pettit*, Philip, 1945–   III. Sylvan, Richard.
IV. Norman, Jean.
B29.M4774 1987   146   87–6619
ISBN 0–631–15043–9

Typeset in 10 on 12 pt Plantin
by Columns of Reading
Printed in Great Britain by T. J. Press, Padstow

Contents

Preface

Recent analytical philosophy is premissed on the assumption of naturalism. This is the assumption, in its contemporary version, that whatever there is in the world, there is nothing which the natural sciences fail to encompass; there is nothing non-natural, nothing preternatural, nothing supernatural.

The assumption is not sharply defined. For example, there are differences over the demarcation of the natural sciences, and differences over what it is for those sciences to encompass an area. It may be required that every entity in the area is recognized by natural scientists or merely that it is definable by some operation on such entities. Again, it may be required that every property ascribed to those entities is reducible to scientific properties or only that it is supervenient on them.

But, however it is construed, the prevailing analytical view is that the assumption of naturalism is sound. This consensus has dictated a problem for philosophy, and an accompanying research programme. The problem is to determine how far a commitment to naturalism undermines our received view of things, our working image of the world. The programme is to develop, where necessary, a naturalistic replacement for that view.

Jack Smart is one of the pioneers of this programme. Consciously or unconsciously, he has worked for more than a quarter of a century on the naturalistic reconstruction of the manifest image of the world. He has led the way in rethinking metaphysical topics like sensations and free will, secondary qualities and time. And, persuaded of the subjectivity of values, he has been one of the first to reopen the exploration of utilitarian moral theory.

The essays in this volume represent both the metaphysical and moral sides of that naturalistic work. They will not be needed to advertise Jack Smart's achievement, for the news has gone well ahead. We shall be happy if they are found sufficiently substantial to mark the respect in which he is universally held. We would like them to serve as a tribute from his colleagues in Canberra, in Australia and in the world of philosophy at large.

P.P.　　　　　　　　　　　　　　Research School of Social Sciences
R.S.　　　　　　　　　　　　　　Australian National University
J.N.　　　　　　　　　　　　　　　　　　　　　　　Canberra

Acknowledgement

We are grateful to Conall O'Connell and Debbie Trew for their assistance in proof-reading.

1

Smart and the Secondary Qualities

D. M. Armstrong

Jack Smart is a world figure in contemporary philosophy, in particular for the part he has played in developing scientific realism. But in Australia it is natural to turn to what he has done for philosophy in this country. There was a sort of pre-established harmony between the man and what he found when he came here.

His completely open and direct way of doing philosophy, springing from his completely open and direct personality, made an instantaneous appeal to students and colleagues. The appeal was all the stronger because it joined hands with Australian values. His philistinism – early in our acquaintance he told me that there was little need to bother about Shakespeare especially if you could look out of your study window at Mt Lofty instead – and his indifference to the history of his subject – why bother about those chaps who are dead? – did him no harm! His writing was straightforward and colloquial, although it did have a great deal of style thus covertly contradicting his declared indifference to aesthetic matters.

To this he has joined disinterested generosity of intellectual spirit, a readiness to praise the good as he saw it as soon as he saw it, and a habit of answering philosophical and other correspondence by return of post. The philosophers of Australia owe him a lot.

One of the topics about which he and I have exchanged letters and papers over many years is that of the secondary qualities. It is to this topic that I now turn. In the first part of this chapter I discuss the development of Smart's views on the secondary qualities, relating this to larger themes in his thought: the development of his scientific realism, his physicalism and his view of the mind. The account of the secondary qualities which he now rests in he had arrived at by 1968, although the paper which contained this account was not published until 1975.[1]

I think that this view is the true one, or close to the truth. So in the second part of this chapter I defend it against objections, in particular against the nagging feeling that it must be rejected because it does not do phenomenological justice to our perception of the secondary qualities.

The development of Smart's view

If one had to sum up Smart's philosophical development in a phrase, one could say that he went from science to scientific realism. He was early inclined to believe that it is pre-eminently scientific investigation that gives us knowledge and rational belief about the nature of the world. But given the Oxford of his graduate studies, and his admiration for the work of Gilbert Ryle, this did not immediately translate into a realistic view of the entities that science speaks of, or appears to speak of.

I begin with the development of Smart's view of the mind. We each believe that it is rational to postulate other minds besides our own. The scientific realist will naturally see this as an inference to unobserved processes and states which are causes of much of the observable behaviour of bodies besides our own. It is a case of inference to the best explanation. The inference is perhaps suggested, and in any case is further supported, by the fact that we are able to observe such processes and states in our own case (introspection), and are even able, apparently, to observe the causal efficacy of some of these processes and states in producing our own outward behaviour.

At Oxford, Smart held no such view. Instead, he leaned to a reductive account which, putting it roughly, identified the mind with behaviour. No doubt, at the time this seemed to him to be the right line for a scientifically minded philosopher to take. For the philosophical orthodoxy of the time took it as obvious that if there were minds which lay behind, and which caused, behaviour, then these minds were immaterial things. At the same time, it seemed that no respectable science of the immaterial could be developed. It might appear that in our own case we have direct awareness of the distinction between our behaviour and our mental states. But this introspective faculty was thought to be a suspicious affair. Orthodoxy, stretching back to Descartes, held that its deliverances were indubitable or incorrigible. It was not easy to see how these characteristics of introspection were to be reconciled with a scientific view of human beings.

But after Oxford Smart made a most important break. In Adelaide, under the influence of U. T. Place, for the case of sensations and the phenomenon of consciousness he reversed what Russell in phenomenalist mood had called the supreme maxim of scientific philosophizing. Unlike Russell, he moved *from* logical constructions *to* inferred entities. But Place and he sought to preserve scientific plausibility by identifying the having of sensations and other conscious experiences with physical processes in the brain.

The Place–Smart view was a half-way house, of course, even if one which Place has continued to find satisfactory. Smart was later to move on to a fully scientific realist, and physicalist, view of the mental, where all mental processes, events and states are identified with physical processes, events and states in, or of, the brain.

A similar development appears to have taken place in Smart's view of the theoretical entities of physics. In his Oxford days he did not take a fully realistic attitude to such entities as molecules. I suppose that the old historical link between empiricism, on the one hand, and positivism and instrumentalism, on the other, was an influence here. That link was certainly present in Ryle's realism about the physical world – a realism about the entities of common sense, but not a realism about the entities that physicists, for the most part, think of as constituting the entities of commonsense.

Here is Smart, in an article published in 1951, apparently poised between denying and asserting the literal reality of molecules:

> unless we recognize the difference of language level between the various uses of 'particle' it might be misleading to say that a gas consists of particles. On the other hand it would not do to retain the use of the word 'particle' for things like billiard balls and refuse to say that a gas consists of particles. How else can we bring out the analogy on which the explanatory power of the theory consists?[2]

This soon changed. Concluding his article 'The reality of theoretical entities', published in 1956, he wrote:

> The modern tendency in philosophy is to be opposed to phenomenalism about tables and chairs but to be phenomenalist about electrons and protons.[3]

However, just before saying this, he had made it clear that he had now repudiated this half-phenomenalism:

> The naive physicist thinks that his science forces us to see the world differently and more truly. I have tried to defend him in this view.[4]

To adopt the physicist's view leads to certain difficulties, of course. For instance, one will be led to say that ordinary physical objects, as opposed to the collapsed, and hugely dense, state of matter found in neutron stars, are mostly empty space. But is not a desk, say, a paradigm of something in which, to use Parmenides's phrase about his One, what is stands close to what is?

This argument from paradigm cases is not very difficult to surmount, as most philosophers would now judge. It is perhaps sufficient to note that something which consistently appears in perception to have a certain character will serve as a perfectly good paradigm of that character for ordinary thought and language (and for teaching a child), even if it in fact lacks that character.

But a much more serious problem is posed by the secondary qualities. In the manifest image of the world, to adopt Wilfrid Sellars's expression, colour, heat and cold, sound, taste and smell, play a conspicuous part. Yet as far back as Galileo (with intellectual precedents stretching back to the Greek atomists) physicists could find no place for these qualities as intrinisic properties of physical things. The trouble is that these properties do not *explain* anything physical. Does the high-pitched sound shatter the glass? To superficial observation it might appear to do so. But investigation reveals that it is vibrations in the air which really break the glass. The secondary qualities do not even help to explain how they themselves are perceived. Contrary to earlier speculations, it is not the sensible species of colours, but rather patterns of light waves, that cause us to see the colours of the surfaces of objects.

What is the scientific realist to do? A traditional solution is to use the mind as an ontological dustbin, or sink, for the secondary qualities. Locke gave us a classical formulation. For him, the surface of a ripe Jonathan apple can properly be said to be red. But what constitutes its redness is only this. The surface has nothing but the primary qualities. In virtue of certain of these properties, however, properties of the micro-structure of the surface, it has the power to produce in the minds of normal perceivers in standard conditions (this last fills out Locke a little) ideas, or sense-impressions or sense-data, mental objects which have a certain simple quality, a quality unfamiliar to persons blind from birth. (Some philosophers, although not Locke himself, might then go on to *identify*, at least token by token, the redness of the surface with the primary qualities of the surface responsible for it having that power.)

This solution does have a phenomenological disadvantage, neatly captured by Berkeley in a little remarked passage: 'Besides, if you will trust your senses, is it not plain all sensible qualities co-exist, or to them appear as being in the same place? Do they ever represent a motion, or a figure, as being divested of all other visible and tangible qualities?[5] By the 'sensible qualities' Berkeley means, of course, the phenomenological qualities. He is surely right that, for example, the sensible quality of redness looks to be an intrinsic (non-relational) property of certain surfaces. Phenomenally, the secondary and the primary qualities cannot be separated. The difficulty can of course be met by embracing a Representative theory of perception of *all* the sensible qualities, primary as well as secondary. But a Representative theory has its own disadvantages.

Here, however, I want to focus upon a much more serious difficulty, much more serious at any rate for one who, like Smart, has accepted a physicalist account of the mind. If we have not merely accepted a scientific realism about the physical world, as Locke did, but have also made the mind part of that world, then there is no hiding place down in the mind for the sensible secondary qualities. The same reasons that made one want to exclude them from the physical world will make one want to exclude them from the mind. So what is the *physicalist* to do with the secondary qualities?

It will help us to appreciate the physicalist's problem if we consider further the phenomenology of these qualities, that is, their characteristics as revealed, or apparently revealed, to observation.[6] In the first place, as we have already noted, they appear to be intrinsic, that is, non-relational, properties of the physical things, surfaces, etc. to which they are attributed. This seems clear enough for the cases of colour and heat and cold. Perhaps it is not so clear for sound, taste and smell. After all, we do have the view of Hume and others that qualities of these three sorts are not spatial. It seems to me on the contrary, as a matter of phenomenology, that sounds have sources and can fill areas, that smells hang around places, and that tastes are intrinsic properties of tasty objects. However, if Hume's view is phenomenologically correct (I do not know how we decide the issue) that will make the existence of the secondary qualities even harder to reconcile with physicalism. (The physicalist will have to say that sounds, tastes and smells *are* spatial but that their spatiality is not revealed to perception.)

Second, the secondary qualities appear as lacking in 'grain', to use Wilfrid Sellars's excellent term. Perhaps Locke was wrong in claiming that they appear to be simple. But they do have a uniformity, a lack of extensive structure, even if they have an intensive structure.

Third, despite the point just made, the different secondary qualities are not merely blankly different from each other. Each determinate quality is set in a logical space, a quality-space it has been called, which psychologists and others are trying (with difficulty) to map for us. Consider, in the case of the colours, the dimensions of hue, saturation and intensity and the resemblance-orderings which these dimensions are associated with.

Fourth, however closely primary and secondary qualities may be correlated, the two sorts of quality appear to be wholly distinct from each other.

So much for the way it seems. Why, now, do these secondary qualities *so conceived* constitute an embarrassment for the scientifically minded philosopher? We have already encountered one reason. The qualities seem to play no part in physical explanations of phenomena. In G. F. Stout's fine phrase, they are not part of 'the executive order of the material world'.[7] And if one takes a physicalist view of the mental, then no relief will be gained by transferring the location of the qualities to the mind.

However, the difficulty that Smart himself emphasized, although not unconnected with the point just made, was a bit different. It was this. If one treats the secondary qualities as qualities *additional* to the primary qualities, and as having the general nature that they appear to have, then one will require *laws* to connect them with the primary qualities. But these laws will have to have a very strange structure.

The laws will be emergent laws. When exceedingly complex assemblages of physical conditions occur (outside or inside the brain will make no difference), then in association with these conditions, relatively simple qualities emerge. Smart says that, as a scientifically minded person, he cannot believe in such laws. He used Herbert Feigl's phrase: the qualities so conceived are 'nomological danglers', excrescences on the organized and beautiful structure of physical law that is beginning to appear. He also said that such laws had a bad smell!

So what solution to the problem does Smart offer? It is very interesting to notice that once again his first reaction was to look for an operationalist/ behaviourist answer. The answer is adumbrated in 'Sensations and brain processes' (1959), expanded in 'Colours' (1961) and repeated in his major work *Philosophy and Scientific Realism* (1963).[8]

Smart's solution has a Lockean element to it, as he points out. Secondary qualities are identified with powers in the objects to which the qualities are attributed, powers which one might then identify with categorial characteristics of the objects. But these powers are powers to cause normal perceivers ('normal' is given a special definition which need not concern us) to be endowed with further powers: *discriminatory* powers. Thus to say something is red is to say, very roughly, that it would not easily be discriminated from, picked out from, a background of ripe tomatoes, but would easily be discriminated from, picked out from, a background of lettuce leaves.

Smart was immediately hit with two objections, objections of a sort very familiar to us today from contemporary discussions of Functionalism. The first was raised by Michael Bradley, and would now be called the 'absent qualia' objection. Is it not possible, asks Bradley, that we should see the world in a uniform shade of grey, and yet be able to make all the discriminations that normally sighted persons make on the basis of the perceived colours of things.[9] The second objection was raised by C. B. Martin, that of the 'inverted spectrum'. Could not the colours of things be systematically inverted (an objectivist form of the inverted spectrum), and yet our ability to discriminate between tomatoes and lettuce leaves remain exactly as before?[10]

Smart originally tried to meet these difficulties by admitting colour-*experiences* into his analyses. To say that something is red *both* says that the thing has the power to furnish a normal perceiver with appropriate discriminatory powers *and* (less important) that it has the power to furnish such a perceiver with the right visual experiences.

But this did not last long at Bradley's hands. Once again, the trouble is caused by Smart's physicalism about the mind. What are these experiences? For Smart they can only be brain processes, as indeed he emphasizes. Furthermore, he maintains, the only introspective notion that we have of these experiences is a topic-neutral one, a notion definable only by reference to the nature of the stimulus that brings the experiences to be. (The idea of a topic-neutral analysis of our mental concepts was, of course, one of Smart's major contributions to developing a central-state physicalism about the mind.) As a result, for something to look red to me (the right sort of experience) is for me to have something characteristically brought about by red things. Red things, however, in Smart's theory, are constituted red by the discriminations they cause, so for him experiences of red must be defined in terms of these discriminations, and cannot vary independently of the right discriminations. As a result, Smart's appeal to experiences adds nothing that will allow him to make sense of Bradley's (and Martin's) case.[11]

In a paper given to a conference at Hawaii in 1968, but not published until 1975, Smart accepts Bradley's criticism.[12] (This paper has not become widely known. I have discovered that many philosophers think that Smart is still committed to the quasi-Lockean quasi-behaviourist view that he held at the time he wrote 'Sensations and brain processes'.) As a result, he finally comes to a realistic account of the secondary qualities. They are objective qualities of objective things. What of the demands of physics, then? He meets these by accepting a suggestion that had been put to him by David Lewis: he identifies a colour, and by implication the other secondary qualities, with a *physical* property of the coloured object. It is a fact that this property is causally responsible for certain discriminatory responses of normal human percipients. It is also a fact that certain colours are associated with certain sorts of physical objects, in particular with their surfaces. When all this is filled out, it will provide identifying descriptions for the colours. Using Kripke's terminology (not that that would please Smart very much) we can say that the descriptions can, if we wish, be used as rigid designators. But the descriptions do not pertain to the essence of the colours.[13]

The only difference in all this from a naive view of colour is that the colour-properties are identified with primary qualities of the micro-structure of the surfaces of the coloured objects. Though realist, the view is reductionist. Smart shows how this account can deal with Bradley's and Martin's cases.

He goes on to explain why he originally rejected Lewis's suggestion. The reason had to do with the particular case of colour, and not the secondary qualities generally. According to Smart, the scientific evidence about the physical correlates of colour is such that a particular shade of colour would have to be a highly *disjunctive* and very *idiosyncratic* property. This, he thought, was a reason to reject the identification. Lewis simply responded by asking him what was wrong with a disjunctive and idiosyncratic property. And by the time Smart came to give his Hawaii paper, he had accepted Lewis's 'So what?'.

Defence of an objectivist physicalism about the secondary qualities

I proceed to defend a physicalist realism about colour and the secondary qualities. The first point I want to make is that there is no difficulty at all in the fact, if it is a fact, that a particular secondary quality is very *idiosyncratic*. In this respect, a certain shade of colour might be like a certain complex, idiosyncratically complex, shape. Such a shape might well be a repeatable, and so a clear case of a property, even though its idiosyncratic nature made it an unimportant property in physical theory. (It might still be important in biological theory. Consider the way that the young of many species of birds automatically cower when a hawk-like shape appears in the sky above.) The physicalist could well admit that, unlike, say, sensible degrees of heat, the colour-properties are not very important physical properties. Perhaps the point of colour-recognition is just to break up the perceptual environment to make it more manageable, or, as Ruth Millikan has suggested, to render more easy the re-identification of individual objects.[14]

That colour-qualities might have to be adjudged ineluctably disjunctive is perhaps a bit more worrying.[15] Certainly, it worried me for a long time. Suppose it turns out that surfaces which we judge by objective tests to be of the very same shade of colour cannot be brought under a genuinely unifying *physical* formula. At one stage, this led me to flirt with the idea that, if the so-called colour-properties really are irreducibly disjunctive in this way, then the proper moral for a physicalist to draw is that, despite their phenomenological prominence, colours do not really *exist*. In Berkeley's splendid phrase, which he of course used pejoratively, they are 'a false, imaginary, glare'.[16]

My problem was compounded in the following way. In the past, I had asserted that all genuine properties are universals. Now there are excellent reasons in the theory of universals to deny that there are *disjunctive* universals. One problem about disjunctive universals is that there would be no identity, no sameness, in the different instances. Let a instantiate universal P but not universal Q. Let b instantiate Q but not P. Both instantiate P *or* Q. But this would appear to yield what Peter Geach calls a 'mere Cambridge' sameness. For this and other reasons I was led to reject disjunctive properties.

But I would now reject the first premiss of this argument. While continuing to reject disjunctive *universals*. I think that we should be prepared to accept disjunctive *properties*. I am influenced by two points here. First, it seems clear that what are *ordinarily* called properties can for the most part only be explicated in terms of more or less tightly knit *ranges* of universals, ranges which must be understood disjunctively. (Wittgenstein on games is relevant here.) Second, I am fortified by the reflection that such properties – which Peter Forrest suggests should be called multiversals – are logically supervenient upon the instantiation of genuine universals, that is, properties and relations which are genuinely identical in their different instances. Given all the non-disjunctive properties of things, then their disjunctive properties are determined. The reflection is fortifying because, I think, what is supervenient is ontologically nothing over and above what it supervenes upon. If that is correct, then we can take disjunctive properties on board without making any addition to our ontology. They are a free lunch.

But what then of the phenomenological point? Suppose that we have two instances of what, despite close examination, appear to be surfaces of exactly the same shade of colour. Could we, if the science of the matter demanded it, accept that the two surfaces instantiate two quite different micro-structural characteristics, where the latter characteristics *constitute* the colour of the surfaces?

I think that we can, as the following simplified neurophysiological thought-experiment is meant to show. Let there be an *or* neuron which is fed by two or more incoming channels. Each channel is activated by a different sort of retinal stimulation, and ultimately by a different sort of distal stimulation: a different sort of surface. Let the neuron be situated at an early stage in the neural processing leading up to the perception of coloured surfaces. Since the neuron is an *or* neuron it will fire, and so pass on its message, even where only *one* incoming channel is activated.

Furthermore, that message will be identical whichever channel is
activated. Different causes, same effect. So for the higher-ups
in the brain it will not be possible to sort out which incoming channel
has fired. Hence different sorts of stimuli must be *represented* as the same
at the higher level, even though they are not in fact the same.

This result will be enhanced by what I call the 'Headless Woman'
effect. Here the failure to perceive something (say the head of a woman,
where the head has been obscured by a black cloth against a black
background) is translated into the illusory perception of seeming to
perceive the absence of that thing. It seems to be illustrated by the case
of introspective awareness. When we introspect, we are certainly not
aware that what we introspect are brain processes. This, by an operator
shift, gives rise to the impression that what we introspect are not brain
processes. This impression is inevitable *even if what we introspect are
actually brain processes*, as we physicalists hold.

In the present case, a failure to perceive the presence of disjunctivity
in a certain property would translate into an impression of the absence of
disjunctivity, that is, an impression of identity. I regret to say that Smart
suggested this application of the Headless Woman principle in the 1975
paper but, as he records there, in correspondence with him I rejected
this particular application. I cannot now see any good reason for my
rejection. I think it was just hostility to disjunctive properties.

There is one other problem about taking colours or other secondary
qualities to be disjunctive properties. The problem has been put to me
by David Lewis, now a little worried about his own suggestion for
dealing with Smart's problem. When we perceive the sensible qualities of
physical things the quality must presumably play a causal role in
bringing the perception to be. But now consider a disjunctive property.
It cannot be thought that the disjunctive property itself plays any causal
role. Only the disjuncts do that. So if sensible qualities are disjunctive,
how can they be perceived?

It seems to me that this problem can be met by a legitimate relaxation
of the causal condition for perception. Provided that each disjunct,
operating by itself, would have produced exactly the same sensory effect,
is it not reasonable to say that the perceiver is perceiving the disjunctive
property? Consider, after all, that although the actual qualities that
things have are determinate, yet they are not perceived as having some
determinate quality. Even if a non-disjunctive account of colour is
correct, it remains true that surfaces are perceived as having a certain
shade of red but are not perceived as having an absolutely precise shade
of red. As a result there will be a disjunctivity in the nature of what is
actually registered perceptually. At the same time, it is the precise shades
which act causally. And whatever account is given of this situation can

presumably be applied to disjunctions of a more 'jumpy' sort.

Returning to the Headless Woman, she seems valuable in explaining two further phenomenological facts: (1) that the secondary qualities appear, if not simple, at least as lacking in grain; (2) that the secondary qualities appear to be quite distinct from the primary qualities.

The particular primary qualities with which Smart, Lewis and myself propose to identify the secondary qualities will fairly clearly be *structural* properties at the microscopic level. But the secondary qualities appear to lack structure ('grain'). How can the structured appear structureless?

What perhaps we need is an *and* neuron. If a cell has a number of incoming channels, each susceptible to different sorts of stimuli, but *each* channel has to fire before the cell emits a *single* impulse, then one could see how a complex structure might register perceptually as something lacking in structure. (It will be a bit more complicated if an irreducible *disjunction* of structures has to register both as a non-structural and non-disjunctive property, but no difficulties of principle seem involved.) Then the Headless Woman effect will explain why the lack of perception of structure gives rise to an impression of lack of structure.

But what of the point that the secondary qualities appear to be other than the primary qualities? The vital point to grasp here, I think, is that, with an exception or two to be noticed, our *concepts* of the individual secondary qualities are quite empty. Consider the colour red. The concept of red does not yield any necessary connection between redness and the surface of ripe Jonathan apples or any other sort of object. It does not yield any necessary connection between redness and any sort of discriminatory behaviour, or capacity for discriminatory behaviour, in us or in other creatures. It does not yield any necessary connection between redness and the way that the presence of redness is detected (eyes, etc.) in us or in other creatures. Finally, and most importantly, it does not yield any necessary connection between red objects and any sort of perceptual experience, such as looking red to normal perceivers in normal viewing conditions.

There may be a conceptual connection between redness and extendedness. But a physicalist, in particular, will think that this gives us little line on its form. There is certainly a conceptual connection between redness and the other colours: the complex resemblances and differences that the colours have to each other. But these conceptual connections do not enable us to break out of the circle of the colours.

With these exceptions, all we have are various identifying descriptions of redness. They identify it all right, but the identification is not conceptually certified. In my opinion, this conceptual blankness is all to the good if we seek to make intelligible a physicalist identification. For it means that there is no conceptual *bar*, at least, to such an identification.

There is topic-neutrality. *Neither* the identity of redness with some primary quality structure *nor* its non-identity with such a property is given us. So if we can find a physical property which qualifies red things (what a good theory will tell us are red things) and bestows the same powers as the powers of red things, including their powers to act on us, then it will be a good bet that this property *is* redness. And I hope it is not overworking the Headless Woman to say that failure to perceive identity with primary qualities gives rise to the impression that that identity definitely does not obtain.

But still one may not be satisfied. Many will think that when we perceive a red surface under normal conditions, perceiving that it is red, we are directly acquainted with a quality, apparently an intrinsic, that is, non-relational, property of the surface, which is visibly different from any physical micro-structure of the surface, or physical micro-goings on at the surface. (And, it may be added, visibly different from any physical goings on in the brain.) I confess that I myself am still not fully satisfied with the physicalist reduction. I accept the reduction; I advocate it. But the phenomenology of the affair continues to worry me.

Here is something that may help to explain further this profound impression of concretely given intrinsic quality. Consider again the relations of resemblance that we perceive to hold between the members of the particular ranges of the secondary qualities. We are not merely aware of the difference in colour of different colour-shades, but also of their resemblances and the degrees of their resemblance. The different hues of red, for instance, do fall naturally together. Any red is more like purple in hue than it is like any blue. As we have already said, the colours exist in a colour-space exhibiting degrees of resemblance along different dimensions. The same holds for the other secondary qualities.

These resemblance relations are, like any resemblance relations, *internal* relations. They hold in every possible world. But if some physicalist account of colour is correct, then despite the rather clear way in which we grasp the resemblances we lack any concrete grasp of the nature of the qualities on which the resemblances depend.

Now I do not think that this creates any epistemological difficulty. It is commonplace for this sort of thing to happen in perception and elsewhere. Smart pointed this out when discussing that famous having of a yellowish-orange after-image which is *like* what goes on in me when an actual orange acts upon my sense-organs. He spoke there of 'The possibility of being able to report that one thing is like another, without being able to state the respect in which it is like'. He went on to say:

If we think cybernetically about the nervous system we can

envisage it as being able to respond to certain likenesses of its internal processes without being able to do more. It would be easier to build a machine which would tell us, say on a punched tape, whether or not the objects were similar, than it would be to build a machine which would report wherein the similarities consisted.[17]

No epistemological problem, then. But I suggest that it is the fact that we grasp these resemblances among the secondary qualities so clearly and comprehensively that generates, or helps to generate, the illusion that we have grasped in a concrete way the natures of the resembling things. In an unselfconscious way, we are all perfectly aware that resemblances are completely determined by the natures of the resembling things. So given resemblances, we automatically infer natures. We know further that in perception what is automatically inferred is regularly felt as directly given, as contrasted with being inferred. (Consider for example the way we pass from hearing words to the semantic intentions of speakers.) So in perception of the secondary qualities, we have a vivid impression of intrinsic nature.

Smart, Lewis and myself share a reductive (physicalistic) and realistic view of the secondary qualities. In the first section of this chapter I traced the path by which Smart reached this conclusion. In the second section I have tried to strengthen the defence of this position.

Notes

1 J. J. C. Smart, 'On some criticisms of a physicalist theory of colors', in Chung-ying Cheng (ed.), *Philosophical Aspects of the Mind–Body Problem*, Honolulu, University Press of Hawaii, 1975, pp. 54–63.

2 J. J. C. Smart, 'Theory construction', *Philosophy and Phenomenolial Research* 11 (1951), reprinted in A. G. N. Flew (ed.), *Logic and Language*, Second Series, Oxford, Basil Blackwell, p. 235.

3 J. J. C. Smart, 'The reality of theoretical entities', *Australasian Journal of Philosophy* 34 (1951), p. 12.

4 Ibid., p. 12.

5 G. Berkeley, 'First dialogue', in D. M. Armstrong, ed., *Berkeley's Philosophical Writings*, New York, Collier-Macmillan, 1965, pp. 157–8.

6 When considering the phenomenology of colours in particular, it is useful to draw a distinction between *standing* and *transient* colours. This is intended as a distinction in the coloured object, and is not perceiver-relative. The distinction may be illustrated by considering two senses of 'spherical' as applied to squash balls. There is a sense in which squash balls, to be any use for squash, must be and remain spherical. They may be said to be spherical in the standing sense. In the transient sense, however, squash balls are

frequently not spherical, for instance when in more or less violent contact with a racquet or wall. To be spherical in the standing sense can be analysed in terms of being transiently spherical. If a ball is transiently spherical when the forces acting upon the ball are those found in 'normal', that is, unstruck conditions, then it is standing spherical.

Now consider a coloured surface such as a piece of cloth with fast dye which is subjected to different sorts of illumination. We often say that it presents a different *appearance* under the different illuminations. This seems misleading. In a standing sense the colour does not change. But *in a transient sense* it really does change colour. The mix of light-waves that leaves the surface is different. A standing colour is thus a disposition to have that transient colour in normal lighting conditions. (See my paper 'Colour realism and the argument from microscopes' in R. B. Brown and C. D. Rollins, eds, *Contemporary Philosophy in Australia*, London, Allen and Unwin, 1969. The terminology of 'standing' and 'transient' was suggested by Keith Campbell.)

We may think of transient colour as the painter's sense of (objective) colour. And if we are considering the phenomenology of colour, it is transient colour upon which we should concentrate.

7   G. F. Stout, 'Primary and secondary qualities', *Proceedings of the Aristotelian Society* 4 (1904), p. 153.

8   J. J. C. Smart, 'Sensations and brain processes', *Philosophical Review* 68 (1959), pp. 141–56; 'Colours', *Philosophy* 36 (1961), pp. 128–42; *Philosophy and Scientific Realism*, London, Routledge and Kegan Paul, 1963.

9   M. Bradley, 'Sensations, brain-processes and colours', *Australasian Journal of Philosophy* 41 (1963), p. 392.

10 J. J. C. Smart, *Philosophy and Scientific Realism*, London, Routledge and Kegan Paul, 1963, p. 81 (acknowledging Martin).

11 M. Bradley, Critical notice of *Philosophy and Scientific Realism*, *Australasian Journal of Philosophy* 42 (1964).

12 J. J. C. Smart, 'On some criticisms of a physicalist theory of colors.'

13 Or so I interpret Smart. In a very interesting recent paper ('Colour and the anthropocentric problem', *Journal of Philosophy* 82 (1985) Edward Wilson Averill appears to interpret Smart differently. He quotes from Smart's 1975 paper ('On some criticisms of a physicalist theory of colors'): 'Colours are the (perhaps highly disjunctive and idiosyncratic) properties of the surfaces of objects that explain the discrimination with respect to colour of normal human percipients, and also the experiences of these percipients, the looking red, or looking blue, etc. of objects'. Averill then seems to take 'explains' here as involving a logical tie. If that is correct, there is still a Lockean or subjectivist element in Smart's account. I, however, take Smart to be cutting all logical links between colours and what happens in the perceivers of colours. (It may be that I do this because I think that a complete objectivity, a complete realism, about the secondary qualities is the true view!)

But there is much of interest in Averill's paper. He points out that Smart assumes that two objects are the (very) same colour if and only if they would appear to be exactly similar in colour to normal human observers under normal viewing conditions. (He fails to note Smart's special definition of a 'normal' observer.) There is no doubt that this is Smart's assumption, even although, I take it, he does not assume that this is conceptual or definitional. But Averill's arguments seem to show that if the assumption is not taken to be a conceptual or definitional truth, then there is no reason to take it to be true *at all*. The moral for the complete anti-Lockean, the complete realist, about colour is that the link between objective colours and the colour-appearances presented to normal perceivers has to be very indirect indeed.

Averill, however, thinks that this is bad news for the full-blooded realist about colours. He thinks that Smart's normality assumption – which is, of course, the assumption generally made – is true, cannot be contingent, and must therefore be conceptual. However, he does concede that the full-blooded realist position might be maintained if the assumption is dropped. (A proposal I had already tentatively made in my 'Colour realism and the argument from microscopes'.) He even points to one advantage that dropping the normality assumption would have. It would become possible to evade saying that the objective colours are disjunctive properties. That would be a considerable gain. It may be noted that Averill's holding to the normality assumption is not without costs. He finds himself forced to say that e.g. yellowness is not (strictly) a colour.

14 Ruth Garrett Millikan, *Language, Thought and Other Biological Categories*, Cambridge, Mass., Bradford Books, MIT Press, 1984, p. 316.

15 Averill's work, cited in note 13, may show that the qualities involved are not after all ineluctably disjunctive. That will be all to the good. But it seems well worth a physicalist contemplating, and trying to deal with, a 'worst case' from the physicalist point of view.

16 G. Berkeley, 'Second dialogue', in Armstrong, ed. *Berkeley's Philosophical Writings*, p. 74.

17 J. J. C. Smart, 'Sensations and brain processes', *Philosophical Review* 68 (1959).

2

Laws, Coincidences and Relations between Universals

L. Jonathan Cohen

In recent years a number of philosophers[1] have come to advocate the thesis that natural laws are (second-order) relations of a certain kind between (first-order) universals or properties. My principal purpose in this chapter is not to refute that thesis, but rather to show that, even if the thesis were true, it would be impotent to resolve the problem that it is intended to resolve. One can state this problem epigrammatically by asking, how is the contrast between laws and coincidences possible? But the best way to clarify what the puzzle is about is to examine some different kinds of attempt to solve it.

I

The problem is sometimes taken, as by Jack Smart recently,[2] to be an issue between extensionalists and intensionalists. On such a view of the problem an extensionalist asserts that statements of laws are like statements of accidental uniformities in being generalizations within which terms of identical extension may be substituted for one another *salva veritate*, but that the former statements differ from the latter in some other way, which concerns their place or function in our reasonings. For example, statements of laws may be said by an extensionalist to formulate rules of predictive inference, or to have explanatory value, or to be derivable within the simplest axiomatization (in some appropriate language) of all true statements of singular facts. An intensionalist, on the other hand, insists that *these* differentiating features are not defining characteristics of laws but merely consequences of laws being what they are. For him or her, laws are intrinsically non-extensional.

Either attitude has strong intuitive support. On the extensionalist side, very many generalizations found in scientific textbooks are most naturally interpreted as plain statements of fact, reporting what goes on, or how things are, in the universe. Those who take daily doses of mepacrine, for example, do not develop malaria. On the intensionalist side, however, it may be pointed out that such a generalization seems to state more than just this because it authorizes the derivation, in appropriate circumstances, of an ampliative counterfactual – a conditional statement where the antecedent posits the existence of at least one more entity satisfying a specified condition than the actual world contains. If the patient had taken a daily dose of mepacrine, he would not have developed malaria. According to the one intuition, laws state no more than what actually happens: according to the other, they tell us also about what might have happened if things had been different from what they actually were.

But in substance both intuitions can be saved. Extensionalism and intensionalism are not opposed to one another, if each is assigned its appropriate analysandum. About the generalized statements of fact that are found in scientific textbooks, the extensionalist account must be correct. The *truth-values* of those statements cannot be altered when terms of identical extension replace one another. But the statements' status as laws may well be affected by this. What is typically non-extensional is not a generalization that has the form 'All *A*s are *B*s' (or a generalization asserting that the values of one quantitative variable are such-and-such a function of the values of another), but rather a statement that asserts a causal connection between being *A* and being *B* or a statement that has the form 'It is a law, or a consequence of laws, that all *A*s are *B*s' (or an analogous statement about a specified correlation between quantitative variables). In these kinds of statement co-extensive predicate-terms cannot be relied on to be exchangeable *salva veritate*. Perhaps it is accidentally the case, with different reasons affecting different people, that all and only those who ever take daily doses of mepacrine in the whole history of the universe are members of the British 14th Army. But we cannot safely exploit the accidental co-extensiveness of these two predicates by substituting the one for the other in the statement that it is a law, or a consequence of laws, or a causal truth, that all those who take daily doses of mepacrine do not develop malaria.

Suppose, for example, a philosopher claims, as many do, that people distinguish laws from coincidences at any one time in virtue of laws being those uniformities that are derivable within the simplest and most comprehensive axiomatization of what is believed to be a fact at that time. Then such a philosopher implicitly grants that any statement of the form 'It is a law, or a consequence of laws, that all As are Bs' is non-extensional. For, if he were to allow any sentences within his axiomatic system to be transformed by the inter-substitution of any two co-extensive predicates, he would thereby be making his axiomatic system less simple without any compensating gain in comprehensiveness. Science does not normally need to use two names for something. So substitutions that preserve the truth-value of 'All As are Bs' may fail to preserve the truth-value of 'It is a law, or a consequence of laws, that all As are Bs.'

But though this point is clear enough in the formal mode of philosophical speech, it is easily enough obscured in the material mode. The claim that all laws are extensional (or that they are all non-extensional) is deceptively ambiguous, and unnecessary controversy is easily engendered when the claim is intended as a claim about statements of the form 'All As are Bs' but is interpreted as a claim about statements of the form 'It is a law, or a consequence of laws, that all As are Bs' (or is intended as the latter and interpreted as the former).

Of course, some philosophers may wish to argue that science can dispense altogether with the non-extensional form of statement. But we shall see, in section V, that this is much easier for a phenomenalist than for a realist, like Jack. And in any case we need the non-extensional form of statement in order to provide the type of premiss from which ampliative counterfactual conditionals are clearly derivable. We need a form of statement that is distinct from mere generalizations of the 'All As are Bs' type, which are ambiguous as to whether or not they can function as premisses for such derivations. Perhaps someone will therefore object that we can dispense also with ampliative counterfactuals. 'So long as we accept such-and-such generalizations as true', the objector will say, 'we can plan our lives on this basis, without ever formulating – let alone deriving – any ampliative counterfactuals. Relevant generalizations, if we have them, will provide us with all the information we need in order to achieve or avoid this or that outcome.' But, unless we can distinguish where an ampliative counterfactual is derivable from where it is not, we shall at the least be unable to distinguish those cases where we have reason to regret (or rejoice at, or praise or blame others for) not having exploited a particular generalization from those cases where we have no such reason. Smith may regret not having taken mepacrine, because, if he had, he would not then have developed malaria, but he need not regret not having been a member of the 14th Army, if it was really only a coincidence that all and only members of the 14th Army took daily doses of mepacrine.

Nevertheless, though the distinction between intensionality and extensionality is important in these contexts, it is powerless to illuminate the difference between laws and coincidences, because statements of the form 'It is a coincidence that all *A*s are *B*s' are in principle just as non-extensional as are statements of the form 'It is a law, or a consequence of a law, that all *A*s are *B*s.' If it were truly a coincidence that members of the 14th Army do not develop malaria, then that truth could be turned into a falsehood by substituting for 'members of the 14th Army' the co-extensive term 'those who take daily doses of mepacrine'. So far as a factual, logically contingent generalization is a statement of a coincidence if and only if it is not a statement of a causal connection or of a law or of a consequence of a law, the substitutivity criterion must operate with equal force in both contexts. If some particular substitution turns a law into a non-law, that is, into a coincidence, the reversed substitution must turn a coincidence into a non-coincidence, that is, into a law.

II

So, if the issue cannot be characterized in terms of a dispute between intensionalists and extensionalists, where else should we look for an explanation of how the contrast between laws and coincidences is possible?

Jack Smart claims that laws are a special kind of cosmic coincidence, namely those that form part of a well-integrated body of theory, or are deducible from such statements, or are such that we think they will one day be so deducible.[3] But how can laws be a kind of coincidence, when the very concept of a coincidence is defined by contrast with that of a law? Jack's claim is of the 'Property is theft', or 'Law is a form of violence', or 'Peace is a continuation of war', variety. It takes a term *G* that in everyday usage implies not-*F*, and then says that *F* is really a form of *G*. Such paradoxical epigrams may have the effect of getting people to reconsider some of their fundamental assumptions. They may even startle people into revising their whole conceptual systems. But they cannot constitute acceptably consistent answers to analytical questions.

Of course, it may be that what Jack himself means by the expression 'coincidence' here is just a bare factual uniformity considered in abstraction from the question whether it is law-based or accidental – that is, the kind of uniformity that I have been referring to as assertible by a statement of the form 'All *A*s are *B*s.' But, if so, another objection comes into play. The trouble now is not that Jack's thesis is inherently self-contradictory but that it does not offer any answer to the question that lies at the heart of the problem. It may be true that, at least in modern science, the generalizations which we call laws (or consequences of laws) either form part of a well-integrated body of theory, or are deducible from such statements, or are such that we think they will one day be so deducible. But this fact does not elucidate why we are normally so ready to assume that, in appropriate circumstances, we may derive ampliative counterfactuals from such generalizations. After all, a body of theory may presumably be well-integrated even if it describes only what happens in the actual world. Why should it then license us to draw conclusions about what would happen in a contingency that never arises in the actual world? It may be tempting to suppose that this licence is underwritten by the fact that the relevant generalization 'All As are Bs' quantifies over a domain that includes possible As as well as actual ones. And so it must, if ampliative counterfactuals are to be derivable. But the awkward question is simply deferred. We have now to ask: how is it possible to generalize over possible As as well as over actual ones?

Nor are ampliative counterfactuals the only relevant type of statements that are left out of account if laws are said to be constituted by those uniformities that are deducible within the simplest axiomatization of what actually occurs. We have also to consider those laws that state relationships which hold good only under idealized assumptions. Thus Nagel, Nowak, Cartwright and others have drawn attention to the existence of laws about the velocity of bodies falling in a frictionless medium, laws about bodies subject to gravitational but not electro-magnetic forces, laws about bodies subject to electromagnetic but not grativational forces, and so on.[4] Such laws establish what would happen in a simpler world than our own – in a world from which one or more familiar categories of properties are absent. But, if suitable allowances are made for the presence of such properties in our own world, such laws enable us to predict or explain certain features of that world. So, even if modern science contained no laws of this kind as yet, we might be well advised not to adopt any philosophical thesis that excluded their possibility.

Of course, such laws do not have to be formulated (though they often are) as correlations that are supposed true of some ideally simplified situations but false of every actually occurring one. Instead we can set them out in conditional form, asserting that at any time, *if* the simplified situation occurs, *then* the correlation operates. But this formulation is not much of an improvement from the point of view of a philosopher who sees all laws as uniformities in what actually occurs, since from that point of view one uninstantiated generalization is indistinguishable from another. Perhaps the safest course for such a philosopher is to claim that the 'real' laws at issue are the uniformities of actual occurrence that are derivable from the idealizations by making suitable allowances and approximations. This strategy consigns idealizing generalizations to an instrumental role. They are not then to be accounted 'real' laws but only theoretical instruments that help us in calculating what the 'real' laws are. But, if an instrumentalist analysis were adopted here, it would reinforce proposals to adopt such an analysis also in regard to the terminology of scientific theories that purport to describe invisible entities or processes. Once you accept that scientific theories can contain at least one kind of formula that functions instrumentally rather than denotatively, it seems less unreasonable to suppose that there are also other kinds. An instrumentalist interpretation of idealizing generalizations would scarcely be congenial, therefore, to realists like Jack Smart. Nor would it sit well with any recognition of the importance of simplicity, conceptual economy, and so on, in the formulation of laws, since the 'real' laws would inevitably be a good deal more complex than the idealizing generalizations.

Nor would anything be gained by specifying that a generalization that states a law is one providing a rule for predictive inference. For if this means just that on the basis of 'All As are Bs' we may predict, in the case of each thing which is actually A, that it will be B, then the generalization does not license the deduction of ampliative counterfactuals. And if what is meant is that on the basis of 'All As are Bs' we may predict, in the case of each thing, that if it were A, it would be B, then the derivability of ampliative counterfactuals is simply being restated, not elucidated.

Moreover, the question is also begged if it is said instead that the relevant generalizations should have explanatory potentials, that is, that the truth of 'All As are Bs' should enable us to explain a thing's being B by its being A. No doubt it is true that laws should always have explanatory potential, whereas coincidences lack it. But an explanation of a thing' being a B could be provided (where the thing is an A) by the truth of 'All As are Bs' only on the assumption that being A is a member (perhaps even the only member) of a set of features such that if a thing did not have one of these features it would not be a B. So, if the explanatory potential of a generalization is cited in an attempt to elucidate why ampliative counterfactuals are derivable from it, our attention is being implicitly directed to the derivability of a different (perhaps the converse) ampliative counterfactual from an equally reliable generalization. Or, if the generalization is said to license the derivation of ampliative counterfactuals because it is itself derivable within a system of explanatory theory, then in calling that system of theory 'explanatory' one of the things being said is that it licenses the derivation of other (perhaps converse) counterfactual conditionals in appropriate circumstances, and the question again arises how such a licence can be given. In

short, any appeal to explanatoriness here begs the question that it is
designed to answer.

I have been arguing that neither the difference between extensionality
and intensionality, nor the notion of derivability within an integrated
system of descriptive theory, nor talk about explanatory or predictive
potential will serve adequately to explain how the contrast between laws
and coincidences is possible. Nor, as I have argued elsewhere, can this
contrast be explained in a non-circular fashion by referring to relations of
similarity or difference between possible worlds.[5] Any general definition
of a selection-function that ranges over possible worlds and selects those
in which a given ampliative counterfactual would be true seems
inevitably to invoke the concept of a law of nature or of natural necessity
in order to require that these worlds be similar in appropriate respects.
Nor is the problem resolved by the Kripke–Putnam thesis that in
statements of laws the terms for natural kinds function as rigid
designators. Even if we agreed that there were some statements of laws in
which such terms functioned thus, we should still have to admit the need
for another category of generalizations entailing ampliative counterfactuals
in order to state identifying attributes, as distinct from essential ones.
For example, if we identify heat by the contingent property of its
producing such-and-such sensations, then we are committed to accepting
that if, say, the radiator had been hot it would have produced those
sensations in anyone who touched it.[6]

III

The view that natural laws are (second-order) relations of a certain kind
between (first-order) properties is ostensibly more promising.

First, it meets all the familiar difficulties about the derivability of
ampliative counterfactuals, because a law-governed linkage between
properties may be supposed to hold good irrespective of where or when
the properties happen to be instantiated. The linkage would be the same
whether the actual number of instantiations was greater or smaller. In
other words its validity is not tied to the particular number of instances it
actually has. It therefore applies to possible instantiations of the relevant
properties as well as to actual ones. So any generalization that is backed
by the right kind of inter-property relations would be capable of
generating ampliative counterfactuals – assertions about possible but
non-actual instances – in appropriate circumstances. Hence the relations-
between-properties analysis can apparently elucidate the derivability of
ampliative counterfactuals in a way that references to simplicity of
axiomatization or to integrated systems of descriptive theory cannot. At

the same time it achieves this elucidation without any of the circularity involved in appeals to explanatory potential or to relevant similarities and differences between possible worlds.

Second, the relations-between-properties analysis clarifies why the subordinate clause in any statement of the form 'It is a law, or a consequence of a law, that all *A*s are *B*s' must be non-extensional. If the truth of the statement rests on the existence of a particular kind of relation between certain properties, this truth may well be adversely affected if the predication of one property in the statement is replaced by the predication of another property, albeit a co-extensive one.

Third, the relations-between-properties analysis seems to clarify why laws have explanatory value. 'Laws figure in the explanation of their instances', as Dretske puts it, 'because they are not mere summaries of these instances . . . The period of a pendulum decreases when you shorten the length of the bob, not because all pendulums do that, but because the period and the length are related in the fashion $T = 2 \pi \sqrt{L/g}$.'[7]

Fourth, if we accept the view that to confirm a hypothesis is to bring forward data for which the hypothesis is the best (or one of the better) competing explanations, then by elucidating why laws have explanatory value the relations-between-properties analysis may also be claimed to elucidate how they admit of confirmation.

So the relations-between-properties analysis deserves very careful scrutiny. If it delivered the goods that it promised, it would be an even more important contribution to the subject than Hume's formulation of the regularity analysis, which is the point of origin for most modern discussions of the subject. But unfortunately the promised goods are not delivered.

Note first that all exponents of the analysis under examination distinguish between assertion of a second-order relation of the kind in question and assertion of a first-order generalization like 'All *A*s are *B*s.' They all hold that the former entails the latter, but not vice versa. They differ a little, though unimportantly, in regard to the nature of the second-order relation. Thus Dretske holds that this may take various forms, depending on whether the law involves quantitative or merely qualitative expressions.[8] Armstrong is less confident than the others about there being second-order relations of exclusion here as well as of necessitation.[9] But I shall mainly follow Tooley's account,[10] because in some important respects it is worked out more fully than the others.

According to Tooley, a statement like 'All *A*s are *B*s' 'expresses a nomological state of affairs if [it] is true in virtue of a contingent, nomological relation holding among universals'. But different types of nomological relations are specified by different functions for mapping ordered sets of universals into propositions about particulars. Thus according to Tooley a relation is one of nomic necessitation if it is of the type specified by the function that maps ordered couples $\lfloor A/B \rfloor$ of universals into propositions of the form $(x)(Ax \rightarrow Bx)$. It is a relation of nomic exclusion if it is of the type determined by the function mapping ordered couples $\lfloor A/B \rfloor$ of universals into propositions of the form $(x)(Ax \rightarrow -Bx)$. But Tooley requires that a relation, to be nomological, should always be irreducibly of an order greater than the order of the universals that enter into it. For, if this requirement were not imposed, he says, every true generalization would get classified as nomological. Suppose that everything with property A just happens to have property B, and consider the relation R which holds between two properties if and only if everything with the one property has the other. Properties A and B then stand in the relation R and do so contingently, and their relationship entails that all As are Bs. But the fact that all As are Bs also entails the existence of the relationship R between the properties A and B. So R fails to satisfy the requirement of irreducibility and is therefore not a nomological relation.

Tooley admits that, unless further qualifications are added, this requirement may be satisfied trivially. Suppose it to be a law that everything with property S has property T, where S and T stand in relation W that is irreducibly of second-order. Then for any two properties A and B one can define a relation R as holding between them if and only if all As are Bs and S and T stand in relation W. So provided there was at least one true nomological statement, all generalizations about particulars would get classified as nomological statements.

But this kind of trivialization may be avoided in various ways, as Tooley points out. What cannot be avoided by such an account is a much more serious difficulty. Suppose it is indeed a mere coincidence that all As are Bs. Then there would be an irreducible relation between the properties A and B, namely the relation that holds between two properties when it is a mere coincidence that everything which has the one also has the other. From the existence of this relation it would certainly follow that all As are Bs (and that there are some As). But it does not follow from the uniformity-stating proposition 'All As are Bs' that it is a mere coincidence that all As are Bs. The uniformity might hold good instead because of a law. Nor does it make any difference here if the generalization is spelt out in the canonical form of a universally quantified truth-functional conditional. The truth of $(x)(Ax \rightarrow Bx)$ will still be a consequence of its being a coincidence that all As are Bs, but the latter will not be a consequence of the former, because $(x)(Ax \rightarrow Bx)$ might hold good because of a law. Moreover, it might instead be a mere coincidence that no As are Bs and then there would be a different irreducible relation between the properties A and B, namely the relation that holds between two properties when it is a mere coincidence that everything which has the one lacks the other. This relation too would be irreducible because, though its existence entails the truth of $(x)(Ax \rightarrow -Bx)$, the converse entailment does not hold.

Indeed, the fact that laws are second-order relations between properties is offered as an elucidation of the non-extensionality of contexts like 'It is a law that . . . '. But, as remarked earlier, 'It is a coincidence that . . . ' is no less a non-extensional context than 'It is a law that . . . '. And such non-extensionality is obviously entitled to an analogous elucidation: if laws are second-order relations between properties, coincidences must be too.

In advocating his version of the relations-between-properties analysis, Tooley has thus failed to notice that coincidentally uniform concomitance and coincidentally uniform non-concomitance are just as much nomological relations (according to his definition of 'nomological relation') as are nomic necessitation and nomic exclusion. His analysis therefore fails to shed any light on how the familiar contrast between laws and coincidences is possible. However, no other version of the relations-between-properties analysis has been any more successful than Tooley's. The hope was that at the higher level – the level of second-order relations between first-order properties – we should be able to define only laws, not coincidences. But in fact we confront an analogous problem at this level to the problem we encounter at the lower level – the level of generalization about particulars. The contrast between law and coincidence reappears, in distinct forms of irreducible relation, and we again want to know how this contrast is possible.

Certainly there is nothing in Dretske's version of the relations-between-properties analysis that enables it to resolve this problem any better than Tooley's does. Nor is there in Armstrong's. Armstrong[11] does list some third-order formal properties of the relation of necessitation – the relation that links first-order properties in the case of a law – and it *might* have been interesting if these third-order properties were different from those belonging to the relation of coincidentally uniform concomitance. But in fact there is no difference.

First, the relation is irreflexive. Just as, according to Armstrong, there is no law by which a property necessitates itself, so too there is no coincidence whereby it accompanies itself.

Second, the relation is non-transitive. Just as, according to Armstrong, it does not follow from there being a fundamental law relating A and B and another relating B and C, that there is also one relating A and C, so too coincidence is non-transitive. It may be a coincidence that all members of the 14th Army take mepacrine and a coincidence that all who take mepacrine are members of the 14th Army but it is certainly not a coincidence that all members of the 14th Army are members of the 14th Army.

Third, according to Armstrong, it does not follow, if *A* necessitates *B*, that not-*B* necessitates not-*A*, because not-*B* and not-*A* are not universals. Of course, it is a little paradoxical to have to conclude thus that laws are not contraposable. But by parity of reasoning a coincidental uniformity would not be contraposable either.

Fourth, just as necessitation is non-symmetrical, so too is coincidental concomitance. It may well be a coincidental uniformity that all *A*s are *B*s without its also being one that all *B*s are *A*s.

IV

The relations-between-properties analysis is thus unfortunately a mare's nest. It may or may not be true, in some important sense, that all laws are relations between properties. But the thesis that they are fails to shed any more light on the problem that it is designed to solve than any of the other circular or question-begging analyses that were mentioned earlier. Nevertheless, there is an intuition behind the thesis that refuses to be ignored. Somehow, according to that intuition, the search for laws investigates the behaviour of properties, not of particulars, whereas conclusions about the existence of accidental uniformities depend on the behaviour of particulars, not of properties. How can philosophy make sense of this?

To do so we must move away from semantic analysis into epistemology. In order to show how the contrast between laws and coincidence is possible we need to look for relevant differences between the pattern of reasoning that is taken to support the existence of a law and the pattern that is taken to support the existence of an accidental uniformity. I do not mean to propose what Armstrong calls an 'epistemic' theory for the semantic analysis of these concepts,[12] because I think it important to distinguish between their semantics and their epistemology. The laws of nature carry on independently of our changing methodologies of research. So it has to be possible for a person to have some way of latching on to the meaning of a statement that such-and-such a proposition states a law, independently of his considering what kind of evidence would support the statement. But at the same time, because the nature of the support has to be tailored to the nature of the statement, a study of the former is bound to provide some help towards an understanding of the latter.

More specifically, as I have already argued elsewhere,[13] what has to be noticed is that natural laws stand in relation to eliminative or variative induction in very much the same way as accidentally true generalizations stand in relation to enumerative induction. Belief in a particular generalization being nomologically, or accidentally, true – as the case may be – is the ideal outcome of the appropriate mode of inductive reasoning.

In eliminative induction we assess the capacity of a low-grade generalization to resist falsification by varying the experimental circumstances in which it is tested, and we assess a high-grade scientific theory by its capacity to explain a variety of accepted lower-grade uniformities and predict some new ones. The better the results, the higher the grade of reliability that we attribute to the generalization or theory. If a generalization resists falsification under every variation of circumstance that we know to have been relevant to some similar generalizations, or if a theory explains every already known uniformity in its field and predicts some new ones, we have as good a reason as we then can for calling it a law. Certainly we shall not gain a better reason by observing more individual instances of the generalization's or theory's application which occur in circumstances that are similar in all relevant respects to already observed instances and therefore occur if and only if the latter occur. We know in any case that like causes produce like effects. Of course, we may well turn out to have been mistaken about what is relevant. Our list of relevant factors to control or uniformities to explain, may turn out to have been incomplete. So if we are looking for absolutely conclusive proof that such-and-such a proposition is a law of nature we shall never get it. A real law of nature is, as it were, the crock of gold at the end of the inductivist rainbow. We can never be sure we have reached it because we can never be absolutely sure that our list of relevant variations or uniformities is complete. Assessments by eliminative induction are thus always empirically corrigible. Nevertheless, to the extent that we are entitled to assume this completeness for a particular domain we are also in a position to determine what is or is not a law for that domain. And because our mode of reasoning here is always to infer from our observations that a generalization applies to such-and-such combinations of circumstances or properties, not to such-and-such individuals, we take ourselves to have obtained a generalization from which ampliative counterfactuals are derivable. So far as the relevant circumstances or properties of the counterfactual instance are appropriate (that is, among those to which the covering generalization applies), the conditional must be true.

In enumerative induction, however, we look only to the number of instances in which a generalization has been favourably satisfied and to the absence of counter-instances. The ideal outcome is reached, not when we have run through all the relevant types of situation that might affect a relationship between the properties or natural kinds in question, but rather when there are only finitely many individual instances and we have run through all those. An exhaustive enumeration of all the actual instances, if favourable, establishes the truth of the generalization; and, when the results so far are favourable and all the instances are independent of one another, the fewer that we have failed to examine the less the chance that our generalization will be mistaken. (When n instances remain to be examined, with $n \geq 0$, and there are k equally possible outcomes on each occasion, there is a $\frac{1}{k^n}$ chance that the generalization will hold good right through to the last instance, e.g. that all the next 7 tosses will land heads.) Naturally, such assessments by enumerative induction are always empirically corrigible in so far as it is an empirical matter whether or not the instances listed as evidence constitute the whole of the class involved. But even to the extent that we are entitled to assume completeness, we are still not in a position to assert that the generalization which has been established states a law in the sense that ampliative counterfactuals are derivable from it. Our mode of reasoning has been to infer from our observations that the generalization applies to this and that individual, not to such-and-such combinations of circumstances. Hence the generalization that all As are Bs, say, gives no warranty for drawing inferences about other individuals than those that are actually As.

Someone may object that enumerative induction, where successful, just establishes the truth of a generalization and leaves open the question whether that generalization states a law or an accidental uniformity. But the objection would be invalid. The use of enumerative induction *does* imply that the generalization at issue is thought not to state a law, as the following argument shows.

The main premiss of the argument is that in an enumerative induction that is going favourably each additionally examined favourable instance counts as further supporting evidence, irrespective of whatever instances have been examined previously. So, if that is how we are treating the outcomes of our investigations, we implicitly reject the possibility that some instances' evidence may be superfluous because they are similar in all relevant respects to already examined instances and therefore occur if and only if the latter occur. And so we imply that a law is not at issue, because if a law were thought to be involved some instances' evidence might indeed be treated as superfluous (as we have already seen) for just that reason.

Thus the contrast between laws and coincidences is made possible by the difference between variative and enumerative induction. Admittedly, if that is the crucial difference between how we assess the generalizations that are hypothesized to state laws and how we assess the generalizations that are hypothesized to state coincidences, it is tempting to suppose that this fact is reflected in the meanings of statements about laws and coincidences, respectively. That is to say, a statement of the form 'It is a law that all *A*s are *B*s' might be supposed to be true if and only if under all variations of circumstance an *A* must be a *B*. And a statement of the form 'It is a coincidence that all *A*s are *B*s' might be supposed to be true if and only if it were true and logically contingent, but not a law, that all *A*s are *B*s. But, of course, as a semantic analysis, this would be just as circular as the analyses discussed earlier in this chapter, since it assumes the intelligibility of the modal auxiliary 'must be' in statements of the form 'Under all variations of circumstance an *A* must be a *B*.' Nor can the modality be eliminated. If 'must be' were replaced here by 'is' we should be back in the situation in which there is no ground for the derivation of ampliative hypotheticals. Nor can we say that 'It is a law that all *A*s are *B*s' means that such-and-such evidence has been found or is available, because a law always predicts more than just the evidence that supports asserting it: its counterfactual instantiations can certainly never be part of the evidence!

In other words, we cannot achieve any analytical escape from the tightly interconnected vocabulary of 'physical possibility', 'law of nature', 'coincidence', 'non-accidental truth', 'causal power', 'explanatory theory', and so on. But why should we expect to be able to do this? After all, there are many other networks of everyday vocabulary into which we cannot be introduced by standardly equivalent locutions or paraphrases. The names for days of the week are a good example. Instead of a paraphrase an ostensive definition – 'Today is Friday' – will give you an entry into the charmed circle, or even a generalization like 'Friday is the day that the rubbish is collected.' But neither definition would suffice at all times and places. Equally perhaps the vocabulary of laws and coincidences has to be picked up initially via examples and extrapolation therefrom, because it cannot be paraphrased into any other area of vocabulary.

By treating the problem as an epistemological one, however, we can get into another such area – the vocabulary of induction. And we can also explain the intuition that laws have something to do with properties in a way that coincidences do not. The relevant point is not that laws are relations between properties, but that in order to assess the extent to which a hypothesized generalization states a law we need to examine the extent to which it resists falsification under varying combinations of relevant circumstances, which is a test that we do not use in the case of a hypothesized coincidence. The relation, in the case of a law, is thus between the properties associated together by the generalization and the further properties capable of entering into this association, rather than just between the properties associated together by the generalization. (Or at least we can explain the intuition thus if the term 'property' in this connection is understood in the quite general sense of 'circumstance' or 'characteristic' – that is, what is representable by a predicate letter in quantification theory – rather than in the narrower scientific sense in which solubility-in-water, say, is a property but being-50-years-old is not.)

An additional advantage of this resolution of the problem is that it applies not only to laws about what happens under conditions actually found in nature but also to laws about what would happen under ideally simplified conditions.[14] The point is that, if certain combinations of circumstances suffice to falsify a generalization, something useful may still be rescued from the wreckage. Instead of assuming the meaning of the hypothesis to be fixed and the level of evidential support to be what is to be discovered, we can instead assume the level of desired support to be fixed and the meaning admissible for a suitable hypothesis with that level of support to be what is to be discovered. In the light of whatever evidence is obtainable, we can adjust the meaning to a specified inductive grading rather than the grading to a specified meaning.

More specifically, in introducing an appropriate qualification into the antecedent of the hypothesized generalization its exposure to falsification by the circumstances in question may be removed. Even if 'All *A*s are *B*s' is false for those *A*s that are also *C*s, 'All things that are both *A*s and *D*s are *B*s' may not be false, if nothing can be both a *C* and a *D*. In testing a generalization within a particular field of enquiry we have to vary certain relevant kinds of circumstance – for example, the patient's age, medical history, and so on in testing the therapeutic efficacy of a drug – and if the hypothesized generalization does not hold good for one variant of such a relevant variable, it may well hold good for another variant of the same variable.

Moreover, where this type of modification affords insufficient protection to a hypothesis, it admits of a natural extension. Instead of specifying one variant of a relevant variable in the antecedent of a generalization in order to exclude falsification by another variant of the same variable, it is possible to require that no variant at all of that variable be present. For example, instead of explicitly confining itself to bodies acted on by a particular species of force, a generalization about the motion of a body may explicitly exclude bodies acted on by *any* external force. Or the generalization may be said to apply only to bodies not acted on by an external force, and the qualification has then gone into the specification of the generalization's intended domain of discourse, rather than into the formulation of its antecedent. In either case we can see how essentially the same procedures of inductive reasoning are used here to justify acceptance of a law about what would happen under ideally simplified conditions as we used elsewhere to justify acceptance of a law about what happens under conditions actually found in nature. In both cases the justification arises from the supposed resistance of a generalization to being falsified under sufficiently wide combinations of relevant circumstances. Idealization, therefore, is an operation that has a legitimate and intelligible role to play within the normal repertoire of inductive procedures.

Some philosophers suppose that recognizing the importance of idealization is incompatible with accepting an inductivist analysis of scientific reasoning.[15] And no doubt this is true on a sufficiently narrow view of induction. For example, it would be true if all induction were enumerative and there were no satisfactory way of letting empirical evidence determine adjustments to the meaning of a hypothesis rather than adjustments to its grading. But, once we accept that any adequate analysis of induction should explore *all* ways of judging the reliability of a generalization against the variety of relevant circumstances that fail to falsify it, we can see that idealization functions characteristically not as a substitute for induction but as a device for increasing support by the variative mode of inductive reasoning. So even where laws are idealizations the possibility of a contrast between laws and coincidences is explained by the difference between variative and enumerative induction as modes of inductive reasoning appropriate to judging the strength of evidential support for a generalization.

V

I have been discussing how the contrast between laws and coincidences is possible, and have argued for a resolution of this problem in epistemological, rather than semantic, terms. A determined extensionalist might still wish to contend, however, that a properly regimented science does not need any non-extensional modes of statement like 'It is a law that . . . ' in its textbooks. Russell long ago argued that the concept of causation was out of place in science,[16] and a thoroughgoing extensionalism would banish all related concepts.

Such a regimentation is undoubtedly possible, though in a somewhat trivial and uninteresting sense. Causal statements and so on could be assigned to 'technology' or 'impure science', and ampliative counterfactuals, though sometimes needed to state reasons for regret, and the like (as already remarked in section I), could be assigned to the language

of action and emotion. But, even if we discount its triviality, this is not a
point that should be congenial to a scientific realist like Jack Smart.
Arguments are available to show, first, that anyone who admits
appropriate modes of non-extensional discourse into science is committed
to a pervasively realist interpretation of theoretical terms, and second,
that anyone who adopts a pervasively realist interpretation of theoretical
terms is committed to including certain modes of non-extensional
discourse in his science.

The first argument incorporates a line of reasoning that I have
developed at length elsewhere.[17] This line of reasoning proceeds by
pointing to the existence of three conditions that cannot be jointly
satisfied by any scientific theory. One – the Descriptive Condition – is
implicit in any anti-realist analysis of theoretical terminology. A theory is
said to satisfy the Descriptive Condition if and only if it is equivalent to a
conjunction of descriptions of all the observable regularities that it
predicts, where the equivalence is underwritten by accepted analytical
truths. Another condition – which I shall call the 'Consequence
Condition' (though it is sometimes known as 'the Special Consequence
Condition') – is that, if a statement of available evidence favours
accepting a given theory, then it also favours at least as strongly each
statement that is entailed by the given theory. The third condition – the
Superior Coverage Condition – specifies that if two equally compendious
and equally well-tested theories, T_1 and T_2, are both unrefuted by the
available evidence, and T_1 predicts or explains all the observable
regularities that T_2 does, plus at least one other observable regularity,
then T_1 is more strongly favoured by the available evidence than T_2.

It is obvious that these three conditions cannot be jointly satisfied.
According to the Descriptive Condition any theory T_1 which predicts
every observable regularity predicted by another T_2 must also entail T_2,
because each theory is equivalent to the totality of what it predicts and so
the content of T_2 must be included in the content of T_1. Hence, under
the circumstances in which the Superior Coverage Condition operates
and the theory T_1 is more strongly favoured than T_2, T_1 must also entail
T_2, and thus the more strongly favoured theory *must* entail the less
strongly favoured one. But according to the Consequence Condition the
entailed theory *cannot* be less strongly favoured than the entailing one. It
follows that anyone who accepts the Consequence Condition and the
Superior Coverage Condition must reject the Descriptive Condition. He
therefore cannot be an anti-realist.

But anyone who admits statements like 'It is a law or a consequence of
a law that . . . ' into his scientific discourse must support them, as we
have seen (in IV), by variative induction. And anyone who employs
variative induction is bound to agree to the Consequence Condition,

since if T is not falsified in certain circumstances then neither is any logical consequence of T and so the evidence must favour accepting such a consequence at least as much as it favours accepting T. Moreover, the Superior Coverage Condition is hardly controversial at all: the search for more powerful theories and greater explanatory or predictive generality is seen as a continuing strand in the intertwining nexus of activities that goes under the name of 'scientific enquriy'. So, admission of the relevant non-extensional contexts into scientific discourse is a commitment, via the Consequence and Superior Coverage Conditions, to favouring a realist analysis of theoretical terminology.

There is also an argument that runs in the converse direction and shows that scientific realism entails the admission of non-extensional contexts into scientific discourse. What can it mean, in general, to say that such-and-such micro-structures or micro-entities are 'real', as when Jack writes that 'there really are electrons'?[18] *Ex hypothesi* this cannot mean that they are observable. It can only mean that they enter into the causal nexus, or – if that sounds too deterministic – that statements about them enter into explanations in distinctive ways. The presence of an appropriate number of the appropriate viruses in the bloodstream explains a patient's influenza; the structure of rubber molecules explains rubber's elasticity; and so on. Could it ever be justifiable to posit these unobservable entities unless they served some explanatory purposes? But in saying such things we bring in the familiar system of non-extensional, or non-extensionality forcing, contexts. First, (as remarked in II) to assert such an explanation is to imply the derivability of an ampliative counterfactual like 'If at least that number of viruses had not invaded his bloodstream, the patient would not have presented influenzal symptoms.' Second, each explanation invokes certain specified properties of the micro-structure or micro-entity involved and only those properties. If it were thought a mere coincidence that two properties always accompanied one another, they would not be supposed to share the same explanatory roles. For example, even if the viruses of a certain disease were the only viruses shared by all the patients in a certain hospital who have names beginning with 'S', it would still not be possible for explanations of the disease to replace a reference to the property of the virus that triggers the symptoms by a reference to the property of being the only virus shared by all the patients in that hospital who have names beginning with 'S'. So a statement that such-and-such is the (or an) explanation of a given phenomenon is intrinsically non-extensional. And, third, knowledge of the explanation allows us also to formulate the usual precautionary counterfactuals, like 'If at least that number of such-and-such viruses had been allowed to invade his bloodstream, the patient would have presented such-and-such symptoms.'

In short, a scientific realist should not only welcome the additional support for his thesis that accrues from arguments for the existence of non-extensional contexts in scientific discourse. He also has to agree that it would be inconsistent of him not to accept the existence of such contexts. He cannot state his realist thesis without implicitly or explicitly asserting that some causal statements or ampliative counterfactuals are true.

Notes

1 F. I. Dretske, 'Laws of nature', *Philosophy of Science* 44 (1977), pp. 248–68; M. Tooley, 'The nature of laws', *Canadian Journal of Philosophy* 7 (1977), pp. 667–98; D. M. Armstrong, *What is a Law of Nature?* Cambridge, Cambridge University Press, 1983, pp. 75–173.

2 J. J. C. Smart, 'Laws of nature and cosmic coincidence', *Philosophical Quarterly* 35 (1985), pp. 272–80.

3 Smart, 'Laws of nature and cosmic coincidence', p. 287.

4 E. Nagel, *The Structure of Science: Problems in the Logic of Scientific Explanation*, London, Routledge and Kegan Paul, 1961, pp. 463–66; L. Nowak, 'Laws of science, theories, measurement', *Philosophy of Science* 39 (1972), pp. 533–48; N. Cartwright, *How the Laws of Physics Lie*, Oxford, Clarendon Press, 1983.

5 L. Jonathan Cohen, 'The problem of natural laws', in D. H. Mellor (ed.), *Prospects for Pragmatism: Essays in Memory of F. P. Ramsey*, Cambridge, Cambridge University Press, 1980, pp. 218–19.

6 Cohen, 'The problem of natural laws', pp. 219–21.

7 Dretske, 'Laws of nature', p. 267.

8 Dretske, 'Laws of nature', p. 253–7.

9 Armstrong, *What is a Law of Nature?*, pp. 143–6.

10 Tooley, 'The nature of laws', pp. 678–81.

11 Armstrong, *What is a Law of Nature?*, pp. 155–7.

12 Armstrong, *What is a Law of Nature?*, pp. 61–4.

13 Cohen, 'The problem of natural laws', pp. 222–7.

14 This point, and the points made in the next two paragraphs, are developed more fully in L. Jonathan Cohen, *The Implications of Induction*, London, Methuen, 1970, pp. 142–55, especially p. 144, and *The Probable and the Provable*, Oxford, Clarendon Press, 1977, pp. 182–7 and p. 186.

15 See for example L. Nowak, 'Idealization and rationalization', *Epistemologia* 2 (1979) pp. 284–6.

16 B. Russell, *Mysticism and Logic*, Harmondsworth, Penguin, 1954, pp. 171–96 (originally published in *Proceedings of the Aristotelian Society* (1913)).

17 'Realism versus anti-realism: what is the issue?' forthcoming in the proceedings of 'The Israel Colloquium for the History, Philosophy and Sociology of Science'.

18 J. J. C. Smart, *Philosophy and Scientific Realism*, London, Routledge and Kegan Paul, 1963, p. 39.

3

Problems in the Explanation
of Action

Donald Davidson

I hold that there is an irreducible difference between psychological explanations that involve the propositional attitudes and explanations in sciences like physics and physiology. In a volume of essays on my work,[1] J. J. C. Smart questioned how conclusive my reasons for this view are. He concluded his comments by saying

> I find [Davidson's] argument congenial but have given some reason for thinking that it may be found to have a sort of circularity by some of those against whom it is presumably directed. This is not surprising. I do not think that there are any really knock-down arguments in philosophy: we need to fall back somewhere on considerations of relative plausibility.[2]

I agreed with this judgement at the time, and I am now if anything even more convinced that Smart was right. This chapter makes no attempt to improve on the reply I gave at the time.[3] My aim here is to provide a larger setting for that reply, and to respond to some related issues that have been raised by others.

Let me begin by answering Wittgenstein's famous question, what must be added to my arm going up to make it my raising my arm?[4] The answer is, I think, nothing. In those cases where I do raise my arm, and my arm therefore goes up, nothing has been added to the event of my arm going up that makes it a case of my raising my arm. Just possibly, however, something must be subtracted from my arm going up to make it a case of my raising my arm; I'll come to this possibility presently.

When I say nothing has to be added to my arm going up to make it a case of my raising my arm, I don't mean no further conditions have to be satisfied to ensure that the rising of my arm is a particular case of my raising my arm; this much is obvious, since it can easily happen that my arm goes up without my raising it. But this is an addition to the description we give of the event, not to the event itself. So what my claim comes to is this: of the many individual events that are risings of my arm, some are cases of my raising my arm; and none of the cases of my raising my arm are events that include more than my arm going up. Nothing is added to the event itself that makes it into an action.

Why should we think otherwise? No one believes something must be added to a tree to make it an oak; some trees just are oaks. One reason we may be inclined to think mere arm-risings can't be arm-raisings is that we want to maintain the distinction between what an agent undergoes – what happens to him or her – and what the agent does, and we think of arm-risings as something that happens to us, while raising an arm is something we do. But the distinction between doing and suffering is not endangered if we allow that some arm-risings are arm-raisings, since we remain free to distinguish between arm-risings that are deeds and arm-risings in which agency plays no direct part.

Still, if we ask what makes a particular case of an arm going up a case of an arm being raised, a natural answer is that the agent made his arm go up. This way of putting it suggests that what the agent did can't be identical with his arm going up: the cause can't be identical with the effect. The effect is the arm going up: the cause is what made it go up. Perhaps this 'making' is the thing that must be added to the arm going up to make *it* the raising of an arm.

There are good reasons for resisting this line. The most obvious is that if what marks the difference between something an agent does and what happens to that agent is a prior act of the agent – a making happen – then for the prior act to be something the agent does, another antecedent is required, and so on. It also will not help to suggest that to do something an agent must do something else, such as try to perform the desired act, for trying is itself an act, and so would require a prior trying, and so on.

It seems clear that it must in general be a mistake to suppose that whenever an event is caused there must be something called a causing. Dropping an egg may cause it to break; here we have one event (dropping the egg) which causes another (the breaking). But there is not a third event which is the causing of the second event by the first. If such a third event were required to relate the original cause and effect, two more events would presumably be needed to relate the original cause and effect with the causing. The difficulty, so far as there is one, is an artifact of grammar. In the sentence 'Smith kicked Jones,' the verb conceals reference to an event: the logical form of such a sentence is made more nearly manifest, in my opinion, by something like 'There was a kicking of which Smith was the agent and Jones the victim.' This makes us think 'caused', as it appears between phrases referring to events, must also conceal reference to still another event. But 'caused' relates events, as do the words 'before' and 'after'; it does not introduce an event itself. Similarly, to say someone made his arm go up (or caused his arm to go up) does not necessarily introduce an event in addition to the arm going up.

However, it may. If I rig up a pulley and rope, I can raise my paralysed left arm by pulling on the rope with my right arm, and in this case I do, of course, raise my left arm by doing something else. So all we can say for sure is that not everything we do can be done by doing something else, or nothing would ever get done. Raising an arm is usually done without doing anything else, but not always.

Suppose that I am right that in the usual case, if my arm went up because I raised it, nothing must be added to my arm going up to make it a case where I raised my arm. To put this slightly less awkwardly: if I raise my arm, then my raising my arm and my arm rising are one and the same event. But how about the less usual case where I raise my arm by doing something else? If I raise my left arm by pulling on a rope with my right, has something been added to my left arm going up to make it a case where I raised my arm? The answer to this question has been much debated. This may seem surprising, since it is obvious that I would not have raised my arm at all if an event clearly separable from my arm going up had not occurred, namely, my pulling on the rope. But all this shows is that my pulling on the rope is not identical with my arm going up; it does not show that something was added to my arm going up that made it a raising of my arm.

The issue is this. We can agree that my pulling the rope and my arm going up are two different events, and one caused the other. We can also agree that, given this causal relation, I raised my arm. The debate concerns the relation between my pulling the rope and my raising my arm. One answer is that these are two separate events, and that therefore I performed two actions: one action involved just the pulling of the rope, while the other includes my paralysed left arm going up. If this is the right answer, then something has indeed been added to my left arm going up that makes it a case of my raising my arm. What has been added is my pulling the rope. My raising my arm is thus the sum of two events, one the cause of the other.

I reject this answer, mainly because it seems to me clear that though I do, of course, perform two sorts of action, a pulling and a raising, there is only one *act* I perform, one act which belongs to two (and no doubt many more) sorts. The single action, the pulling of the rope, is, on my view, the very same action as my raising my arm (by pulling the rope). If this is right, then the answer to Wittgenstein's question for a case like this is that nothing is added to the rising of my arm that makes it a case of my raising my arm, because the rising of my arm is not part of my action at all. So once again, though in a very different way, the answer to Wittgenstein's question is 'nothing'.

It is no objection to my 'identity' thesis that I might have pulled on the rope without raising my arm. The two descriptions of what I did are not logically equivalent, and so one description might have applied to my action and the other not; the point is that in this case both descriptions do apply. There is, however, a more serious difficulty with the identity thesis; it concerns times and places. In the story I have been telling, my pulling the rope and my raising my arm occur at the same time and in (almost) the same place. But suppose I thank someone for a pleasant evening by telephoning and leaving a message on her answering machine. Then my act of phoning and her getting thanked take place at different times and places. If my acts of phoning and thanking her are one and the same, I must have finished thanking her long before she was thanked. How can this be? My reply (which I have made at greater length elsewhere) comes in two parts. First, we need to notice that the verb to thank, like very many others, is a causal verb: x thanks y if and only if there are two events, call them e and e', such that x is the agent of e, e' is a being thanked by y, and e caused e'. In other words, x did something that caused y to be thanked. So the time-lapse between my phoning my friend and her being thanked does not show I performed two actions; what it shows is that the one action I performed did not have its desired consequence until later.

This leads to the second point. To say I thanked my friend entails that I did something that caused her to be thanked. But while what I did could correctly be described as my phoning and leaving the message at the time I performed this action, that same action could not be described as thanking my friend until she received the message. So although my telephoning and my thanking her were the same action, what I did can't be described in both ways until long after the performance. In the same way, my great-great-grandfather in the paternal line could not have been described in just these terms during his lifetime, but that does not show he was not the same person as Clarence Herbert Davidson of Inverness.[5]

The topic of this chapter is the explanation of action; it may seem that the discussion so far is only remotely connected with explanation. But this appearance is misleading. In fact the causal character of the concepts used in talking about action is an essential part of what must be grasped in coming to a clear view of the nature of action explanation. What I have emphasized so far is the way we very often identify actions by referring to their consequences. Thus thanking someone is doing something that causes that person to be thanked; killing someone is doing something that causes that person's death; building a house is doing something that causes a house to be built; and so on.

One form the explanation of action can take is what we may call explanation by redescription. So if you ask me why I am pulling on the rope or telephoning, I can answer by saying I am raising my paralysed arm or thanking my friend. Not any redescription will serve. If I had no idea that the rope was tied to my arm, but thought it was tied to a bag of groceries, then my pulling the rope would still be my raising my arm, but this fact would not explain my pulling the rope. The difference between explanatory and non-explanatory redescriptions is that the explanatory redescriptions supply a purpose with which the agent acted, an intention. Though the redescription characterizes the action in terms of a consequence of the action, that consequence is seen as intended when the redescription is offered as an answer to the question 'Why did you do that?'

Perhaps it will now seem that after all something is added to an event to make it an action, namely an intention. Certainly it is true that if some event, say my arm going up, is an action, then there must also be an intention. But in my view, the intention is not part of the action, but a cause of it. Just as nothing is added to my telephoning my friend when that act becomes a thanking, so nothing is added to my arm going up if that event is caused by an intention.

At one time (about 25 years ago, when I wrote 'Actions, reasons and causes',[6]) I thought there were no such states as intending; there were just intentional actions. This was, I now believe, an error. This is clear in the case where an intention is formed long before the intended action is performed, and even clearer in the case where the intended action is never performed. Intentions are also required to explain how complex actions are monitored and controlled.[7]

Although intentional actions are caused by intentions, it is not enough to ensure that an action was performed with a certain intention that it was caused by that intention. For example, I might intend to meet my daughter at a certain restaurant on her birthday. Believing her birthday is tomorrow, I go to the restaurant today to make a reservation, and there I meet my daughter. Her birthday, it turns out, is today. So my intention to meet her at the restaurant on her birthday has caused me to do that very thing – but by lucky accident, and therefore not intentionally. Deviant causal chains of this kind present a problem in the explanation of action, since we would like to be able to say what the conditions are that must be satisfied if an action is to be intentional. Several clever philosophers have tried to show how to eliminate the deviant causal chains,[8] but I remain convinced that the concepts of event, cause and intention are inadequate to account for intentional action.

I come now to a delicate issue about which I have no firm conviction; another problem area. The issue concerns the stages in the emergence of an intention. An intention to act (or to refrain from acting) requires both a belief and a desire or pro-attitude: a desire or pro-attitude toward outcomes or situations with certain properties, and a belief that acting in a certain way will promote such an outcome or situation. The emergence of an intention requires two transformations on the belief–desire couple. The first is obvious. The belief and the desire must be brought together; a course of action must be seen by the agent as attractive in the light of the fact that it promises to bring about a desired state of affairs. This transformation is what is usually thought of as 'practical reasoning', reasoning from the perceived value of the end to the value of the means. But this is not enough; we do not perform every action that we believe would promote some good or satisfy some obligation. We don't, if for no other reason because we can't, since acting to promote one good will often prevent our acting to promote some other good. And of course many actions that we know would promote some good we also know would produce much greater evils. When an intention is formed we go from a stage in which we perceive, or imagine that we perceive, the attractions and drawbacks of a course of action to a stage in which we commit ourselves to act. This may be just another pro-attitude, but an intention, unlike other desires or pro-attitudes, is not merely conditional or prima facie. If it is to produce an action, it can't be simply an appreciation that some good would come of acting in a certain way.

This story about how beliefs and desires cause an action is arrived at not by introspecting a process of which agents are generally aware, but by reflecting on the nature of beliefs and pro-attitudes on the one hand, and on the nature of action on the other. As a result, it is easy to question the claim that these 'steps', which logic seems to demand, correspond to anything in the actual psychology of action. It is clear that most of our actions are not preceded by any conscious reasoning or deliberation. We don't usually 'form' intentions, we just come to have them. And it is striking that in explaining why we did something we usually say nothing about the attractions of the alternatives we passed up, or the drawbacks that were outweighed by the positive feature or features we mention in giving our reasons. One is attracted by the simplicity of Aristotle's account of action done for a reason, which corresponds exactly to the explanations we most commonly give of actions; he treats the contents of a belief and a desire as providing the premises of an argument, and performing the action as drawing the conclusion. Aristotle is right, I think, in treating the explanation of an action as the retracing of a course of reasoning on the part of the actor. But I do not see how the 'reasoning' can be as simple as Aristotle wants it to be. And the more complex we find the logic of the reasoning, the more strain we put on the idea that the causality of action corresponds to the reconstructed logical steps.

Doubts have often been expressed (for example by Philippa Foot and Thomas Nagel[9]) about the need for a pro-attitude or desire in explaining action. The suggestion is that belief alone is often adequate to spark off an action. Thus, someone may perform a disagreeable task simply because he promised to, while finding nothing desirable or attractive about it. It is true that in explaining an action there is usually no need to mention both the belief and the pro-attitude. If it is asked why someone lowered his foot, the answer may be that he believed that by putting his foot down he would crush a snail; if this is the answer, it is obviously assumed that he wanted to crush the snail. But in the same way one could mention only the desire; the belief would then be obvious. A more important issue is involved, for to deny the need for a pro-attitude in the aetiology of action is to lose an important explanatory aid. If a person is constituted in such a way that, if he believes that by acting in a certain way he will crush a snail then he has a tendency to act in that way, then in this respect he differs from most other people, and this difference will help explain why he acts as he does. The special fact about how he is constituted is one of his causal powers, a disposition to act under specified conditions in specific ways. Such a disposition is what I mean by a pro-attitude.

Intentional actions are, then, by their most common descriptions seen as sandwiched between cause and effect. If we know that someone intentionally crushed a snail, we know some action of his was caused by a desire to crush a snail, and a belief that by performing the action he would promote the crushing of a snail; and we also know that the action so caused itself caused a snail to be crushed.

The way explanation is built into the concepts of action, belief and desire has understandably raised doubts, both about how truly explanatory reason-explanations are, and about whether they are genuinely causal. The first doubt is engendered by the Molière factor. How can the appropriate belief and desire *explain* an action if we already know, from the description of the action, that it must have been caused by such a belief–desire pair, and we know that such an action is just what such a belief–desire pair is suited to cause? A small part of the answer is that Molière was wrong; it may explain why a pill put someone to sleep to advert to its dormative power, since a pill without such a power might put still someone to sleep (it might have acted as a placebo). But we also realize that we learn little about why someone crushed a snail by being told he wanted to crush a snail and believed . . . and so on – we learn little more than that the action was intentional under the given description. However, most reason-explanations do not take this form. It may be far from obvious that the reason someone put his foot down was to crush a snail. The more interesting point involves the cause. It is true that someone who has a desire that he believes he can realize by acting in a certain way will have a *tendency* to act in that way. But, as we noticed, most such tendencies are not realized. Much of the explanatory force of reason-explanations comes from the fact that they specify *which* pair, from among the vast number of belief–desire pairs that were suited to cause the action, actually did cause it.

There can be no doubt, however, that reason-explanations, by virtue of the features I have been depicting, are in some sense low-grade; they explain less than the best explanations in the hard sciences because of their heavy dependence on causal propensities. The fact that beliefs and desires explain actions only when they are described in such a way as to reveal their suitability for causing the action reduces the power of the explanation, and so does the fact that the explanation provides no reason for saying that one suitable belief–desire pair rather than another (which may well also have been present in the agent) did the causing. These two facts are connected, for both are due to the unavailability of accurate laws for reason-explanations.

If laws were available to back up reason-explanations, the latter would consist in a specification of the law and naming the relevant belief and desire; the condition would automatically be satisfied that the belief and desire caused the action. Lacking a law of the right kind, it is essential to advert to the causal relation, since the belief and the desire might be present, and the action take place, and yet the belief and the desire not explain the action. If adequate laws were available, there would be no need to describe the cause in terms of the effects it tends to produce, just as, when sophisticated laws are in hand, we can dispense with reference to such dispositions as being soluble or frangible in explaining why an object dissolved or broke.

At one time it was widely thought that just because there are no serious laws linking reasons with actions, the relation between reasons and actions could not be causal, whereas I have been suggesting that appeal to causal concepts is appropriate to the explanation of action in part precisely because strict laws are not available. The two apparently opposed views can be reconciled if we hold that causal relations obtained between events however the events are described, while laws deal with *types* of event, and hence with particular events only as they have the properties that earn them membership in a type. One can then maintain that cause and effect must in principle be describable in terms that instantiate a law, but can be mentioned in explanatory contexts in other terms. Thus beliefs and desires may really cause actions, even though the actions, beliefs and desires are not types that lend themselves to treatment by serious laws.

This view, which I have developed over the years in a number of papers,[10] has seemed unsatisfactory to a number of philosophers, and I would like to discuss some of the difficulties they have found, or think they have found.

A difficulty which unites many critics concerns explanation. How, they wonder, can beliefs and desires explain an action if no law is invoked? It is one thing to say that singular causal statements ('this event caused that event') are extensional, and so remain true no matter how the events are described; it is quite another thing to accord such statements explanatory force no matter how things are described, for explanation is intentional. Of course, reason-explanations don't explain no matter how cause and effect are described; there is the very strong requirement that the belief and desire be described in terms of their semantic contents, and that these contents imply the desirability of the action as seen by the agent. So the complaint continues, the explanation copes with the reasons in so far as they show how the action was reasonable for the agent, but it fails to explain the causality.

Carl Hempel, proponent of the 'covering law' theory of explanation, has proposed a solution.[11] He suggests that the laws of action state what a *rational* agent will do. The rational agent will do what, in the light of his beliefs and desires, is his optimal course of action. To explain the agent's actions, we describe his attitudes in terms of their contents, we refer to laws that specify how any rational agent acts in various circumstances, and add as a premise that the agent was rational. To deal with the problem that even a rational agent often has reasons for doing incompatible things, Hempel proposes to accept some version of decision theory, which supplies a way of weighing competing claims. I shall pass over, in this discussion, the question of how adequate decision theory is, and the related problem of giving such a theory a clear empirical interpretation. There remains this oddity in Hempel's proposal: the 'laws', so-called, of decision theory (or any other theory of rationality) are not empirical generalizations about all agents. What they do is define what is meant (or what someone means) by being rational. Application of Hempel's scheme depends on knowing that the agent is rational, but there is no way of determining this except by establishing that the 'laws' fit the agent. The 'explanation' in terms of rationality therefore lacks explanatory force.

Dagfinn Føllesdal claims that he agrees with Hempel that explanation requires laws, and complains of my account of reason-explanation that it divorces such explanation from laws that would make it truly illuminating.[12] He agrees that explanation often succeeds although strict laws covering the case are not known, and so the descriptions of cause and effect that would instantiate the laws are also not known, but he insists that 'To say that *A* is a cause of *B* does not contribute to an *explanation* of the occurrence of *B* unless there is a law which is instantiated by *A* and *B* under approximately these descriptions.'[13] In my opinion, though I think not in Føllesdal's, the difference between us here is largely terminological; but when terminology is adjusted, an important difference may be discovered in the background.

First, what is to count as a law? Since I was interested in the question whether reason-explanations are or ever could be just like the best explanations for which physics strives, I set very high standards for what I called 'strict' laws. They were to be 'closed' in the sense of requiring no *ceteris paribus* clauses; they were to come as close to allowing the unconditional prediction of the event in question as the perhaps irreducibly probabilistic character of physics allows. I was also prepared to interpret the concept of law as strictly as had all those philosophers who claimed there were no laws to back up reason-explanations. Føllesdal takes a slacker view of laws; for him, it is a law that 'Any severely dehydrated person who drinks water will improve.' He then points out that a person might instantiate several such 'laws' at the same time, and these laws might predict contradictory results; we would then have to 'balance the laws against one another'.[14] I had assumed that laws had to be true, and so couldn't lead to contradictions; but, as I say, this is just a matter of terminology. Many philosophers of science consider the ascriptions of tendencies, propensities, and causal powers to involve laws, and the laws they involve, while perhaps not properly stated in the form that Føllesdal suggests, certainly provide most of our everyday understanding of the world and of people. As I have already pointed out, beliefs and desires have causal powers, and that is why they explain actions. If 'Someone who wants to crush a snail has a tendency to do what he believes will result in crushing a snail' is a law, I agree that reason-explanations require, and appeal to, laws. But I wonder whether or not Føllesdal agrees with me that this 'law' adds nothing to what we already understand if we know what a want or desire is; and whether he agrees that the relevant belief and desire explain the action only if the belief–desire pair caused the action in the right way.

The interesting matter on which Føllesdal and I differ concerns the question whether reason-explanations and explanations in physics constitute two different kinds of explanation, neither being reducible to the other (which is my view), or whether 'our theory of the mental and our theory of nature are both parts of one comprehensive theory'.[15] Of course, explanations of mental events must include reference to physical causes (as in perception, for example), and, as we have seen, actions are typically characterized in terms of their physically described consequences. So any 'theory' of the mental must cover interactions between the mental events (that is, events described in mentalistic ways) and physical events (events characterized in physical ways). The basic difference that I think exists between reason-explanations and the explanations of an ultimate physics can therefore put this way: laws relating the mental and the physical are not like the laws of physics, and cannot be reduced to them. Since action explanations require such laws, the former are not like explanations in physics, and cannot be reduced to them. The laws of many physical sciences are also not like the laws of physics, but I do not know of important theoretical (as opposed to practical) reasons why they cannot be reduced to the laws of physics. But there *is* a reason why psychological concepts like belief, desire, and intentional action, and the laws containing them, cannot be reduced to physical concepts and laws. I shall come back to this point.

Ted Honderich has raised a related question about my account of action explanations.[16] His complaint is that one event causes another only in virtue of certain properties, and these are the properties that instantiate a law. Therefore, he argues, if the only real laws are physical, mental events and states cannot cause or be caused by physical events and states. The conclusion Honderich seems to draw is that either there are strict psychophysical laws, or mental events are not identical with physical events. In my opinion Honderich has failed to note the difference between events described in terms that allow the application of laws without *ceteris paribus* clauses, laws that make no use of causal tendencies, potentialities or dispositions, and laws that, by using such devices, allow us to choose what we call the cause according to our special explanatory interests. (This distinction can be maintained even if there are no laws altogether free from appeal to such concepts, for there will be laws as free as possible from using such concepts, and laws that do not come close.) Laws of these different sorts all yield explanations, but explanations of different sorts. Explanation in terms of the ultimate physics, though it answers to various interests, is not interest relative: it treats everything without exception as a cause of an event if it lies within physical reach (falls within the light cone leading to the effect). Every event in this area is *a* cause of the effect, no matter how causes and effect are described. Special sciences, or explanatory schemes, take note of more or less precise correlations between effects of certain kinds and far more limited causes of certain kinds. These correlations, of the sort we find in economics, geology, biology, aerodynamics and the explanation of action, depend on assumptions about other things being more or less equal – assumptions that cannot be made precise. We can agree with Honderich to this extent: depending on the sort of explanation we are interested in, different properties of events are treated as causally efficacious. But, interest aside, every property of every event is causally efficacious.

Some have denied this. Lars Bergström, for example, says

> The fact that a system is open (in the sense, I suppose, that some of its components are influenced by factors outside the system) does not prevent the existence of strict laws describing (parts of) the system. For example, consider an electronic calculator: the numerals displayed are strictly determined by the buttons pressed even though factors outside the system determine which buttons are pressed.[17]

The quotation emphasizes how easily we disregard factors we are not interested in. For of course the 'law' mentioned above fails (to mention one of a thousand possibilities) if the current goes off between the button being pressed and the numerals being displayed.

In these remarks, I have made no distinction between a science like geology and the explanatory scheme of 'folk psychology'; the big distinction came between physics and the rest. If there is a distinction between reason-explanation and the rest, it must depend on some further feature of reason-explanations. (And of course there may be a significant sense in which geology, for instance, cannot be reduced to physics.) Let me say what I think this special feature is that sets reason-explanations, and psychological concepts generally, apart.

Let me first make clear that in my view the mental is not an ontological but a conceptual category. Mental objects and events are at the same time also physical, physiological, biological and chemical objects and events. To say of an event, for example an intentional action, that it is mental, is simply to say that we can describe it in a certain vocabulary – and the mark of that vocabulary is semantic intentionality. Reason-explanations differ from physical explanations because they are couched (in part) in an intentional vocabulary, and the basic concepts of this vocabulary cannot be reduced, or related by strict laws, to the vocabularies of the physical sciences.

The reason mental concepts cannot be reduced to physical concepts is the *normative* character of mental concepts. Beliefs, desires, intentions and intentional actions must, as we have seen, be identified by their semantic contents in reason-explanations. The semantic contents of attitudes and beliefs determine their relations to one another and to the world in ways that meet at least rough standards of consistency and correctness. Unless such standards are met to an adequate degree, nothing can count as being a belief, a pro-attitude, or an intention. But these standards are norms – *our* norms – there being no others.

The point to emphasize is not that we as explainers and observers employ our norms in understanding the actions of others; in some sense we employ our norms whatever we study. The point is rather that in explaining action we are identifying the phenomena to be explained, and the phenomena that do the explaining, as directly answering to our own norms; reason-explanations make others intelligible to us only to the extent that we can recognize something like our own reasoning powers at work. It would be a mistake to suppose that this is merely a sign of lack of imagination, or perhaps of soft-heartedness. It is a central, and irreplaceable, feature of the intentional. We have noticed the obvious fact that a belief and a desire explain an action only if the contents of the belief and desire entail that there is something desirable about the action, given the description under which the action is being explained. This entailment marks a normative element, a primitive aspect of rationality. Similar remarks can be made about the identification of particular beliefs and desires.

There is, I think, a strong tendency on the part of many psychologists today, and perhaps of many philosophers of psychology, to think that rationality itself can somehow be reduced to non-normative, perhaps formal, characteristics. I have in mind some of the work of Jerry Fodor, of Fred Dretske, and even Dagfinn Føllesdal's remarks about a single unitary system for explaining both the physical and the mental. Let me conclude by sketching briefly, and with no attempt at serious argument, where I believe these efforts at reduction, if they were successful, would lead.

Imagine that there were spaces in the universe, persistent over time, but moveable and changeable in shape, spaces within which nothing could be observed from outside, even with the use of the most sophisticated instruments. Let us call these spaces black holes. Obviously our explanations of what goes on in the observable world will be incomplete unless we know something about the black holes. For these holes absorb observable material and energy and spew it out, they move relative to other objects, they change shape, they help mould gravitational fields.

We build up a theory about these black holes. Since the aim of the theory is to complete our explanation of the rest of the world, the theory must be comprehensive – it must deal with every relevant aspect of change and force. It must, in a word, be a physical theory. This theory will aim to describe, on the basis of what goes on outside, what is going on inside a black hole.

Would there then be something we could call a science of black holes? Certainly not, as distinct from physics generally, for all we did to complete our scientific account of the world was to fill in the physical description of what was in the hole. Using our knowledge of what happens outside, we extrapolated in.

As far as I can see, a science of animal behaviour that aimed to be continuous with physics would be no different: it would merely substitute black boxes for black holes. It would describe what went into such boxes in physical terms (as it is sometimes said 'stimuli' should be described), and it would describe the output in terms of physical motion (as it is sometimes said 'responses' should be described). Would this science differ from, or add to, ordinary physics? Not in any way. The laws would be those of physics, and all the phenomena treated would be described in physical terms. But what would such a science tell us about intentional action?

Notes

1 *Essays on Davidson: Actions and Events*, Bruce Vermazen and Merrill B. Hintikka (eds), Oxford, Oxford University Press, 1985.
2 J. J. C. Smart, 'Davidson's minimal materialism', in Vermazen and Hintikka (eds), *Essays on Davidson*, p. 182.
3 Ibid., pp. 224–7.
4 L. Wittgenstein, *The Blue and Brown Books*, New York, Harper and Brothers, 1958.
5 I discuss this issue at greater length in 'Adverbs of action', Vermazen and Hintikka (eds), *Essays on Davidson*, pp. 230–41.
6 D. Davidson, 'Actions, reasons and causes', reprinted in Davidson, *Essays on Actions and Events*, Oxford, Oxford University Press, 1980.
7 This change of mind and the reasons for it are recorded in 'Intending', reprinted in my *Essays on Actions and Events*.
8 For examples, see David Armstrong, 'Acting and trying', *Philosophical Papers* 4 (1975), pp. 1–8; Christopher Peacocke, 'Deviant causal chains', in *Midwest Studies in Philosophy* IV, Peter French, Theodore Ueling, Jr., and Howard Wettstein (eds), University of Minnesota Press, 1979.
9 P. Foot, *Virtues and Vices and Other Essays in Moral Philosophy*, Oxford, Basil Blackwell, 1978; T. Nagel, *Mortal Questions*, Cambridge, Cambridge University Press, 1979.
10 Particularly in essays 6–10 in *Essays on Actions and Events*.
11 Carl Hempel, 'Rational action', in *Proceedings and Addresses of the American Philosophical Association*, New York, The Antioch Press, 1962, pp. 5–24, and *Aspects of Scientific Explanation*, New York, Free Press, 1965, pp. 463–89. I have discussed this suggestion further in 'Hempel on explaining action', in Vermazen and Hintikka (eds), *Essays on Actions and Events*.
12 Føllesdal's comments appear in 'Causation and explanation: a problem in Davidson's view on action and mind', in *Actions and Events: Perspectives on*

the Philosophy of Donald Davidson, Ernie LePore and Brian McLaughlin (eds), Oxford, Basil Blackwell, 1985.

13 Ibid., p. 315.
14 Ibid., pp. 318–19.
15 Ibid., p. 321.
16 See Ted Honderich, 'The argument for anomalous monism', *Analysis* 42 (1982), pp. 59–64; 'Psychophysical lawlike connections and their problem', *Inquiry* 24 (1981), pp. 277–303; 'Nomological dualism: reply to four critics', *Inquiry* 24 (1981), pp. 419–38.
17 The passage is quoted with approval by Føllesdal from Lars Bergström, 'Føllesdal and Davidson on reasons and causes', in Wlodzimierz Rabinowicz (ed.), *Tankar och Tankefel: Tillägnade Zalma Puterman*, 50 ar, 1. oktober 1981 (Filosofiska Studier utgivna av Filosofiska Föreningen och Filosofiska Institutionen vid Uppsala Universitet, nr. 33), Uppsala 1981, pp. 9–21.

4

The Ontology of
Scientific Realism

Brian Ellis

Scientific realists believe that an ontology adequate for science must include theoretical entities of various kinds, and that it is reasonable to accept such an ontology as the foundation for a general theory of what there is. J. J. C. Smart elaborated this doctrine in his *Philosophy and Scientific Realism*.[1] The theory he proposed was mainly about what really exists, that is, it had an *ontological* orientation. Theories with a similar orientation have been defended recently by Nancy Cartwright[2] and Michael Devitt.[3] The theory I have called 'scientific entity realism'[4] is also a theory of this kind. These theories may be contrasted with those semantically oriented versions of scientific realism which often seem to be more concerned with the theories of truth and reference than with what there is.

The ontology of scientific realism is supported by an argument from the best explanation: if the world behaves *as if* entities of the kind postulated by science exist, then the best explanation of this fact is that they really do exist. Properly understood and used, this is a good and powerful argument. But there has been little attempt made to find out what its scope and limitations are; and scientific realists have generally presented it crudely as an argument for the existence of 'things like atoms and electrons' – as if this were all that needed to be said. However, the argument is *not* a good argument for the existence of *some* kinds of theoretical entities (such as space–time points), and it *is* a good argument for the existence of certain kinds of properties and relationships which many scientific realists do not believe in.

The aims of this chapter are: (1) to discuss the scope and limitations of the main argument for scientific realism; (2) to spell out some more discriminating criteria for the existence of theoretical entities than this argument provides; and (3) to use these criteria to elaborate and defend a sophisticated realist ontology for science. I shall not, however, attempt to argue that this ontology is adequate as the foundation for a general theory of what there is.

Scientific realism

Scientific realism and descriptivism

Smart's original scientific realism was realism about certain kinds of theoretical entities, such as atoms and electrons. His opponents were the *instrumentalists*, who regarded the theories which postulated these things as just more or less powerful instruments for prediction, and the *logical positivists* who sought to reduce all talk about atoms, electrons and the like to talk about observables. It is not that Smart was opposed to ontological reduction. On the contrary, much of his book argues for the reduction of mental events to brain processes.[5] It was just that the attempts, particularly of the logical positivists, to construe the theoretical entities of science as logical constructions out of observables seemed to him to be entirely wrong-headed. The theoretical entities of science *explained* the world as we observed it, just as he thought the micro-processes of the brain would eventually explain our experience of it. Therefore, their existence must be ontologically more fundamental, and any ontological reduction must be in their direction. I think Smart was quite right about this.

Some more recent versions of scientific realism are: (1) the *successful achievement version*, that the laws and theories of the mature sciences are mostly approximately true; (b) the *goal-directive version*, that science aims to give us a literally true story of what the world is like; (c) the *semantic version*, that non-observational terms in scientific theories typically refer; and (d) the *descriptivist version*, that the theoretical statements of science are, or purport to be, true generalized descriptions of reality. In these versions of scientific realism, the issue is seen as being concerned directly with the referentiality of theoretical terms, or the truth or meaning of theoretical statements, and only indirectly with ontology. The four versions also have this in common: they all regard the laws and theories of science as more or less accurate, more or less general, descriptions of reality. They are all descriptivist theories.

By 'descriptivism' I mean the view: (1) that the aim of science is to give a true, generalized description of reality; and (2) that the laws and theories of science should be evaluated, as descriptions generally are, by their truthfulness, objectivity and economy. I think that this is wrong, both about the aim of science, and how scientific theories should be evaluated. The primary aim of science, I want to say, is to *explain* what happens, not just to describe it, or even to say what always, or usually, happens. It is true that some explanations are, and are intended to be, descriptive of underlying events or processes, or of general features of the world which the facts to be explained instantiate. But many explanations are not like these, and cannot plausibly be interpreted as descriptions of things. Accordingly, I think descriptivist criteria for evaluating theories are not always the most appropriate. In particular, they do not include what I think is the most important of all criteria for evaluating theories, namely their *explanatory power*.

However, there is no denying that many scientific theories were originally offered as descriptions of things or processes which are not directly observable. For example, the atomic and molecular theories of nineteenth-century chemistry, and the Bohr theory of the atom, were clearly intended to be taken literally as descriptions of unobservable physical structures and processes. The entities postulated in these theories were assumed to have certain properties, similar in some ways, but different in others, from things we already know about, and to participate in various causal processes to give rise to the phenomena to be explained. I call such theories 'causal process theories'. For these theories, the usual arguments for realism concerning the entities postulated in them are mostly sound. However, to argue as though all, or nearly all, scientific theories were causal process theories, as some scientific realists seem to do, is to show no awareness of the variety of aims of theory construction, of the diversity of kinds of theoretical entities in science, or of the different roles that scientific theories may have. There are many important, indeed fundamental, theories which plainly are not intended to describe hidden structures or processes, and realism about the theoretical entities postulated in these theories may not be at all reasonable.

It is commonly assumed by scientific realists that a language without modalities or counterfactual conditionals should be adequate for science, perhaps because it is thought that such a language should be adequate for the descriptive purposes of science.[6] In fact, scientific laws and theories *are* often expressed in such a language. But the language of science may be somewhat misleading in this respect. The more basic sciences are at least as much concerned with *possibilities* as with actualities, and many of the terms they use do not name actual systems, or kinds of systems of which there are any real instances, but systems which are variously simplified or idealized. Many a paragraph in a physics text, for example, will begin by inviting us to consider some arbitrary system of such-and-such a kind (although it is clear from the context that there are no such systems), and end by formulating, in declarative language, some derivative law concerning its behaviour. Despite the language used, however, the terms occurring in these formulations typically do not refer.

This is not just a debating point. For science is fundamentally concerned to *explain* what happens in nature, not just to describe it. If Hempel's theory of explanation had been sound, then laws would be true generalizations about reality, and a descriptivist theory of science would be tenable, because explaining would then be just a matter of subsuming events under laws. But for reasons which are too well known to need re-stating, it is clear that Hempel was wrong, both about the nature of laws, and about scientific explanations. For one thing, to understand why an event or process occurs, we often need to know what contributions are made by various factors to its production; and this frequently involves having a knowledge of counterfactuals, and sometimes even of counterlegals. For what we need to know is what would happen in the absence of this or that factor, even if the factor is never, or cannot ever, be absent. It is essential to the task of science to develop the framework for such explanations, and many of the laws and theories of science, particularly of physics and cosmology, do just this.

Physical geometries, for example, are constructed to systematize the range of *possible* spatial or spatio-temporal relationships. In doing so, they postulate an infinite set of *possible* locations, or points in space or space–time, and construe the actual world as consisting of things or events occupying some or other of these points. However, it is not obvious that such theories should be interpreted realistically. First, physical things and events may not be precisely located. Therefore, the actual spatial or spatio-temporal relationships between them may not be exactly like those postulated to hold between geometrical points. The theory may thus idealize actual physical relationships. Second, it is at least arguable whether physical geometries are, or are intended to be, causal explanatory theories. If not, then we may not need an ontology which includes infinitely many space or space–time points *in addition* to the physical entities which we suppose may occupy them. If points in space or space–time have no causal explanatory roles, it is not clear how we can argue that the world behaves *as if* they existed.

Other theories appear to describe how certain *ideal* systems would behave in various specified circumstances, for instance in the absence of certain forces (which may never in fact be absent). Thus, the laws of conservation of energy and momentum apply strictly only to closed and isolated systems (although there are no macroscopic systems other than the universe as a whole which are like this, and whether these laws apply to the universe is at least problematic); the principles of special relativity tell us how things would behave in inertial systems (although general relativity implies that no such systems can exist); certain of the laws of thermodynamics apply only to perfectly reversible heat engines (which other principles of thermodynamics clearly prohibit). Now theories of this kind are not at all unusual, and the laws they contain are among the most fundamental in science. Therefore, they cannot be dismissed as anomalies. On the other hand, they cannot be taken to be true, generalized descriptions of nature either, for then the theories would all be vacuous. I think these fundamental laws and theories, which apparently refer to idealized systems of various kinds, which we know on other grounds could not possibly exist, have to be understood as *framework principles*.

Framework principles have been discussed extensively in the literature; so I shall be brief. The best-known example of such a principle is Newton's law of inertia. This law is clearly not just a vacuously true generalization about how bodies not subject to the action of forces actually move. If it were, it would be of no conceivable interest. Its role is not to *describe* the motions of things as we find them, but rather to provide a framework for *explaining* them. It does this by setting up an ideal of force-free motion with which the actual motions of things may be compared, and so partly explained. That part of the motion which may be considered to be force-free is explained by subsumption under the law of inertia. What then remains to be explained is the *difference* between this motion and the motion which actually occurs. In the context, this difference is the *effect* which requires causal explanation. Now the laws of conservation of energy and momentum, the principles of special relativity, and some of the laws of thermodynamics all have roles similar to the law of inertia. They do not themselves offer causal explanations of events; rather, they serve to identify and gauge the effects which need such explanations. That being the case, there may be no good argument from the best explanation for the existence of *any* of the theoretical entities postulated in these theories.

These points about the variety of kinds of laws and theories in science, and the inability of descriptivist theories to deal with the full range of cases, are well known and widely accepted. Yet many descriptivists are inclined to be dismissive of this criticism, and insist on regarding the laws and theories for which their account fails as just more or less crude approximations of the truth. They envisage that these laws and theories will eventually be replaced by *better* ones which will *more accurately* describe reality. The case of Boyle's law being replaced by van der Waals's equation is often cited as an example of such progress. But Boyle's law has not been replaced by van der Waals's, and the modified law is better only in the sense that it gives a more accurate account of the behaviour of real gases. From the point of view of physical theory, *Boyle's law is still the more fundamental one*, because it defines the standard with which real gases are compared, and their characteristic ways of behaving are measured and explained. In general, the more fundamental law or theory is not necessarily that which is descriptively the more accurate, and modifications of fundamental laws designed merely to increase their descriptive accuracy are, in themselves, of little scientific interest.

The point can also be made with regard to laws which apply strictly only in certain ideal situations. Galileo's laws of projectile motion, for example, tell us how things would move in inertial systems in uniform gravitational fields without air resistance. Yet Galileo's laws are still theoretically important. The corrections we need to make because the earth's gravitational field is not uniform, because the earth is not an inertial system, or because there is air resistance, are theoretically unimportant. Of course, if we wish to apply physical theory to solve practical problems, we must know how real things behave in practice. Industrial or military engineers who want to predict the behaviour of real gases or projectiles, must know how to modify the fundamental laws appropriately. *But science is not engineering*, and it is a mistake to try to evaluate scientific laws and theories by criteria which are more appropriate to engineering than to science.

Boyle's law and Galileo's laws of projectile motion are admittedly not very fundamental. So the view that these laws are just approximations to the truth that will eventually be replaced by laws which are descriptively more accurate may have some force. But the more fundamental laws of Newtonian mechanics from which they may be derived (in the case of Boyle's law, the kinetic theory of gases) by making some simplifying assumptions apply strictly only to *point masses* moving under the influence of forces in *inertial systems*. So they too idealize reality. Hence, if these more fundamental laws are to be evaluated by descriptivist criteria, they will also be found wanting. It is true that Newton's laws of motion have been replaced by those of the Special Theory of Relativity, and that Einstein's laws yield more accurate predictions, detectably so where high velocities are involved. But Einstein's theory is not just a modification of Newton's made in the interest of greater realism, as van der Waals's modification of Boyle's law was. It is a radically different theory which idealizes reality no less than Newton's. It is valued, not just because it yields more accurate predictions than Newton's theory, which it does, or because the entities it apparently refers to are more realistic, which they are not, but because it explains the Lorentz invariance of Maxwell's equations, which Newton's theory was unable to do. In all this, there is no evidence of a trend to greater realism concerning postulated theoretical entities. Point masses and inertial systems are no more realistic in Special Relativity than in Newtonian mechanics.

The main argument for scientific realism

The most important argument for scientific realism is an argument from the best explanation. It would be 'too much of a coincidence to be believed', Smart claimed,[5] if the world were to behave just *as if* the entities seriously postulated by science existed, if they did not really do so.[7] Now, for causal process theories, this argument for the existence of the theoretical entities they postulate is always a good argument. If *A* is agreed to be the best causal account that can be given of the occurrence of some event *E*, and *A* is otherwise a satisfactory theory, then the entities postulated in *A* as the *causes* of *E* must also be thought to exist. To say that it is just *as if* they existed is always to weaken the explanation, for it immediately raises the further question why this should be so; and the realist answer, 'because they *do* exist', appears to be the only satisfactory one. We should, therefore, always be realists about the theoretical entities postulated to exist in the causal process theories we accept.

This argument, which is the main one for scientific realism, applies strictly only to the theoretical entities of *causal process* theories. For it gains its strength from the roles these entities are supposed to have in bringing about what is to be explained. The world has to be *as if* these things existed. This is why the argument is a good one for the existence of things like atoms and electrons, as its proponents claim. However, there are theoretical entities occurring in other kinds of theories which are not supposed to have any such causal roles, and the argument simply does not apply to them. Therefore, it is not a strong argument for any form of scientific realism which does not distinguish between different kinds of theoretical entities. It is not even a convincing argument for wholesale realism about those entities which are postulated as causes in the causal process theories we accept. For, as the paradox of the preface shows, 'each' does not epistemically imply 'all'. Scientific realists may therefore concede that probably some of the entities they believe in do not exist.

To determine the scope of the main argument for scientific realism, we need to be able to distinguish clearly between those entities which are supposed to be involved in causal processes and those that are not. I do not know precisely how to do this, but one distinguishing mark appears to be that they should have effects other than those they were introduced or defined as having. The point derives from James Clerk Maxwell who held that a quantity must be related to other quantities, independently of how it is defined, if it is to count as a genuine physical magnitude. Otherwise, he said, it is a 'mere scientific concept'. Maxwell made this distinction in the course of a discussion of Lord Kelvin's analogy between the laws of electrostatics, and those of heat conduction.[8] Kelvin observed that, in certain circumstances, the two sets of laws are formally the same; so that concepts used in the one field have formal analogues in the other. Maxwell argued, however, that these formally analogous concepts do not have the same *ontological* status. In particular, he claimed that the electrical potential at a point in a field, which is the formal analogue of the temperature at a point in a conductor, is not, as temperature is, a genuine physical magnitude. Physically, he said, it is only potential *difference* which has effects, whereas temperature has effects independently of temperature differences.

Whether Maxwell was right about this particular case does not matter. What is important is Maxwell's insight that causal connectivity is what characterizes real things. That is, real things should have a range of different properties, and so be capable of participating in various causal processes. Therefore, we should not expect the properties of a real thing to be given wholly by definition, or to be just those it is postulated as having in some particular theory. Rather, we should expect it to have properties, and hence effects, other than these, and so to manifest itself in different ways. Consider place, time and direction, for example. If mere position in space and time has no effects, and space is isotropic, then place, time and direction are all 'mere scientific concepts' by Maxwell's criterion. The physically real quantities here (assuming a Newtonian world) are just distance, time-interval and angle; for these are the properties which make a difference in physical causal processes.

While the main argument for scientific realism is thus limited in its applicability to certain of the entities postulated in our causal process theories, it is important to appreciate the full strength of the argument. It is not, as I see it, just an argument for the existence of material particles, and things that are constituted of them. It is also, prima facie, an argument for the existence of certain properties, for example the properties that these particles are supposed to have. For, we may ask, 'Why do the fundamental particles behave *as if* they had these properties?' The only satisfactory answer seems to be: 'because they *actually do* have these properties'. To try to reduce them (the properties) to sets of material particles, as Smart was (and I believe is still) inclined to do, is to make a mystery of the similarity of behaviour of these particles. For this fact could hardly be explained by their common set membership, if it is being denied that there is anything which unites the members of this set, save that they have the same general name.

The set-theoretic reduction of particle properties to sets of particles thus seems contrary to the spirit of scientific realism. Indeed, such a reduction is more in keeping with logical atomism than scientific realism, because it seeks to cut our ontology to fit our logic rather than our science.

The main argument for scientific realism is also, apparently, an argument for the existence of forces, fields, spatio-temporal relationships, and many other kinds of things. If we are not to embrace *global* scientific realism, we must at least show how its application is limited to what we may reasonably believe in. Unfortunately, this is not an easy task, because the main argument for scientific realism is not a sufficient guide. The difficulty is in deciding when the world behaves as if entities of such-and-such a kind existed, and when postulation of entities of this kind is necessary to explain this fact. Consider the question of whether forces exist. It seems clear enough that the world behaves as if forces both existed and acted more or less as they are supposed to act. But it is doubtful whether we must suppose them to exist to explain this fact. Or again, what about points in space–time? Here there seems to be a clash of intuitions about whether the world behaves as if they existed. Certainly, they are postulated to exist in most physical geometries, but they are not considered to be causes. So my inclination is to say that the main argument does not apply to them.

The aim of the remaining sections of this chapter is to sketch the kind of ontology I think the main argument for scientific realism implies, given the current state of scientific knowledge.

The ontology

Ontological reduction

We say that things of a kind *A* can be reduced ontologically to elements of the kinds *B* if and only if it can be shown (1) that *A*s would not exist unless elements of the kinds B existed; and (2) that *A*s consist of elements of just these kinds. That is, the existence of elements of the kinds *B* must be severally necessary and jointly sufficient for the existence of *A*s. If *A*s can be so reduced, then we may say that the existence of *A*s *depends on* the existence of elements of the kinds *B*. If elements of these kinds cannot themselves be ontologically reduced, then we may say that they *exist fundamentally*. The aim of ontology is to say what kinds of elements must be supposed to exist fundamentally. In other words, what kinds of things do we really need for an ontological reduction of everything there is?

I do not require that things which exist fundamentally should also be capable of existing independently of each other. For it is possible, given these definitions, that the elements to which a thing may be reduced should turn out to be ontologically *interdependent*. For example, it is consistent to hold that the universe consists of fundamental particles and their basic properties, although neither could exist without the other. Some philosophers will take a different view on this, and insist that things in the basic categories should be capable of existing independently of things in other categories. However, I can see no good reason to insist on the independence assumption – at least across categories. A good deal of ontological reduction is possible without it, and, as we shall see, it would prevent the construction of some very neat and satisfying ontologies to demand it.

For reasons to be given shortly, we should expect an ontology to be highly reductive in each of the basic categories of existents it assumes. I stress, however, that the economy required concerns *kinds* of things rather than their individual instances. This is because the reductiveness of an ontology is unaffected by how many individual things we may have to suppose there are of any given kind. David Lewis has argued this in his defence of modal realism.[9] I endorse the point, without endorsing the theory he was defending.

The basic items in any given category must be simple, that is, not constituted of, or divisible into, other things in this category. For if they were not simple, they would be reducible to these other things, and so would not exist fundamentally. For example, if quarks are postulated as basic items in the category of physical entities, then it must be supposed that they are not reducible to any more fundamental things in this category. Nor can it be that the basic items of a given category are reducible to things in other categories. For example, if we have an ontology that includes fundamental particles as basic items, we cannot consider the particles to be just co-instantiations of particle properties at points in space. For this would be to make points in space and particle properties the more fundamental categories.

Comprehensiveness, reductiveness and explanatory power

An ontology seeks to establish a system of categories of the sorts of things which exist fundamentally, and to explain how other things either fit into these categories, or depend ontologically on the sorts of things that do. To be acceptable, it should be a good theory by the usual criteria for theory evaluation. However, because an ontology must be a supremely general theory to be any good, comprehensiveness must be a very important consideration in evaluating an ontology. Other kinds of theories can afford to be more restricted in scope. On the other hand, we should not expect an ontology to be predictive, as we would a scientific theory, because such a general theory as an ontology must be, is bound to be programmatic. It would be an extraordinary ontology if it were able to predict the existence of some new kind of entity, although I do not say that this is impossible. However, a good ontology should be able to influence our beliefs about what there is in the sort of way that a good moral theory should be able to influence our beliefs about what is right. That is, by systematizing, and seeking to explain and justify our beliefs, it should ultimately correct them.

An ontology should also be highly reductive, not only because we want it to be as simple as possible, but also because differences between supposedly fundamental existents must be held to be inexplicable. For example, when there were just a few fundamental particles known to exist, they could be all be accepted as basic items in an ontology. But when the number grew to 100 or more, we should have had to suppose that all this diversity could exist without any underlying structure which would explain it, if we still wished to accept all of these particles as ultimate constituents of matter. Some diversity, somewhere in the fundamental categories, is needed to explain the diversity we know exists. But too much leaves too many differences at the fundamental level unexplained; and to accept the ontology is to suppose that these differences are finally inexplicable. Consequently, it is a considerable virtue of an ontology, if the number of basic items posited for each category is small.

As with any theory, the most important virtue of an ontology is its explanatory power. Consequently, there is not much point in eliminating a category of things from an ontology, if it does not increase our understanding to do so. The Humean reduction of causes to regularities, for example, made possible an ontology without a category of causal relationships. But it did so at the expense of our understanding of reality. Hume's own psychological account of the genesis of our causal concepts is certainly unsatisfactory, and epistemological theories about the nature of causal laws do not explain their apparent necessity to everyone's satisfaction. An ontology which included a category of causes, and explained more, might be better than one which was more highly reductive, but explained less. Reductiveness is not an autonomous virtue, but is derivative from considerations of simplicity, and the concern of ontologists not to leave too much diversity unexplained at the fundamental level.

According to the mechanistic ontology which was commonly accepted after Newton as sufficient for the material world, all physical changes are fundamentally changes of position. Even for Descartes, the world consisted just of matter in motion. Consequently, the regularity theory of causation would allow all causal relationships to be understood as being fundamentally spatio-temporal. This mechanistic ontology had the advantage of being highly reductive. However, since the advent of quantum theory, mechanism is no longer tenable, and the prospect of reducing all changes to changes of position no longer exists. Therefore, other kinds of changes must be envisaged as at least as primitive. In particular, the sorts of interactions which occur between fundamental particles, which cannot be analysed simply as changes of position, may be in a category of their own, and not reducible to anything else. If so, then perhaps we can reduce all causal processes to these primitive causal interactions between the fundamental particles. I shall consider this possibility in the section 'The ontology of causation' below.

The ontological reduction of physical entities

In the category of physical entities I include everything that is thought to possess energy. The category includes all material objects, all of the fundamental particles, and all of the force fields of the kinds recognized in Quantum Field Theory. It does not include numbers, sets, propositions, sentences, or other abstract particulars. It does not include properties or relationships. And it does not include forces. If we believe that any of these sorts of things exist, and are not reducible to things in the category of physical entities, we must say to what other category or categories they belong.

Until quite recently, some philosophers of science argued against the existence of fields. For example, P. W. Bridgman did so in his book *The Logic of Modern Physics*.[10] Bridgman sought to eliminate fields and to construe statements about them as being strictly about the dispositions of charged particles, or whatever they are supposed to act upon, to behave in certain characteristic ways, depending on where they are in relationship to other particles.

There are, however, good reasons to be realists about fields. One such reason derives from the main argument for scientific realism. The best theory we have of the causal interactions which take place between particles is Quantum Field Theory. This is a causal explanatory theory; for the fields are required as mediators in interactions between particles, and they are essential to the explanation, because they are the carriers of the energy which is transferred in these interactions. Without them energy would not be conserved in these processes. Therefore, by the main argument for scientific realism, we should be realists about fields.

Next, an ontology of fundamental particles, interacting without the mediation of fields, is untenable, given that some of the fundamental laws of quantum mechanics are expressed as wave equations, and that the energy transfer processes involved in particle interactions are best described by these equations. Indeed, an ontology of fields, in which particles are understood to be more or less stable wave packets, is now generally accepted. Moreover, the distinction between particles and resonances is hard to make,[11] and particles are coming to be seen as field phenomena, which cannot exist, except in the fields in which they are embedded. Therefore, the direction of ontological reduction that now seems most plausible is from particles to fields.

Even classically, there is good reason to believe in fields, since they have always been required as the bearers of potential energy. When opposite charges are separated, it is conventional to say that they each acquire a certain amount of potential energy. But in a classical ontology of particles, moving under the influence of mutually attractive or repulsive forces, potential energy can only be understood dispositionally if fields are not considered to be real. For the particles are not *changed* in any way as a result of being separated. Therefore, if we do not have fields in our ontology, we must say that, in acquiring potential energy, the particles simply gain a disposition to accelerate towards each other. To explain a disposition, however, we need a categorical basis for it. A field which is created in the process of separating the particles, and which bears the potential energy, is the best explanation we have.

If fields are the more basic kinds of physical entities, this raises important questions about their nature. What sorts of things are they? The evidence seems to be that they are entities that are propagated as waves, but act as particles; the probability of a field acting at a point being a function of the wave amplitude at that point. The difficult question is how this is possible. If the energy is localized somewhere in the field, then there is a problem of explaining the interference phenomena that are observed (for instance in the 'two slit' experiment). If the energy is dispersed throughout the field in the process of propagation, then there is the problem of explaining how the field can collapse, apparently instantaneously, in the process of particle interaction. For this would seem to imply that energy localization may occur instantaneously, or at least at superluminal velocities. I favour the second view, despite its apparent conflict with relativity theory, because a probability field seems more like a mathematical fiction than a physical entity. What is physical has energy, and if fields are physical entities, then the energy must be dispersed throughout them. In any case, the empirical evidence is that there is an upper limit to the speed of energy *transmission*, not that there is an upper limit to the speed of energy *localization*. These two kinds of processes must be just fundamentally different.

The ontological reduction of events

Scientific realists must suppose that all events are physical events, where these events are changes in physical systems. Such events always involve changes in the form or distribution of energy. So, without loss of generality, we may define a physical event as any change of distribution of energy in any of its forms. Of course, many events, so understood, will be phenomenologically indistinct parts of larger events, and so not thought of as separate events. Nevertheless, this definition of 'physical event' fits well with our conception of a physical entity and it does not include any changes which are clearly not physical. It does not include mental events, for example, if these are not changes in the distribution of energy in the universe.

Not all physical events have the same ontological status. Changes of shape, for example, are ontologically reducible to systematic changes in the relative positions of parts of things; and changes which occur in them are ontologically reducible to changes in their parts, and so on. But not 'and so on' indefinitely. For we now know that there are many physical changes which are not reducible to changes of position. The question for ontology, then, is what sorts of physical events must we consider to be those which occur most fundamentally.

Changes of position within physical systems are certainly physical events by the definition we have given; and there is no reason to suppose that they are reducible to any more fundamental physical changes. All attempts to develop causal theories of space–time, which would permit the reduction of spatio-temporal relationships to causal ones, have so far been unsuccessful, and the prospects for their success in future are not good.[12] The temporal order is perhaps identical to the causal order, and hence reducible to it, as Hans Reichenbach once argued.[13] But the complete reduction of spatio-temporal relationships to causal ones does not seem to be possible. Therefore, we should, at least provisionally, recognize changes of position occurring within physical systems as a primitive category of events.

In addition to changes of position, I think we also need to recognize that there are some essentially different kinds of changes occurring in the interactions between fundamental particles. On present theory, as I understand it, these interactions can be reduced to four basic kinds – the strong, the weak, the electromagnetic and the gravitational – although there is reason to think that some reduction in the number of kinds of basic interactions may be possible.[14] These basic kinds of interactions are thought to be governed by characteristic conservation and symmetry principles, and the general theory of particle interactions based on these principles is elegant, comprehensive and highly reductive. Therefore, it is reasonable to speculate that all physical events are ultimately reducible to interactions of these kinds, and the characteristic wave/particle emissions they produce.

The ontology of causation

The ontology of events I have now outlined immediately suggests an ontology for causal relationships, for it is plausible to suppose that all causal interactions are reducible to basic interactions between fundamental particles. Thus, if the billiard ball A collides with the billiard ball B, then this event is presumably just the sum of the interactions between their particles; and the subsequent motions of A and B are the continuing consequences of these interactions (compounded by those of any further interactions there may be between the balls and the table or other things in their surroundings).

I postulate that no causes are required to sustain a continuing consequence of a causal interaction – such as an inertial motion, or the propagation of an electromagnetic wave. These chains of events will continue indefinitely, or until they become involved in some new basic interactions. The only causes involved in these processes, I wish to say, are the interactions which would initiate, change or destroy such motions or waves. The case for regarding inertial motion as a kind of 'natural' motion, not requiring any cause to sustain it, has been argued at length in the literature.[15] The case for taking a similar view of electromagnetic radiation is also compelling, although I have never seen it argued. It is that there is no good reason to distinguish radically between electromagnetic (such as gamma) radiation, on the one hand, and alpha, beta, and other forms of radiation resulting from particle interactions, on the other. If the motions of the latter are considered to be inertial, then those of the former should be too. Let us call any motions like these, which require no causes to sustain them, 'energy transfer processes'.

A basic problem for the theory of causation is to say how causes are related to their effects. Plausibly, the answer is that they are related somehow by energy transfer processes. Certainly, many causes act positively to produce their effects by these processes. But, while I think this answer is on the right track, it will not do as it stands. For there are some causes which produce their effects, not by transferring energy to the sites of these effects, but by blocking or modifying energy transfers to them which would otherwise have occurred. (For example, I may darken my room by pulling the blinds.) Let us say that causes which act in these ways do so negatively. The issue is further complicated by the fact that an effect may be produced by a combination of positively and negatively acting causes, which may be acting either in series or in parallel. However, it would seem to be at least a necessary condition for an event A to be causally related to an event B that it be serially related to B by some such combination of processes.

This ontological account of causation is comprehensive, highly reductive and offers a satisfying explanation of the nature and variety of causal relationships. It identifies their direction as that of the energy transfer processes involved; it explains why there is an upper limit to the speed with which causal influences may be transmitted (because there is an upper limit to the speed of energy transfer); it explains how there can be unique, never to be repeated, cause-and-effect relationships, which regularity theories cannot satisfactorily account for; and it explains how causes may operate in an indeterministic world, which no regularity or natural necessitation theory of causation can do. According to my ontological theory, *all* causal influences are transmitted by processes which are fundamentally indeterministic.

These energy transfer processes are also said to transmit the *forces* which are involved in particle interactions. Thus, the electromagnetic force is supposed to be transmitted by photons or electromagnetic waves; the strong force is thought to be transmitted by gluons, gravitation by gravitons, and so on. All of the changes which occur in particle interactions are said to be produced by the actions of these forces. Now, this way of speaking suggests that forces are just kinds of causal influences, and, so conceived, there is good enough reason to believe in them. If there are four basic kinds of causal interactions between particles, there are four basic kinds of causal influences.

There is another way of speaking about forces, however, which suggests that they are necessarily present when the effects they are said to produce occur, and are necessarily productive of these effects. This is the classical conception of force as an entity which intervenes between a material cause and its effect, but is not itself a material cause. For reasons I have given elsewhere, I see no reason to believe in forces of this kind.[15] In principle, they are eliminable from physics,[16] and if we have an ontology which includes primitive causal influences, we are not left having to believe in a Humean world. When we know how fields and particles interact, and how the effects of their interactions are transmitted, we know what there is to know about primitive causes, and how they are related to their effects.

Properties and relationships

The main argument for scientific realism requires us to be realists about physical properties and relationships as well as about forces (conceived as modes of causal influence). For there are infinitely many effects which such forces may have, depending on the physical properties and relationships of their sources and objects. These physical properties and relationships must therefore be part of the causal story of why things behave as they do. Thus, we must say that the world behaves *as if* things had these physical properties, and were related physically to each other in these ways; and the best explanation of this fact must be that they really do have these properties, and are in fact so related.

It is not easy to say what sorts of things physical properties and relationships are. Consider properties. Some would simply identify them with sets of individuals (every set being a property); others would say that they are universals which individuals may or may not instantiate; and some would say that there are no property-universals, only property-instances or tropes, which may in fact be similar. However, I am unhappy with all of these accounts of the nature of properties. For reasons to be given presently, I am sure that properties are not just sets of individuals; and the other two theories cannot easily account for the structure we find in the system of the most fundamental properties we know about. For example, how does one explain the relationship between *different* properties of the *same* kind, like spin $^1/_2$ and spin $^3/_2$, on a theory of universals or tropes? What seems to be needed for science is an ontology which recognizes the fundamentally *quantitative* nature of the most basic properties of particles and fields; and such an ontology must somehow include such multi-valued properties or their values as primitive.

I do not know how to construct such an ontology, because I have no adequate theory of what quantities, or more generally, what multi-valued properties, are. They are not universals as they are usually understood, because universals are not multi-valued. Universals may be multiply *instantiated*; but different instances of a property-universal must be *the same* in respect of this property, that is, they must be single-valued. In *Basic Concepts of Measurement*, I argued that quantities are the objective linear orders into which things possessing them may be arranged, and that the measurement of quantities consists in assigning 'numerals' to things according to their positions in these linear orders.[17] By doing so, I sought to avoid the extremes of operationism, which would pointlessly have divided our quantitative concepts according to how they were measured, and a naive realism, which would have located quantities and their magnitudes wholly in the objects possessing them – independently of the existence of anything else. However, I no longer find any of these accounts completely satisfying.

It is easier to say what physical properties and relationships are not than what they are. In formal logic, it is usual to represent a property as a set of individuals, and an n-place relationship as a set of ordered n-

tuples of things – thus leaving the question of what sort of thing a property or relationship is wide open. This is fine for the purposes of logic, but it would be a mistake to make too much of the usefulness of this particular representation, and suppose that properties are nothing more than the sets of individuals which possess them, or that relationships are nothing more than the sets of ordered *n*-tuples which instantiate them. For what has to be explained is what the various members of these sets have in common, and it is not at all helpful to say that they all satisfy the same predicates, for this leaves the point of having these predicates wholly unexplained.

Moreover, to regard properties just as sets of individuals, and *n*-place relationships as sets of ordered *n*-tuples of individuals, is to make nonsense of the idea of *discovering* a new property or relationship. Sets are defined or constructed, not discovered; and there is nothing easier than defining a new set. Yet scientists surely *do* discover new properties and relationships, and what they do is by no means trivial. Murray Gell-Mann, for example, was awarded the Nobel Prize for Physics for his discovery of the set of relationships among certain properties of the fundamental particles known as the 'Eightfold Way'. A consistent scientific realist must hold that this symmetry existed before it was described.

Whatever general account of properties we may eventually give, we may define a *physical* property as one whose value is relevant, in some circumstances, to how a physical system is likely to act. It is a property which thus makes a physical difference. The most fundamental physical properties we know about are the multi-valued properties of fields and fundamental particles. They include such quantities as mass, charge, spin, interaction potential, hypercharge, strangeness, colour, charm, flavour, and many others. But perhaps the most important of all multi-valued properties is energy itself. I think a scientific realist must believe that energy exists, and is conserved in all fundamental interactions.

The account we give of physical properties should give us the lead for an account of physical relationships. For the most important physical relationships are also quantitative. In many cases, the quantitative relationships we speak about are ontologically dependent on the physical properties of the things related. This is normally the case, for example, when we speak of two things being equal or unequal in respect of some quantity. Therefore, we do not need to have an independent theory of relationships like this, if we have an ontology of quantitative universals. However, there appears to be at least one class of relationships which cannot be so reduced, namely spatio-temporal relationships. For position in space-time does not appear to be a physical property in the sense in which I am here using this term. The laws of nature are supposed to be invariant with respect to position in space–time; therefore, mere position in space-time cannot make a difference to the propensity of a physical system to act in any way. Therefore, we must recognize that there is at least one ontologically irreducible class of physical relationships, namely the spatio-temporal ones.

The theory of multi-valued universals I have proposed as a possible solution to the problem of ontologically reducing the category of properties and relationships to its most basic elements is so far not much more than a suggestion. But if it can be made to work, it promises to yield a theory no less reductive or comprehensive in its own sphere than the reduction of all physical entities to particles and fields.

This ontology is probably not yet complete. For, in addition to the various categories of things I have described, we probably also need a category of numerical relationships – since there is no reason to suppose that these relationships can be reduced to any of the other categories. And no doubt there are other kinds of things that have not yet been accounted for. However, realism about numerical relationships does not require realism about numbers. For numbers, abstractly considered, belong to the theory of *possible* numerical relationships, and so are not supposed to be causally effective. They are like geometrical points in this respect. Therefore, a scientific realist is not required to believe in them.

There is also no good reason for a scientific realist to be realistic about sets. For sets are idealized heaps or collections. They have determinate membership; heaps do not. The membership of a set may not vary; but a thing may at one time be, and at another time not be, something that belongs to a given heap. The things that belong to a given collection must belong to the same ontological category; sets are not so restricted. But sets are not supposed to have any causal roles. Like numbers, they are incapable of changing or being changed. Therefore, a scientific realist is not required to believe in them. It may be useful to postulate them for certain purposes, just as it is useful to speak of other sorts of idealized systems. However, a sophisticated scientific realist should not be realistic about every sort of thing it is useful to postulate, but only those things they have to believe in to accept the causal process theories they do.

Smart probably disagrees with me about whether a scientific realist should believe in sets, since I know he was once inclined to believe in an ontology which included sets of things, like the set of all negatively charged fundamental particles, along with the fundamental particles themselves. However, his own argument for scientific realism does not require him to do so. The world does not behave *as if* there were such sets, because the sets *must* exist if and only if all their members exist, and they are, therefore, ontologically reducible to them. But it *does* behave as if there were certain properties, like that of being negatively charged, and this is reason enough to believe in such properties, as well as in the things which possess them.

The ontology to which a scientific realist is committed does not, therefore, include all of the categories of things Smart would wish to include, and it does include some kinds of things which Smart may not wish to have in his ontology. Nevertheless, Smart's original argument for scientific realism is a powerful one, although it cannot be deployed indiscriminately. We need to understand its scope and limitations to apply it correctly. When we do, we can use it to develop a comprehensive and highly reductive ontology for science. It has been the aim of this chapter to show how this can be done.

Notes

1 J. J. C. Smart, *Philosophy and Scientific Realism*, London, Routledge and Kegan Paul, 1963.

2 Nancy Cartwright, *How the Laws of Physics Lie*, Oxford, Oxford University Press, 1983.

3 Michael Devitt, *Realism and Truth*, Princeton, N.J., Princeton University Press, 1984.

4 Mentioned in Brian Ellis, *Rational Belief Systems*, Oxford, Basil Blackwell, 1979, pp. 45–6, and discussed briefly in 'What science aims to do', in *Images of Science*, Paul M. Churchland and Clifford A. Hooker (eds), Chicago, University of Chicago Press, 1985. An earlier development of the position, which I now wish to revise, is to be found in 'The existence of forces', *Studies in the History and Philosophy of Science* 7, (1976) pp. 171–85.

5 Smart, *Philosophy and Scientific Realism*.

6 Smart endorses Quine's position on this. See W. V. O. Quine, 'The scope and language of science' in *Ways of Paradox and Other Essays*, New York, Random House, 1966, pp. 215–32, and J. J. C. Smart, *Between Science and Philosophy*, New York, Random House, 1968, p. 164.

7 Smart, *Philosophy and Scientific Realism*, p. 47.

8 J. C. Maxwell, *Elementary Treatise on Electricity*, William Garnett (ed.), Oxford, Clarendon Press, 1881, paras 65 and 66.

9 See David Lewis, *Counterfactuals*, Cambridge, Mass., Harvard University Press, 1973, p. 87.

10 P. W. Bridgman, *The Logic of Modern Physics*, London, Macmillan, 1954, p. 59.

11 See Eyvind H. Wichmann, *Berkeley Physics Course* 4, New York, McGraw Hill, 1971, for an excellent discussion on this point.

12 See Adrian Heathcote, 'Causal theories of space and time', unpublished Ph.D. thesis, La Trobe University, Melbourne, 1984.

13 Hans Reichenbach, *The Philosophy of Space and Time*, New York, Dover, 1958, para. 21.

14 This possibility is discussed by Daniel Z. Freedman and Peter van Nieuwenhuizen in 'Supergravity and the unification of the laws of physics', *Scientific American* 239 6 (February 1978), pp. 126–43.

15 See Brian Ellis, 'The origin and nature of Newton's laws of motion', in *Beyond the Edge of Certainty*, R. G. Colodny (ed.), Englewood Cliffs, N.J., Prentice Hall, 1965, pp. 29–68.

16 See Brian Ellis, 'The existence of forces' for a proof of this.

17 Brian Ellis, *Basic Concepts of Measurement*, Cambridge, Cambridge University Press, 1966, ch. 2.

5

Why Moral Language?

R. M. Hare

Jack Smart tells us in *Ethics, Persuasion and Truth*[1] that if he said someone was a good philosopher, one might gather that that person was not an existentialist or phenomenologist, wrote lucidly, possessed originality or was an inspiring teacher. That he himself exhibits to a very high degree not just the disjunction but the conjunction of these properties is obvious to all who know him. But what impresses me most about him is his transparent integrity. I use the word, not in Bernard Williams's somewhat off-beat sense,[2] in which Hitler was a paradigm of it – the sense in which someone displays integrity if he pursues his own 'projects' regardless of all other considerations – but in its usual sense of the honesty which, whether in someone's writing or in anything else that they do, one can trust absolutely. We know, when reading Smart's work, that, pleasant though that experience is, he will not indulge in any rhetorical tricks; that he will expose himself to criticism by coming absolutely clean on what he thinks and by expressing it with complete clarity; and that if he feels an argument is suspect he will tell us so. I wish there were more philosophers like him. He may have suffered some disadvantages from this integrity (for example in his encounter with Williams); it is obviously easier to win dialectical battles if one exposes oneself less. But anyone who goes through Smart and Williams's *Utilitarianism: For and Against* looking for positive and definite theses that stand a good chance of being right and, even if mistaken, are stated clearly enough for the discovery of the mistake to advance the subject, will find the higher proportion in Smart's contribution.

I am not going, however, to write about that book, but about just one chapter, the third, in *Ethics, Persuasion and Truth*. In the Preface Smart says that I will profoundly disagree with his treatment of some central issues; and this is true.[3] I have chosen one on which I disagree most profoundly, and which at the same time gives me an opportunity to discuss the very important question there raised of whether we could do without moral language. I shall take issue, not only with Smart's views, but also with those of M. Zimmerman, whose paper of 1962[4] Smart says is 'one of the most stimulating papers that have been written on moral philosophy for more than twenty years'.[5] I shall also say something about a related topic, discussed by Peter Singer in another good paper, namely 'Need we make a fuss about whether "ought" is derivable from "is"?'.[6] It is one of the many merits of Smart's book to have brought these questions again into the open.

As a preliminary to the discussion of these main issues, I shall first enter a complaint against Smart's use of the term 'pragmatics'. The triad 'semantics', 'syntactics' and 'pragmatics' was first put forward in a laudable attempt to make some distinctions within the rather general concept of 'meaning'. Unfortunately, the terms are not now always used to mark the same distinctions, and some important distinctions escape this classification. For example, some writers (mainly linguists) seem to distinguish semantics as having to do with meaning in some quite general sense, and syntax as having to do with rules of sentence-formation not affecting meaning; but others (mainly philosophers) follow the original distinction and allow that there may be syntactic features which have to do with meaning. Thus the transformation which generates the imperative mood might be called in one sense a syntactical or grammatical transformation, but in another it might be called a semantic change because it obviously affects the meaning of sentences.

This distinction need not here concern us. But the expression 'pragmatics' has created enormous confusion in moral philosophy which, since the work of J. L. Austin, there is no excuse for prolonging.[7] The same confusion has sometimes resulted from the indiscriminate handling of the Wittgensteinian expression 'the use' of words and sentences. Austin distinguished between illocutionary and perlocutionary acts, and within the former between different kinds of illocutionary force. The word 'pragmatics' might have been designed to blur these distinctions, and, as is well known, it confused the emotivists. When Stevenson called part of his book 'Pragmatic Aspects of Meaning,' he treated what were perlocutionary features of moral language as if they were constitutive of its meaning, and as a result became an irrationalist, because perlocutionary acts are not subject to logical rules.[8]

But illocutionary acts *are* so subject (Searle and Vanderveken have recently published a book on these rules[9]). It is perfectly in order to claim, as the emotivists did, that moral judgements have a different sort of illocutionary force from that of ordinary 'constative' speech acts, but yet, as they did not but as I have done, to claim that they are subject to rules of consistency and other logical rules, and that rational moral argument is therefore possible.[10] Talk about pragmatics obscures this possibility, because it leads people to say, as Smart does, that chapter 3, which I am going to discuss, was concerned with the pragmatics of 'ought' and not with its semantics;[11] and this might be thought to imply that the questions discussed by Smart in that chapter, following Zimmerman, have nothing to do with logical consistency. It also implies that what is discussed in chapter 4, the semantics of 'ought', does have to do with logical consistency. But, as I shall show, although some of the issues raised by Zimmerman have to do with the perlocutionary effects that we produce by making moral judgements, it is impossible to sort out these issues without an understanding of the *logical* properties of the illocutionary acts we perform in making them. As we shall see, through neglecting these logical properties, Zimmerman is led to underrate grotesquely the importance of having such a language, and thus totally misconceives even its 'pragmatics', in the sense of what we can achieve by using it, and what we would fail to achieve if we did not have it. What we can do *by* saying things must depend on what we are doing *in* saying them, and this is determined to a large extent by the logical properties of the words we use.

I will try to summarize Zimmerman's thesis, which Smart accepts, as accurately as I can in a few sentences. Zimmerman thinks that we could do without the word 'ought', and thus avoid the tiresome disputes which have arisen about whether 'ought'-statements are logically derivable from 'is'-statements. We could, he says, make do simply with 'is'-statements. By 'make do' he means 'achieve our object'. He takes it for granted that the object of making 'ought'-statements is to persuade people to do things. But we could persuade them just as well, he thinks, by making the 'is'-statements which give the reasons why doing those things will bring about what *they* want to bring about. If these reasons do not persuade them, then saying to them that they ought to bring about those things will not persuade them either. So why not dispense with the 'ought'-language and just give the reasons, using only 'is'-statements.

As Kenneth Hanly sees, the word 'want' which occurs in this argument is crucial (perhaps more crucial than even he realizes).[12] To want something to happen is to be in a state of mind which, if it had to be put into words, could be expressed by saying that one accepts the prescription that it happen. The acceptance itself does not have to be verbalized (dumb animals can want things); but if it *were* verbalized, that would be a way of doing it. So Zimmerman's contention amounts to this: instead of persuading people by saying something prescriptive ('You ought'), we could persuade them by showing them that *they*, in wanting something, accepted a prescription. The most essential item among the 'is'-statements that Zimmerman says will do instead of the 'ought'-statement (which is a prescription) is thus a statement that somebody (the addressee) accepts a prescription.

Suppose I say to the judge in Zimmerman's example,[13] not 'You ought to sentence the prisoner', but 'You want (or will want when I have given the facts about the case which will make you want) to sentence the prisoner.' I am then attributing to the judge the acceptance of a prescription, or predicting that he will accept one, instead of issuing one to him. And Zimmerman is quite right in thinking that to get the judge to act as I intend, *he* has to accept the prescription. This way of putting Zimmerman's point may not please him, but it begins to make clear how the logical properties of prescriptions are important.

It may become clearer still if we consider a simpler kind of prescription, the ordinary imperative. Zimmerman could equally well have said that we could do without this. For if (as so many people wrongly think) the meaning of imperatives is constituted by their function of getting people to do things, one can more successfully get someone to shut the door by giving him (in indicative sentences) the reasons which will lead him to want to shut the door than by saying to him 'Shut the door.' So is not the imperative mood dispensable too?

There are two things wrong with this argument. The first is that it relies on the 'verbal shove' theory of the meaning of imperatives. I have explained at length elsewhere why this is wrong.[14] We have here the same confusion between illocutionary and perlocutionary acts. A school-master has said the same thing, *in* saying 'Keep quiet' to the boys in his class, whether his object is to get them, *by* saying this, to keep quiet, or to get them to make a noise so that he may have the pleasure of thrashing them.[15] What makes the utterance of the imperative *that* illocutionary act is nothing about what the speaker is trying to achieve by saying it, but the fact that compliance with it would consist in keeping quiet. His intention *in* saying it is to make it the case that the boys will not be complying if they make a noise. *In* saying what he says, he makes this the case; and *by* thus making it the case he may achieve the object of getting the boys to expose themselves to his eccentric, but now authorized, *amours*.

It is thus the logical properties of the speech act, in the sense of what it implies, or what compliance with it would have to consist in, which give it the perlocutionary effect that it is intended to have. If the boys did not know that they had to keep quiet in order to comply, their natural inclination to mischief would not cause them to make a noise. They would not know what, in this situation, mischief would consist in. (Suppose, for example, that they thought that 'Keep quiet' was not a command addressed to them, but a way of trying out the acoustics.) Thus we see that to perform the illocutionary act of commanding is a means to performing the perlocutionary act of getting the boys to keep quiet or to make a noise (as the case may be); but the two acts are not identical. As the example shows, they can come apart.

I have used an uncommon example to illustrate the difference between illocutionary and perlocutionary acts. But if we ask, by analogy with Zimmerman's and Smart's question, whether we could do without the imperative mood, we can think of ordinary examples without limit to show that it would be very awkward. The basic reason (which applies to sentences in the indicative mood too) is that we do not want to, and indeed cannot, give reasons for everything that we say. If asked for reasons we can normally provide them; but a programme that required us always, *instead* of saying something, to give the reason for saying it, would be impracticable.

Just as we need a means of making statements without then and there giving reasons for them, so we need a means of giving instructions, making requests, praying, issuing invitations and an enormous variety of other prescriptions, without on each occasion supplying the reasons. It would be not merely inconvenient but in practice impossible to do so. The kinds of situation in which we need the imperative mood are much more various than some philosophers, who concentrate their attention on military orders, seem to realize. There are cases, for example, where the speaker is an acknowledged expert ('Take two pills three times a day'); cases where someone has to be in charge ('Take in the jib sheet'); cases where we just want to know what somebody wants us to do and are disposed to do it ('A double pink gin on the rocks, please'); cases where we *hope* that somebody is disposed to do our bidding ('Give us this day our daily bread'). This list could go on for a long time. The imperative mood is a very useful and in practice necessary part of our language, and if somebody told us we could do without it we should be unlikely to believe him, and should think he had some philosophical axe to grind.

The usefulness of the imperative mood lies in the fact that we can use it to communicate prescriptions without going into the reasons for them. It is interesting, also, that the prescription that is communicated may be complied with for different reasons by different hearers. The Fabric Committee chairman says to the College Meeting, 'Our recommendation is: Reface the Old Library in Clipsham stone'; one fellow may vote in favour because he thinks that otherwise stones will start falling on people's heads from the decayed façade; another because he likes the look of new stonework; another because he has shares in the Clipsham quarries. But the recommendation (which is a kind of prescription) to which all three assent is the same. If the chairman had had to dispense

with the imperative form he used and its equivalents, and actually give
the reasons, no single motion could have been put before the college
meeting which would have secured the votes of all these three people.
The virtue of the form he actually used was that it made clear what the
recommendation was (that is, what would be involved in complying with
it) without having to give a lot of reasons. No doubt in the committee's
report a lot of reasons would be given; but the fellows did not have to
accept *those* reasons in order to accept the recommendation.

Returning to the case of the more complicated prescriptions which
'ought'-sentences express, we can now appreciate the possibility that the
perlocutionary effects of moral language are brought about because it has
the logical properties that it has, and therefore can be used to perform
the illocutionary acts called moral judgements. If this were so, it would
be less likely that moral language was dispensable.

It is paradoxical if someone who thinks he is talking about 'pragmatics'
pays as little attention as Smart does to the actual perlocutionary effects
of the use of moral language in our society. I am going to list some of
these. The most basic is that it serves as an engine for producing
agreement on how people should behave. This is the truth after which
contractualist theories are groping. If we had only plain singular
imperatives but nothing equivalent to 'ought', agreement would be
harder to reach. What makes people agree on the moral principles that
most of us accept is that we are looking for prescriptions we can all
universalize; they have to cover cases, both actual and hypothetical, in
which we ourselves occupy the positions of those affected by the
adoption of, and therefore at least partial compliance with, the
prescriptions. This is the essence of the Kantian argument that I have
used in constructing a system of moral reasoning.[16] If we had only
singular imperatives available, and not the universalizable 'ought', we
should have to look for very large sets of singular imperatives, directing
in detail how each of us should behave; and how could we easily agree on
these? But if what are proposed to us are much simpler universal
prescriptions, it may be that we can agree on them as a compromise,
when we see what the effects of adopting them would be — that is, the
effects of cultivating *these* moral principles.

It may be said that we could do this without using 'ought'; we could
just use universal imperatives, which certainly exist. But they would not
serve. In order to conduct the argument we have to consider hypothetical
and past actual cases; and in the ordinary imperative mood we cannot
talk about the latter, and would find it at least difficult to talk about the
former. We need a language in which properly universal prescriptions
can be framed, applicable to all logically possible cases identical in their
universal properties, no matter what individuals occupy the roles in

them.[17] Otherwise there will be loopholes in the argument (for example, somebody may say 'I can readily accept that principle, because I am powerful enough to protect myself against the evil consequences for some others of its adoption').[18] If, to overcome these difficulties, we set about expanding the imperative mood to cover the past tense and all persons, as I once tried (whether or not successfully) to do,[19] what we shall be doing, in effect, is to reinvent the word 'ought'. This can hardly be an argument for saying that we can do without it.

One of the advantages, then, of having 'ought' in our language is that it reveals, to anyone who cares to look, the logical basis of the general agreement, which undoubtedly exists, on a standard set of moral principles that has been found serviceable. It also enables us to revise these principles by mutual discussion. In order to secure agreement on moral principles, all kinds of arguments are needed, relying no doubt on the production of a lot of 'is'-statements, above all about people's desires or preferences. But the reasons for the proposal are not the proposal itself. We adopt a moral principle because of the consequences of having it; but it is not itself a statement of those consequences. And if we had to do without the principle and just catalogue the consequences, we might never reach agreement. To start with, we should not know what the proposal was that we were trying to agree on. Next, the catalogue of facts would not itself carry with it the logical requirement that the principle agreed on had to be a universal prescription; and this, as we have seen, is an essential part of the argument by which we can reach agreement. Further, different people may have slightly, or even radically, different reasons (in the form of different facts) for agreeing on the same principle.

But this is only the beginning of the benefits we get from having in our language a form of words with these logical properties (prescriptivity combined with universalizability). Once we have the agreed principles, we can set about propagating them. Here we must avoid a trap set for us by Zimmerman. He seems to argue that the use of 'ought' is to 'persuade' or 'get' people to do things; but there are better ways of doing this; so we do not need 'ought'.[20] But the *illocutionary* use of 'ought' is not to persuade or get people to do things; it is to express universal prescriptions. Persuading or getting people to adopt them is another matter. Maybe there are more effective ways than just saying 'You ought.' Adducing reasons in the form of facts about consequences is only one of these.

What we are talking about here is moral education in a broad sense.[21] Part of this, no doubt, is teaching people the reasons for the principles (which involves their understanding, not just the facts, but the logical properties of moral judgements). But normally this comes much later than an inculcation into our offspring of moral principles which we ourselves think sound (and perhaps can even defend in argument, if we have prepared ourselves to do so). Later they will themselves, we hope, come to appreciate the arguments. But the process could never have begun unless we started by teaching them the word 'ought', which, as we have seen, expresses a universal prescription *without* giving the reasons for it. Children can be got (indeed have to be got) to internalize *some* universal prescriptions before they are given the reasons for them; and different parents and teachers may have quite different reasons. Later the children will come themselves to examine these reasons, decide between them, or even amend the principles if they see good cause. But to start with they have to understand what it is to follow universal prescriptions without having the reasons for them. And for most of our day-to-day adult lives the same applies to all of us; that is why we need the level of thinking which I have called 'intuitive'.

Very few of the advantages of moral education could be realized if we did not have a language for pursuing and later defending it: a language with the logical properties which 'ought' has.[22] So the effects of a genuine abandonment of 'ought' from our language (and not just the substitution of some equivalent expression) would be catastrophic for our society. We can actually see the beginnings of such a development; but I am old enough to have seen this happen before,[23] and optimistic enough to believe that they will never be more than beginnings, because 'ought' and similar words are too essential to our survival for us to succeed in giving them up.

In recent years (in fact just when Zimmerman was writing his 1962 paper) it became quite common to advocate the abandonment of morality. Zimmerman has not been the only philosopher to echo, wittingly or not, this popular trend among intellectuals. The argument was that we can get along without morality if only we attend to our own and other people's feelings and especially desires.[24] If there is enough love around, what need for justice?

Aristotle was familiar with this move, which was made in ancient times too.[25] He seems to have agreed with it, but was percipient enough to see that it was not enough as a basis for good living, which involves 'desiring and acting in accordance with a [sc. universal] principle', instead of being, like children, 'guided in life by feeling and following particular whims'.[26] And, even if each individual could reconcile his own disparate and conflicting feelings, the snag for society is that interests, and therefore desires, of different people diverge and conflict, and something other than attention to them is needed to produce the kind of *modus vivendi* that makes living in one society tolerable or even possible. This something is morality. If attention to others' feelings were to be widespread enough to achieve this, it would have become a morality.

The anti-moralist movement, and other similar ones before it, only started because people had forgotten this conciliatory purpose of morality, and thought of it as *nothing but* a set of rules for which no reasons could be given. In this way they were abetted by some deontologist moral philosophers who were acquainted with only the intuitive level of moral thinking. Against such a background of ossified morality, both the anti-moralist movement and the arguments of Zimmerman are easy to understand.[27]

Is it an obstacle to the process of rational agreement I have been describing that 'ought' cannot be logically derived from 'is'? Zimmerman might affect to think so. He has in his paper a straw man who, on hearing that it cannot be derived, says 'Disaster! We can never justify ethics and morality!'[28] I say 'might affect', because I do not think that this is Zimmerman's real view. His real view is the same as mine, that we can get on perfectly well without *such* a justification of morality. He goes further than me, and implies that we can do without morality altogether, and therefore without a justification of it; but that is a mistake, as we have seen. He is quite right, though, to think that 'is'-'ought' derivations have nothing to contribute to the avoidance of disaster.

The thought of the straw man is this: if nobody ever believed anything that could not be supported by 'is'-statements, and nobody believed that 'ought'-statements could be supported by 'is'-statements (that 'is'-'ought' derivations were possible), then nobody would believe any 'ought'-statements, and morality would collapse. But we can see how absurd this is if we consider the analogous case with imperatives. If we believed, as most people do, that imperatives are not derivable from 'is'-statements,[29] would we therefore give up using imperatives (ordering, instructing, asking, inviting, urging, begging or praying people to do things)? It seems that the imperative mood has a use in language which does not depend on the derivability of imperatives from 'is'-statements; so why should not the same be true of 'ought'-statements, if they, like imperatives, express prescriptions?

Is it irrational to voice requests, for example, without being able to derive them from 'is'-statements? The thought that it is so stems from a misconception about reason-giving which I have exposed before.[30] Suppose I say 'Give me a double pink gin on the rocks, please', and somebody is impertinent or philosophical enough to ask me 'Why?' I may come out with some 'is'-statements. Let us avoid the pitfall of supposing that I could make do with 'want'-statements. If I said 'Because I want it' (or even 'Because it would be to my liking'), I should be missing the point; my desire or wish for it is precisely what I was expressing when I said 'Give me . . . please'; it does not give the reason for saying it. The questioner would go on 'But why do you want it?' I would then have to answer, as I should have answered before, with a more helpful 'is'-statement: 'It would taste like *that* (if you don't know what cold gin and angostura tastes like, you can try one yourself); and the degree of intoxication that a double gin produces, which is my second reason for wanting it, is like *that* (you can try that too). I am assuming that your taste-experiences and susceptibility to alcohol are much the same as mine. If they aren't, then I can't tell you what it is like for me, but that is an old philosophical problem we needn't argue about now; at least I have produced as my reason a conjunction of "is"-statements which *I* know how to support'.

If I say 'Give me . . . because it will taste and feel like *that*', I am not *deriving* the imperative from the 'is'-statement. The 'is'-statement gives my reason for voicing the request, but does not entail the request. We often utter sentences of the form '*q* because *p*', even when both constituents are 'is'-sentences, without the statement that *q* being *derivable logically* from the statement that *p*. For example, I can say 'It is poisonous because it contains cyanide', although the statement that it contains cyanide does not *entail* that it is poisonous.[31] It would entail it if conjoined with the premiss that everything containing cyanide is poisonous; but that premiss itself is not logically nor even analytically true.

So, if I can say 'Give me . . . because . . . ' without there being derivations of imperatives from 'is'-statements, why cannot the judge say 'I ought to sentence the prisoner, because . . . ' without there being a corresponding derivation? The 'cyanide' example yields a clue here. There is, no doubt, a universal, synthetic, *prescriptive* premiss which the judge accepts, namely that he ought to sentence prisoners who have been found guilty by due process. If this in turn were questioned, the kind of reasoning which I invoked earlier would provide a means of justifying it.[32] This kind of reasoning does not involve 'is'–'ought' derivations. What it involves is asking judges and others to choose one of a set of alternative prescriptions to accept, on the condition that they be universal (and therefore applicable whatever role the chooser were to play – of a judge, or a prisoner, or one of the many victims of crime), and in full knowledge of what that would be like (a knowledge expressible in 'is'-sentences).

What is in evidence here is a fundamental mistake about rationality.[33] To have a reason for what we say does not involve being able to derive it logically from an 'is'-statement which does not entail it. It involves having something in mind which is our reason. This could, but need not be, expressed in an 'is'-sentence. That it is a reason is another way of saying that there is some universal synthetic premiss which we accept, and which, in conjunction with the aforementioned reason, *does* entail what we said. All this applies to imperatives, moral statements and factual statements alike. Even the man who asks for the gin because it would be like that to drink it must be accepting, at any rate for the time being, the premiss that he should, *ceteris paribus*, on occasions like this, when he is in this kind of mood, take drinks which would have that effect on him. He is being incontinent, as Aristotle put it, 'in obedience, in a manner of speaking, to a principle coupled with a factual belief'.[34] The justification of the universal premiss is an entirely different matter. I have dealt with it as regards moral arguments,[35] and I leave it to philosophers of science like Smart to deal with it as regards factual statements.

The next question that Smart will want to ask is about my use in the last few paragraphs of the analytic–synthetic distinction. Because he likes Quine's views on this more than I do, he might think that I shall be in trouble because I use these suspect terms.[36] But I am in no trouble at all. The first thing I wish to say about this (which is worth saying, although it could be accused of being rhetoric) is that I do not think it profitable to argue with people who deny that there is a distinction between analytically and synthetically true statements. The reason why I do not think it profitable is this: 'analytic' is one of a set of expressions (others are 'synonymous', 'consistent' and 'follows from') which are essential to the assessment of arguments. For example, if somebody does not know the difference between one statement following from another and its not following, what could ever be achieved by arguing with him? And since 'analytic' and 'follow from' are interdefinable, if he is prepared to use one he must be prepared to use the other.

Perhaps that was just rhetoric. So, for the sake of argument, I am going to assume that the word 'analytic' *is* suspect, and try to see what would happen in my own moral philosophy if I dispensed with it. It seems to me that I should not suffer much; and the reason for this is important. It is, that the method of moral reasoning that I advocate is entirely formal. It can make use, therefore, of the notions '*logically* true', '*logically* follows' and the like, and does not have to use the suspect expression 'analytic'. Those who like completely formal systems can construct a system of deontic logic having the same properties as I say ordinary moral language has. In this formal system the sign corresponding to 'ought' will be defined in terms of the universal quantifier and the imperative mood-sign, and will not need to import any of the kind of notions that Quine wants to ban. If the formal logical relations between statements in this system are as I say the formal relations between statements in English are (and I can see no reason why they should not be), then I could in principle do all that I want to, by way of introducing the system of reasoning, without using the notions of synonymy and of analyticity between statements in English. Of course, the English-speakers that I am trying to communicate with and help would have to learn the new language; but they could as easily do this as they can learn any other formal language. Personally, because I do not have the fastidious scruples that Quine has, I prefer to go on talking English; but it makes no fundamental difference.

Actually, it is not I but my opponents in moral philosophy who are likely to be in trouble. They really do need to claim, at any rate if they are naturalists, that certain expressions are synonymous as used in ordinary English (for example, 'good' and 'satisfying basic human needs'); or that certain statements made in ordinary English are analytically true (for example, that the gratuitous infliction of pain is wrong). By all means let them try out those on Quine: my withers are unwrung. If I were a follower of Quine, I would say that the synonymy or analyticity cannot be established, because the notions themselves are shaky. Not being a follower of Quine, what I shall actually do is to challenge the naturalists to show that they *are* analytic or synonymous, in the confidence that they will fail. But I myself can take refuge in the safety of a system of reasoning which does not need to use such suspect notions.

If, for the sake of argument, we accept Quine's thesis that there is no hard and fast line between the analytic and the synthetic, we shall still have a spectrum with deeply entrenched theses at one end and easily discardable ones at the other. In terms of such a view, we can ask the naturalists where on this spectrum they would put their favoured moral judgements. Obviously they will try to put them at the entrenched end. But on any controversial question of morality, what is at issue is precisely whether such and such an opinion *should* be so entrenched. So a naturalistic theory can never be used to settle any controversial moral question. Like intuitionism, it may seem to work for questions to which we all think we know the answers, but not with those that really bother us. The fraudulence of both these theories consists in trying to make out that questions are settled by our intuitions, or by an appeal to language, or by some Quinean entrenchment, when they are not.

I can usefully end by dealing with a difficulty raised by Peter Singer, which, though not discussed directly by Smart, is relevant to matters that he does discuss.[37] Singer uses an argument very similar to one that I remember using myself in early lectures to show that we cannot derive 'ought' from 'is'; but he turns it on its head. I used to argue, and would still argue, that since the main point of moral judgements is to guide actions, and since they cannot do this without having imperatives as their consequences, they cannot themselves be derivable from pure non-moral 'is'-statements, since *these* do not have imperative consequences. If statement R does not follow from statement P, but does follow from statement Q, then Q also cannot follow from P; for if it did, then R could be made to follow from P via Q, which is contrary to hypothesis. So if P is an ordinary statement of fact, and Q a moral judgement, Q cannot follow from P.

Though this argument is valid, I gave up using it because objectors tended to deny one of its premisses, namely that moral judgements entail imperatives. I still think that they do, if used prescriptively (this is indeed a tautology); but the matter obviously needed more discussion, which I duly gave it.[38] Singer's argument is very similar, but in reverse. He accepts that what we need to have is something to guide actions. He accepts that non-moral facts do not by themselves do this, in the sense that there is no logical bar to agreeing with the facts and not acting. So there is a 'gap' between the factual statements and the decision to act. The question is whether a moral statement or judgement put in between the two can bridge the gap; and Singer argues that it cannot, because whatever view we take of the status of the moral judgement, a gap will still be left one side of it or the other.

He distinguishes two extreme views about the logical character and relations of moral judgements, and then goes on to consider an intermediate view, which he attributes not unfairly to me. None of these views, he says, will bridge the gap. At one extreme we have what he calls the form-and-content neutralist, or for short the *neutralist*, position. (Since my own position is content- but not form-neutralist, the abbreviation might mislead, but I will accept it.) The neutralist holds that 'there are no limits on the kind of principle which can be held as a moral principle'.[39] This cannot be what Singer really means, because nobody would want to maintain that sentences of absolutely any kind could express moral principles. For example, 'No pigs have wings' could not. What Singer means is rather that, as he says a few sentences further on, according to the neutralist 'to count as a moral principle, a principle does not have to satisfy any of the formal requirements *that have sometimes been proposed*, such as being able to be willed as a universal law, being acceptable to an impartial observer, being able to be formulated without the use of proper names, personal pronouns, or other singular terms'.[40]

So Singer's 'neutralist' is not exempting moral principles from *all* formal restrictions. In fact, Singer goes on to say that it is a strength of neutralism 'that it provides a very close *logical* connection between the moral principles a man holds and the way he acts'.[41] This is to say that moral principles have to be prescriptive, which is a formal property. He has also said earlier that they have to be overriding according to the neutralist; and this too is a formal requirement.

The descriptivist, on the other hand, makes no such formal connection between moral principles and decisions to act. But he does (at least if he is a naturalist) make a *logical* connection between moral judgements and the facts which are the reasons for them. This is because he puts on moral principles restrictions of both form *and* content. For example, he may say that 'moral judgements are logically tied to suffering and happiness' and that they must not 'arbitrarily place more importance on the suffering and happiness of a particular person or group of persons than on the suffering and happiness of any others'.[42] The first of these restrictions is on the content, the second on the form. In virtue of the first, the descriptivist should be able in principle, once someone has agreed that to give money to famine relief would prevent more suffering than spending it on a new Mercedes, to compel him to conclude that he ought to give the money to famine relief.

The two extreme positions exhibit, as Singer shows, symmetrically opposite weaknesses. The descriptivist can get the reluctant donor to agree that he *ought* to give the money, but has no way of bringing him to the decision actually to give the money. The neutralist, on the other hand, can bring him to this decision once he has accepted the moral judgement that he ought to give it, because of the neutralist's logical link between moral judgements and action; but the reluctant donor remains at liberty not to accept the moral judgement, even though he has agreed on the non-moral fact that a gift would relieve more suffering. So neither the descriptivist nor the neutralist can get all the way by logical means from non-moral facts to decisions to act; for both of them there is a gap: for the descriptivist between values and actions, and for the neutralist between facts and values.

Singer concludes that the dispute between these extreme positions is of no practical importance; and he supports this conclusion by pointing out that, faced with the reluctant donor, both would use essentially the same means of getting him to go all the way, though they might use different words. The reluctant donor would say to the descriptivist that, although he agreed that he ought to give the money, that was no reason for giving it. The descriptivist's next move would be to try to get him to 'take notice of morality' by 'appealing to the feelings of sympathy and benevolence which, in common with most of mankind, he probably has to some extent'.[43] The neutralist, on the other hand, will seek to overcome his gap, though it is in a different place, by appealing to the same feelings. He knows that the reluctant donor, *if* he accepted the moral principle that one ought to relieve suffering, would give the money; and therefore he will use the very same appeal to human sympathy to get him to accept the principle.

The similarity is obvious between Singer's conclusion and the contention of Zimmerman which I discussed earlier and which attracts Smart. Singer, however, does not go to the extreme length of denying that we need to use 'ought' at all; he merely says that we need not make so much fuss about whether it is derivable from 'is', because that is a trivial, verbal question which depends merely on how we define the moral words, or the word 'moral'. I agree with both Singer and Zimmerman that some of the reasons sometimes given for worrying about the gap between 'is' and 'ought' are bad ones. We do not need to worry, so much as to give an account of how, although 'ought' is not logically derivable from 'is', we can still reason about moral questions. This I have tried to do.

Zimmerman's contention is that we can do without 'ought' and appeal instead to desires. Singer's argument, if pursued to its limit, would have the same consequence. For if, in the argument from 'is' via 'ought' to action-decisions, there is going to be a gap one side or the other of the 'ought', and the gap can be bridged only by an appeal to sympathetic and benevolent feelings (which are kinds of desires) then why not dispense with the 'ought' and just appeal to the desires, as Zimmerman suggests? Singer still differs from Zimmerman, because he would appeal to a special kind of feeling which one might even dignify by the name of 'moral feeling'; and nobody could deny that this is from the moral point of view an improvement. But both writers make it look as if we should stop worrying about the logic of moral language and whether 'ought' is derivable from 'is'.

I am going to counter Singer's argument in the same way as I countered Zimmerman's; and I can best do so by considering what he says about the 'composite' or 'middle' position, which is my own.[44] This is content-neutral but not form-neutral. That is to say, it puts formal restrictions on what can count as a moral principle, but no restrictions on content. As we saw, even what Singer calls 'neutralism' puts some formal restrictions on this, namely prescriptivity and overridingness. I only need add to these a requirement of universality or universalizability. Singer expounds this position very fairly, and I have already sketched it in this paper, so I will not explain in detail how universalizability helps bridge the gap, but will simply consider Singer's objection to the manœuvre. I must add that Singer's paper was written some time before my *Moral Thinking*, and that our positions are now much closer to each other; for this, see his contribution to the forthcoming volume of essays on my ideas and my comments, and also his books *Practical Ethics* and *The Expanding Circle*.[45] In what follows I shall not be trying to controvert Singer's present views, but only to deal with the difficulty raised in his paper.

His objection consists in producing the character whom in my books I have called the 'amoralist'. This is 'a person whose overriding principle of action is non-universalizable – for instance a person who acts on the principle of pure egoism'. I dealt with the amoralist at some length in my *Moral Thinking* and more briefly but on the same lines in *Freedom and Reason*.[46] My tactic is to admit that there can be amoralists, and that I cannot refute them by logic, provided that they are consistent in their amoralism; but then to produce prudential reasons why we should not be amoralists. In particular, I argued that if we were educating a child with only the child's interest at heart, we would be well advised not to bring him up as an amoralist, but to give him a normal moral education, and in so doing both teach him the moral language with its logic, and cultivate in him the firm intuitive principles which would be most likely to make him both happy and an acceptable member of society.

Into this argument I shall not go at length. But I do want to emphasize as I did when answering Zimmerman, the importance for moral education of having a moral language. It is very hard to imagine what moral education would be like if it had to be conducted without one. I discussed earlier the recent (indeed recurrent) tendency among intellectuals to say that we could do without morality. If we tried to do this, we should have to reinvent it under another name. The same holds for the moral language; for it would be hard to practice morality without some way of expressing moral opinions. These opinions are, after all, one of the things that we are trying to get people to have when we are educating them morally. They will have in addition to acquire dispositions to act on these opinions; but before they do this they have to have the opinions.

As both Singer and Zimmerman see, we could not do without some appeal to people's feelings or desires. Singer adds to this, but Zimmerman does not, that the desires will have to be sympathetic and benevolent ones. Suppose we ask, then, how such feelings or desires will be expressed. The words we use in moral discourse are designed for this very purpose. That is why I said that the project of doing without morality would lead to its reinvention.

But there is more to it than that. To acquire impartially benevolent desires is to come to accept one kind of universal prescription (not the only kind, because there can be fanatical universal prescriptions which are not benevolent – some are even malevolent).[47] Moral judgements are the way language provides of expressing these prescriptions. But it goes further; it also provides them with a logic. Moral education, which, I have argued, it is in our interest to have, brings this logic with it. The logic is based on the features of prescriptivity and universality. It has these features just because it is designed to express the impartially benevolent feelings that Singer wishes to appeal to. If we assume that people are nearly always at least benevolent to *themselves*, and therefore prescribe what they think is for their own good, and if we then require them to universalize their prescriptions, they will have to treat the good of other people as if it were their own and prescribe for others as if they were prescribing for themselves. It is crucial for this argument that moral language has the features both of prescriptivity and of universality.

If this is so, then we can see why in spite of what Singer says, it does matter very much that 'ought' is not derivable from 'is'. For prescriptivity is a necessary part of the argument. If moral judgements were not prescriptive, one move in it would be barred, namely the move which asks whether we are prepared to prescribe that what we are proposing to do to somebody else should be done to us were we in his position. But if moral language is prescriptive, and prescriptions are not logically derivable from non-moral facts, then moral judgements are not derivable from them either; and conversely, if they were derivable, they could not be prescriptive. So it is very important whether they are derivable. We have come back to my original argument.

The importance is not merely theoretical. If moral judgements were derivable from factual statements, and therefore not prescriptive, morality would lose its grip on people's conduct. We would have, as we have already in some quarters, a 'So what?' morality.[48] By this I mean the morality of those who can say 'Yes, I know I ought; but so what?' Singer uses such people as an argument against the descriptivist, quite rightly, and says that this prescriptivity is the strength of the neutralist position. It is one strength of my own sort of neutralist position too. If morality is universally *prescriptive*, one cannot say 'So what?', because to accept the moral judgement is already to accept its bearing on our conduct. In order to avoid the bearing on our conduct, we have to stop making the moral judgement. I have not denied that it is possible to do this, and become an amoralist. But I have argued that there is a price to be paid for it – a price which we would be imprudent to pay.

In his latest writings Singer presents arguments to show why the scope of morality gets extended beyond the tribe and the race to the whole of humanity, and beyond the human species to other sentient creatures.[49] I hope that these arguments will be successful. As I have argued in reviewing one of his books, moral language, and its natural tendency to extend the range of universalization, plays an even bigger part in this than Singer suggests.[50]

What would Smart say to all this? I hope that he would agree that the 'pragmatics', as he calls them, of moral language extend a good deal further than he has followed them in his book. Once we start looking at the process of moral education, and see how difficult it would be in default of a language with the logical and illocutionary features which alone make the pragmatics possible, we can see that the whole cohesion of our society depends on having such a language.

Notes

1 J. J. C. Smart, *Ethics, Persuasion and Truth*, London, Routledge and Kegan Paul, 1984, p. 90f.
2 See J. J. C. Smart and B. A. O. Williams, *Utilitarianism: For and Against*, Cambridge, Cambridge University Press, 1973, p. 108. and R. M. Hare, 'Ethical theory and utilitarianism', in H. D. Lewis (ed.), *Contemporary British Philosophy 4*, London, Allen and Unwin, 1976, p. 120n.
3 Smart, *Ethics, Persuasion and Truth*.
4 M. Zimmerman, 'The "is–ought": an unnecessary dualism', *Mind* 71 (1962); reprinted in W. D. Hudson (ed.), *The Is–Ought Question*, London, Macmillan, 1969.
5 J. J. C. Smart, 'Why moral language?', *Essays Metaphysical and Moral*, Oxford, Basil Blackwell 1987.
6 P. Singer, 'The triviality of the debate over "is–ought" and the definition of "moral"', *American Philosophical Quarterly* 10 (1973).
7 J. L. Austin, *How to Do Things with Words*, Oxford, Oxford University Press, 1962, p. 100. See also R. M. Hare 'Freedom of the will', *Aristotelian Society Supplementary Volume* 25 (1951); reprinted in R. M. Hare, *Essays on the Moral Concepts*, London, Macmillan, 1972.
8 C. L. Stevenson, *Ethics and Language*, New Haven, Yale University Press, ch. 3. See J. O. Urmson, *The Emotive Theory of Ethics*, London, Hutchinson, 1968, p. 131.
9 J. Searle and D. Vanderveken, *Foundations of Illocutionary Logic*, Cambridge, Cambridge University Press, 1985.
10 See R. M. Hare, *The Language of Morals (LM)*, Oxford, Oxford University Press, 1952, p. 15f.
11 Smart, *Ethics, Persuasion and Truth*, p. 64.
12 K. Hanly, 'Zimmerman's "is–is": a schizophrenic monism', *Mind* 73 (1964).
13 Zimmerman, 'The "is–ought"', p. 53.
14 See R. M. Hare, 'Wanting: some pitfalls' in R. Binkley, R. Bronaugh and A. Marras (eds), *Agent, Action and Reason*, Oxford, Basil Blackwell, 1971, second half; reprinted in R. M. Hare, *Practical Inferences*, London, Macmillan, 1971.
15 I remember using this example in discussion with Mr Norman Doenges in 1949.
16 See Hare, *Moral Thinking (MT)*, Oxford, Oxford University Press, 1981.
17 See Hare, *LM*, pp. 187ff. and 'Universal and past-tense prescriptions: a reply to Mr Ibberson', *Analysis* 39 (1979).
18 See Hare, *MT*, pp. 112f. and *Freedom and Reason (FR)*, Oxford, Oxford

University Press, 1963, pp. 188–90.

19 Hare, *LM*, pp. 188–90.

20 Zimmerman, 'The "is–ought"', pp. 54–6.

21 See Hare, *MT*, pp. 191ff., and Hare 'Adolescents into adults', in T. Hollins (ed.) *Aims in Education*, Manchester, Manchester University Press, 1964; reprinted in R. M. Hare, *Applications of Moral Philosophy*, London, Macmillan, 1972.

22 See Hare, 'Language and moral education', in G. Langford and D. J. O'Connor (eds), *New Essays in the Philosophy of Education*, London, Routledge and Kegan Paul, 1973; reprinted in D. B. Cochrane, *The Domain of Moral Education*, Paulist Press and Ontario Institute for Studies in Education, Toronto, 1979, with criticism by G. J. Warnock and reply by R. M. Hare.

23 See Hare, *LM*, pp. 72ff.

24 See Hare, 'Satanism and nihilism' (forthcoming).

25 Aristotle, *Nicomachean Ethics* 1155a 26 (reference to Bekker pagination given in margin of most editions and translations).

26 Ibid., 1095a 7–10.

27 See Hare, *LM*, p. 149, and 'Nothing matters', in R. M. Hare, *Applications of Moral Philosophy*, London, Macmillan, 1972.

28 Zimmerman, 'The "is–ought"', p. 53.

29 See Hare, *LM*, p. 78.

30 See Hare, 'What makes choices rational?', *Review of Metaphysics* 32 (1979).

31 See Hare, 'Descriptivism', *Proceedings of the British Academy* 49 (1963), *s.f.*; reprinted in R. M. Hare, *Essays on the Moral Concepts*, London, Macmillan, 1972.

32 See Hare, *FR*, pp. 115–17, 124f., and R. M. Hare, 'Punishment and retributive justice', *Philosophical Topics* 14 (1986).

33 See Hare, 'What Makes Choices Rational?', and 'Come decidere razionalmente le questioni morali', in E. Lecaldano (ed.), *Etica e diritto: le vie della giustificazione rationale*, Rome, Laterza, 1985, forthcoming in English.

34 Aristotle, *Nicomachean Ethics*, 1147b 1.

35 See Hare, *MT*.

36 W. V. Quine, *From a Logical Point of View*, Cambridge, Mass., Harvard University Press, 1953, ch. 2.

37 Singer, 'The triviality of the debate over "is–ought"'.

38 See Hare, *LM*, ch. 11 and *FR* pp. 26f.

39 Singer, 'The triviality of the debate over "is–ought"'; p. 52.

40 Ibid., p. 52; my italics.

41 Ibid., p. 58; my italics.

42 Ibid., p. 53.

43 Ibid., p. 53.

44 Ibid., p. 55.

45 P. Singer, 'Reasoning towards utilitarianism', in N. Fotion and D. Seanor (eds), *Hare and Critics*, Oxford, Oxford University Press, forthcoming; *The Expanding Circle: Ethics and Sociobiology*, Oxford, Oxford University Press,

1981; and *Practical Ethics*, Cambridge, Cambridge University Press, 1979, ch. 1.
46 Hare, *MT*, pp. 182ff.; *FR*, pp. 100f.
47 See Hare, *FR*, ch. 9; *MT*, ch. 10.
48 See Hare, 'The practical relevance of philosophy', in my *Essays on Philosophical Method*, London, Macmillan, 1971, p. 113.
49 See Singer, 'Reasoning towards utilitarianism', *The Expanding Circle*, *Practical Ethics*.
50 *New Republic*, February 1981.

6

Group Morality

Frank Jackson

Lerner and Lowe wrote *My Fair Lady*. But Lerner did not write *My Fair Lady*, and nor did Lowe. They each participated in writing *My Fair Lady*, they together wrote it, but neither wrote it himself. Writing *My Fair Lady* was a *group action* – an action performed by a group of people but not by any member of that group – whereas the actions performed by Lerner and those performed by Lowe were *individual actions* – actions performed by an individual.

Obviously, group actions and individual actions are closely related. Group actions are made up of individual actions. When a group of people do something together, what they do together is an aggregation or amalgamation in some sense of what each does separately. For in order for a number of people to have done something together, it is clearly necessary for each to have done something separately, and it is implausible that the whole they achieve together – the group action – is somehow greater than its parts – the individual actions.[1]

If we distinguish group actions from their constituent individual actions, we can distinguish the question of the moral status of a group action from those of its constituent actions. The general thrust of this chapter is that it is important to distinguish these two questions. More particularly, in the first section I argue that attending to this distinction resolves otherwise baffling problems surrounding what I will call the difference principle. In the second section I employ the distinction to sort out a puzzle about obligation and time raised by examples akin to those sometimes brought against the Kantian principle that 'ought' implies 'can'. The final section is devoted to some brief, programmatic remarks about the implications of the discussion in the first two sections for ethical theories in general.

But first three preliminary matters need to be settled. The moral status I will be mainly talking about is whether the actions, individual or group, are *objectively* right, wrong or neutral, not whether they are *subjectively* right, wrong or neutral, and not whether they are performed with good, bad or neutral motives. Thus, in the sense we are concerned with, an action performed with admirable motives and every justified expectation of being the right thing to do may nevertheless be the wrong thing, the objectively wrong thing, to do. At one point I will say something very brief about the bearing of our discussion on moral responsibility, while the question of subjective rightness and wrongness will not be touched upon at all – though I think it will be obvious how, in broad outline, at least parts of my discussion might be reformulated to cover it. My reason for concentrating almost exclusively on objective rightness and wrongness is to corral the discussion. It is not because I think that the objective notion is more fundamental to ethical theory than are its neighbours.[2]

The second preliminary concerns how to refer to group actions. A convenient feature of Lerner and Lowe's most famous group action is that it has a ready-made singular term in English, namely, 'the writing of *My Fair Lady*'. But many group actions lack ready-made labels. Suppose I open the red wine and you open the white wine. Neither 'my opening the red wine' nor 'your opening the white wine' refers to our group action. The first refers to what I do, my individual action, and the second to your individual action. If it happens that the red wine I open and the white wine you open is all the wine on the table, 'our opening all the wine on the table' does the trick.[3] For then, though neither you nor I open all the wine on the table, we together do so, and, therefore, opening all the wine on the table is what we together do. It is our group action. But clearly we need to have, at least sometimes in reserve, a more fool-proof and mechanical device for picking out group actions, these events that are aggregations of individual actions. I will use 'together with' between terms for the individual actions. Thus, 'my opening the red wine together with your opening the white wine' refers to our group action, to what we do together, and, in the happenstance, to the same action as 'our opening all the wine'.

Our device for referring to group actions must, of course, be read as sometimes referring to possible but non-actual group actions. Our opening all the wine is the right thing to do whether or not we actually do it. A similar attitude is, of course, equally required for reference to individual actions in the context of discussions of moral status. Standing up to Hitler is what Chamberlain ought to have done, and, in granting that, we perforce cannot read 'standing up to Hitler' as referring to what Chamberlain actually did. I set aside the question as to whether such reference should in the final analysis be read as reference to possibilia, as reference to types of acts rather than tokens, as mere putative reference, or as . . .

The final preliminary concerns how liberal we should be about what counts as a group action. My use of 'together' in forming expressions to refer to group actions suggests that it is essential to an action being a group action that the agents involved in the various constituent individual actions co-operate, or at least interact. But I think that this suggestion should be ignored. Suppose – *contrary* to fact – that Lerner and Lowe never exchanged a word. They worked quite independently in ignorance of each other – one on the words, the other on the music – and by an incredible fluke the two independently produced parts fitted together to make up *My Fair Lady*. It would still be true that they together wrote *My Fair Lady* without either writing it alone. Writing *My Fair Lady* would still have been something they did together, without it being the case that they had a common goal, or indeed that one's action in any way affected the other's.

Or consider two tunnellers working in complete ignorance of each other on opposite sides of a mountain, who amaze each other by meeting in the middle. Isn't opening a tunnel through the mountain a group action of theirs despite their failure to co-operate or interact, or even despite not having completing the tunnel as a common purpose – perhaps each intended to go only half-way through?

These two examples do not show that any old aggregation or mereological sum of individual actions counts as a group action. There is, in some pretty broad sense, a common or unifying element though no common intention in them – *My Fair Lady* in the one case, the completed tunnel in the other. But surely a common element can always be found – or cooked-up (grued-up)? Hence, I am inclined to count any old mereological sum of individual actions (or of group actions) as a group action (or as a *further* group action). My last eye-blink together with Nero's burning of Rome is a group action, a highly heterogeneous one of no particular interest to anyone, but a group action nevertheless. But I know that this will disturb some. There is a similar issue about objects instead of events. My desk is an object; the sun is an object; but is the mereological sum of my desk and the sun an object? Why not; why cannot disjointed, heterogeneous, uninteresting objects be objects none the less? The easy-going stance about objects will disturb much the same people as my easy-going stance on group actions. This is not the place to debate the issue. I think it will be clear that, although some of the examples I give later reflect my easy-going stance, substitute examples palatable to all parties could be constructed.

I now turn to putting the distinction between individual actions and group actions, and the attendant distinction between their moral status, to work.

The difference principle

Typically our actions make a difference. Had they not been performed, things would be different from the way they in fact are. Indeed, there would be little point in acting if this were not so. Why do something if things would be exactly the same whether or not you did it? If making a difference gives point to acting, it is plausible that it also determines the morality of acting. For surely moral action is at least pointful action. The rightness or wrongness of an action depends on the difference it does or would make.

Examples bear this out. It is not the goods or bads that actions cause that matter most immediately for whether they are right or wrong, but whether the differences they make are good or bad. A dentist may cause pain, that is, a bad, yet do what is right, because had she not acted, more pain later would have been the case. Though causing something bad, she makes a difference for the better. And the fact is what makes her action right.

Or consider (to borrow from Derek Parfit[4]) what is involved in deciding whether or not to join a rescue party to save trapped miners. It is wrong to consider merely what would happen if you joined the rescue party. What is crucial is how many *more* miners would be saved were you to join the rescue party by comparison with how many would be saved if you were not to join the rescue party but instead worked by yourself. Only if the former number is greater than the latter, should you join the rescue party. It is the difference that matters. Causing good does not make an action right if you could do better elsewhere.

We can state the difference principle as follows: the morality of an action depends on the difference it makes; it depends, that is, on the relationship between what would be the case were the act performed and what would be the case were the act not performed.

The difference principle as stated says nothing about how to evaluate the differences, and nothing about what kinds of differences matter morally. The principle is properly neutral with regard to pleasure utilitarianism, ideal utilitarianism, natural law theories, duty theories, and so on and so forth. The principle says to look to the differences, but which ones are important and just what to do with them when you've found them is another thing altogether.

I grant that, at first hearing, the difference principle does not sound as neutral between the various ethical theories as I have just made out. It sounds, rather, like a broadly consequentialist principle. But in fact a non-consequentialist can consistently embrace the difference principle. Suppose I have promised to send a certain sum of money to the Brotherhood, but that I could break my promise and send the money to the Society instead. The money would do exactly the same amount of good in either case, and there would be no other relevant effects in either case – we have, that is, the sort of situation often envisaged in discussions of 'death-bed promises'. Many non-consequentialists insist that, despite the equality in consequences, I ought to honour my promise and send the money to the Brotherhood. And this they can do without departing in any way from the difference principle. Were I to send the money to the Brotherhood, it would be the case that I honoured my promise and produced good consequences; on the other hand, were I to send the money to the Society, it would be the case that I dishonoured my promise and produced equally good consequences. Thus, there is a difference between what would be the case for the two actions, namely the difference between good results together with honouring a promise, and equally good results together with dishonouring a promise – and it is open to these non-consequentialists to hold that this difference matters morally. Similarly, difference theorists may consistently insist that the moral issues raised by 'by-product' killing are quite distinct from those raised by 'directly intended' killing, even if the killing is equally certain in both cases. Their view is that the *difference* between doing something which incidentally leads to someone's death as opposed to directly intending their death matters for the morality of the actions in question.

Thus, the difference principle should appeal to both consequentialists and non-consequentialists. What is perhaps true is that the difference principle should be especially appealing to consequentialists. (Except for those consequentialists who think that it is the consequences of *everyone* doing something that determine whether *my* doing it is right.) This makes it all the more puzzling that there are plausible *consequentialist* counter-examples to the difference principle. These putative counter-examples are consequentialist in the sense that it is pretty clear that, wherever you stand in general, in these particular cases it is only considerations of a consequentialist kind that are morally relevant. The puzzle is that these examples seem to run counter to the difference principle. Here is a simple one.

The over-determination case[5] Suppose that X and Y jointly cause unjustified pain in Z. Both what X does and what Y does play a role in causing Z's pain. We may suppose, nevertheless, that we have over-determination in the following sense. Had X done nothing, Y would still have acted and Z would have experienced pain which would have been just as bad as the pain Z actually experienced – whether it would have been the very same pain does not matter for our purposes. Likewise, had Y done nothing, X would still have acted and Z would have experienced equally bad pain as the pain Z actually experienced.

It is clear that something wrong is done here. (Remember that here and throughout we are talking about objective wrong: it thus does not matter that I haven't told you anything about X or Y's states of mind, about whether, for instance, they intended Z's pain.) But, according to the difference principle, nothing wrong is done by X, because X does not make a difference for the worse. Had X not acted, things would have been no better for Z. Similarly and obviously, the difference principle implies that Y does nothing wrong. But X and Y are the only agents in our little story, so the difference principle implies that nothing wrong is done in the over-determination case, and that is absurd.

It is, thus, entirely understandable that Derek Parfit should regard the over-determination case as a refutation of the difference principle, at least as I have stated the principle. Parfit's view is that we – or at any rate we consequentialists – must enlarge our notion of what makes an action wrong. An action may be wrong because it makes a difference for the worse, and *also* because, though it itself does not make a difference for the worse, the aaction belongs to a collection of actions which makes a difference for the worse. Thus, X's action is wrong because it belongs to the collection consisting of X and Y's actions, and this collection makes a difference for the worse; for had neither member of it been performed, things would have been better. Had neither X nor Y acted as they did, Z would have experienced no pain. Similarly, Y's act counts as wrong, according to Parfit, because it too belongs to this collection consisting of X and Y's actions.[6]

Here is a second example which points in the same direction, and which clearly played a major role in influencing Parfit.

The beans example[7]   A thousand villagers each has a thousand beans. A thousand bandits have two ways of stealing the beans from the villagers. Each bandit can steal all the beans of exactly one villager, or each bandit can steal exactly one bean from each villager. Call the first vertical stealing, and the second horizontal stealing. The overall effect of vertical stealing and of horizontal stealing is exactly the same – no beans for any of the villagers, and a thousand beans for each bandit – and thus a very attractive position is that the moral status of what each bandit does is totally unaffected by whether he steals horizontally or vertically. In either case, what he does is wrong. Moreover, it seems to be quite consistent with this position to hold (1) that each bandit acts independently of each other bandit, and (2) that to be left with no beans is no worse than to be left with one bean; indeed, possibly one bean is worse than none – a solitary bean would only remind you of what you are missing out on.

The problem for the difference principle is that it implies that, in the case as I have just described it, a bandit who steals horizontally does nothing wrong. For it is true of each bandit that had he not acted as he did, each villager would have ended up with exactly one bean (remember, the other bandits would still have stolen), and ending up with one bean is no better, and may be worse, than ending up with no beans. If the bandits steal horizontally, no bandit makes a difference for the worse, and so, if the difference principle is correct, none does anything wrong.

There are two ways difference theorists might try to avoid conceding that each horizontally stealing bandit does nothing wrong. First, they might point out that, though no horizontal stealer increases the suffering of any villager, each horizontal stealer ends up with a whole lot of beans that do not belong to him; and having something which does not belong to you is a difference for the worse. But clearly this is an incidental feature of the beans example. The beans might not have belonged to the villagers anymore than to the bandits – that is, what's wrong with *vertical* stealing, regardless of what should be said about horizontal stealing, might have been that the villagers *needed* the beans more than the bandits. A second more interesting avoidance strategy would be to draw on the notion that *who* it is that produces a certain result may matter in and of itself. When evaluating an action of mine that produces something good or bad, it may be necessary to take into account not only the good or bad produced, but also, as an ineliminable extra, the fact that it is I myself who produce it. Accordingly, difference theorists might urge that each horizontally stealing bandit does make a relevant difference for the worse, not in the suffering of the villagers, but in *who* is involved. As for each bandit it is true that had he not taken one bean from each villager, he would not have himself been involved. But involved in what? Not *ex hypothesi* in making things worse for the villagers – each bandit may in fact be making things better for them. In *this* case, how can the fact of direct involvement be relevant in itself? We should grant as a possible ethical position for difference theorists that, in negatively evaluating an action, not only the harm resulting from it but also how directly the agent was involved in producing the harm is relevant, particularly, perhaps, when it is the agent's own evaluation of the action that is in question. We should not, though, grant as a possible position for difference theorists that, *when no harm at all results*, how directly the agent was involved matters. Who did it may be relevant *in* itself, but not *by* itself. Similarly, it does not help difference theorists to make play with the fact that each horizontally stealing bandit is joining a group of wrong-doers. For precisely what is at issue for difference theorists *is* whether they are wrong-doers.

I conclude that there is no escape for difference theorists. They must hold that each horizontally stealing bandit does, in horizontally stealing, nothing wrong.

It is again entirely understandable that Parfit should reject this consequence of the difference principle, and so the principle itself, and urge that each bandit's horizontal stealing is wrong by virtue of belonging to a collection of actions, namely, that made up of every case of a bandit's horizontal stealing; which collection itself, unlike its members, makes a difference for the worse.[8]

It is time to stop being understanding. I think that neither the over-determination case nor the beans example refutes the difference principle, because I think that reflection shows that the difference principle's answers for the two cases are, despite initial appearances, the right answers. What X does is not wrong; what Y does is not wrong; and what each horizontally stealing bandit does is not wrong.

I will try to convince you that these answers, the difference principle's answers, are the right ones: (1), by arguing that Parfit's treatment of the two cases faces a major difficulty, and thus the only plausible way of making out that X, Y and the horizontally stealing bandits do something wrong, despite not making a difference for the worse, fails; (2), I will bring to bear an intuition about choice in support of the answers given by the difference principle; and, finally, I will tell you how to explain away the intuition that the answers given by the difference principle are wrong.

(1) I will develop my argument against Parfit's treatment of the two cases in the terms of the over-determination case. It will be obvious how to direct it against his treatment of the beans case. Parfit, remember, wants to count X's and Y's actions as wrong because of their membership of a collection of actions which together make things worse, a sort of 'guilt by association' view. The fundamental problem with his approach comes out when we consider a modification on the over-determination case.

The modified over-determination case As before, X and Y jointly cause pain to Z; they act independently: had one not acted, the other still would have; and had neither acted, Z would have experienced no pain. The modification is that had X not acted, Z's pain would have been much worse; that is, the best thing would be for neither X nor Y to act, no pain in that case; the next best thing is for both X and Y to act (as in fact happens), some pain in that case; and the worst thing would be for Y to act alone, much worse pain in that case.

I put it to you that it is obvious that X is right to act, for Y is going to act regardless. Think of it from Z's point of view. If Z knows the situation, won't he be hoping like mad that X will act? Indeed, we can imagine that Z pleads with X to act, pointing out that if he doesn't, Y will act alone and he, Z, will suffer worse pain. Is Z pleading and hoping for something immoral to be done? Surely not! It seems, however, that Parfit must declare X's act wrong in our modified over-determination case. For X's act belongs to a collection of acts that together makes things worse – had neither X nor Y acted, Z would have experienced no pain – and, according to Parfit, an action's membership of a collection that together makes things worse makes that action itself wrong.

How might Parfit evade this disastrous result?[9] He might give an exemption to acts which, while being members of collections of acts that together make things worse, themselves make things better. We might put it this way: an act which collectively makes things worse is wrong unless it individually makes things better. Obviously, cases like our modification on over-determination, except with pleasures for pains, would force Parfit to add what is anyway needed on symmetry grounds: an act which collectively makes things better is good unless it individually makes things worse.

This is a very unattractive position to end up in. The position is that individual score overrides collective status *except* where individual score is zero. That looks like making zero unbelievably special. It is, if you like, a form of 'zero worship'. If individual score has the whip hand when it is positive or negative, how does it mysteriously lose its power when it is zero? Clearly, if a positive individual score makes an act good, and a negative one makes it bad, zero should make the act morally neutral.

(2) There is an intuition about choice that supports the answers given by the difference principle in the over-determination and beans cases. This time I will develop the point in terms of the beans example.

One's initial reaction to the beans example is that a bandit's horizontally stealing a thousand beans and his vertically stealing a thousand beans are morally on a par; but reflection on a point about choice shows that this cannot be right. Suppose a bandit has the choice of horizontally stealing a thousand beans as in our original case, or of stealing a thousand beans from some quite different villager not involved in our original case. It is obvious that the bandit should stick with horizontally stealing a thousand beans from the original villagers, otherwise there will be a thousand and one unhappy, hungry villagers instead of one thousand; and, remember, it is not the case that the one thousand villagers are each even a tiny bit better off than the one thousand and one would be. Thus, we can see immediately that there must be something wrong with our initial intuitive reaction to the beans case. For if the choice had been between *vertically* stealing a thousand beans from one of our original villagers, or of stealing one thousand beans from our new villager, it would be a toss-up. Therefore, substituting 'vertically' for 'horizontally' makes a dramatic difference, and so there must be something radically amiss with one's initial reaction that the horizontal and the vertical stealing are morally on a par.

Moreover, the choice argument can obviously be extended to yield the conclusion that the horizontal stealing is not only not as bad as the vertical stealing, but is in fact morally neutral. For suppose the choice had been between horizontally stealing 1000 beans or stealing 900 beans from the new villager. This change would not alter the fact that for each bandit the right decision is to steal horizontally the thousand beans from our original villagers, rather than the beans from the new villager. It remains the case that stealing from the new villager would create an additional unhappy villager without compensating gain for the original one thousand villagers – they would be just as badly off as before. Obviously, essentially the same is true with 800 beans instead of 900, or with 700 instead of 800, or with . . . We end up with the conclusion that the horizontal stealing is to be preferred to doing anything else bad, even if the alternative is only marginally bad, and so with the conclusion that the horizontal stealing is morally neutral.

(3) What can we say in place of what Parfit says? It is evident that something wrong *happens* in both the over-determination case and the horizontal version of the beans example; but more than that is evident: something wrong is *done*. (It would be quite wrong to think of either case as being one of a natural misfortune, like a flood.) But if what X does and what Y does is not wrong in the over-determination case, and if what each horizontally stealing bandit does is not wrong, what actions *are* wrong in these cases? The answer is the group action as opposed to the individual actions. It is what X and Y do together that is wrong in the over-determination case, their group action, and what the horizontally stealing bandits do together, their group action, that is wrong in the beans example.

What foxes us when first presented with the over-determination case and the horizontal version of the beans example is tunnel vision. We are immediately struck by the intuition that something wrong is done; we then search around for a wrong action, restricting ourselves, without fully realizing it, to the individual actions in the cases, and so have no choice but to say that X's and Y's actions, and each horizontally stealing bandit's action, are wrong. There are no other starters among the individual actions. But if we enlarge the class of actions which may be morally evaluated to include group actions as well as individual actions, we can say that the agents' group actions, though not their individual actions, are wrong. And the intuition that something done in the horizontal version of the beans case is morally on a par with something done in the vertical version can be accommodated by insisting that the group actions, what the bandits do together, are in both versions indeed morally on a par. Switching from the vertical to the horizontal version makes not one iota of difference to the moral status of the group action; it is only the standings of the individual actions that are affected.

Parfit wants to enlarge our conception of what makes an action wrong with his guilt by association theory. We have seen its difficulties. I am suggesting that we respond to the difficult cases for the difference principle by enlarging our conception of what kinds of actions can be wrong (and right).

Two objections to my suggestion here will leap – will already have leapt – to mind. The first is that I am giving a recipe for making it easy, *too* easy, to avoid moral responsibility. This objection might be fleshed out for the over-determination case as follows. 'You must endorse as morally acceptable an obviously outrageous bit of collusion between X and Y. Suppose X and Y independently both want Z in pain, but neither wants to do anything wrong. They get together and jointly over-determine Z's pain, each saying consolingly to himself that he has done nothing wrong because he has not made a difference for the worse.'

Part of the answer to this objection lies in the fact that their individual acts of preparation make a difference for the worse. Though neither individual act at the time of carrying out the plan makes things worse for Z, the prior preparatory acts do. Nevertheless, intuitively, we want to be able to blame X and Y for something more than preparing to inflict pain on Z; we want to blame them for *what* they prepare to do as well. But, of course, I can do exactly this. What they prepare to do is their group action, and that group action *is* wrong on my view.

The second objection is that if a group act is wrong, surely at least one of its constituent acts is wrong. How can they *all* be neutral? How could the morality of a group act be so much at variance with the morality of its constituent acts?

In fact, however, the moral standing of a group act can be partially or totally at variance with the standings of its constituents. Here follow some cases to illustrate the point. These examples have been kept as simple as possible, and partially as a result of this it is arguable that some of them involve prudential 'oughts' more than moral 'oughts'. I think, though, that it will be obvious that this is inessential, and I will talk as if the 'ought's were all clearly moral ones. (After all, prudence can be turned into morality by adding dependents.)

The intersection case You and I approach an intersection from different directions. I have the right of way, so that what ought to happen is that you give way together with my driving straight on. What in fact happens is that you do not give way, and would not regardless of what I do; so that were I to drive straight on, there would be an accident. What ought I to do? Drive straight on, consoling myself with the thought that I will be able to say from my hospital bed that I was in the right? Obviously, what I ought to do is stop. The position, then, is that the right group action is your stopping together with my driving on; the right action for you is to give way, and the right action for me is to stop. But if the right action for me is to stop, the wrong action for me is to drive on. Hence, we have a group action – your stopping together with my driving on – which is right, which nevertheless has a constituent action – my driving on – which is wrong.

I have been surprised by how often I have met the following response to this sort of example. 'The argument turns crucially on the claim that I ought to stop. But I ought to stop *only because* you do not do as you ought, namely, give way, and so all that is really true is that I ought to stop given you do not give way.' However, the sketched alternative position is inconsistent: '*P* only because *Q*' entails *P*! To grant that it is true that I ought to stop is true only because you do not give way is *ipso facto* to grant that it is true that I ought to stop.[10]

I have just given an example of a right group action with a wrong constituent. But we can have more extreme variance between the moral status of a group action and those of its constituents. We can, for instance, have a group action which is wrong, yet every constituent act is right; and a group action which is right yet every constituent act is wrong. One example will serve to illustrate both possibilities.

The morning traffic example There is a steady stream of traffic going to work. Everyone is driving at 80 kilometres per hour. It would be safer if everyone was driving at 60. The right group action is for everyone together to drive at 60. But what about each person, should he or she drive at 60? The answer may well be no; for it may well be the case that if he or she were to drive at 60, everyone else would still drive at 80, and so a lot of dangerous overtaking would result. For each individual the right action is to keep driving at 80, so avoid dangerously disrupting the traffic flow; yet the right group action is for everyone to drive at 60. Thus, we have in this example a right group action – everyone together driving at 60 – with each and every constituent individual action – each action of a person driving at 60 – wrong. And also we have a wrong group action – everyone together driving at 80 – with each and every constituent action – each action of a person driving at 80 – right. We see, therefore, that not even the attractive-sounding principle that if a group action is right, at least one of its constituent acts is right, is valid.

Although it is perhaps initially surprising that there should be such marked disparities between the moral properties of group actions and those of their constituents, the explanation on reflection is really quite straightforward. There is no great mystery here. Take the intersection case. The options available to you and the options available to me are different from the options available to us together. You can give way or not, and the better of those two is giving way; hence, you ought to give way. I can drive on or stop; the better of these two is to stop (as you won't give way); hence, I ought to stop. But there are four instead of two options available to you together with me: you can give way together with my stopping, you can give way together with my driving on, you can fail to give way together with my stopping, or you can fail to give way together with my driving on. The second – your giving way together with my driving on – is the best of the four; hence, it is what you together with me ought to do. The marked disparities that can obtain between the moral properties of group actions and their constituent individual actions are a reflection of the differences in the options available to groups of people as opposed to the options available to the members of those groups.

Time and obligation

Here is a second puzzle to which to apply the distinction between group and individual actions, and the attendant distinction between their moral properties.

The pilot case I am a jet pilot who is scheduled to fly on Tuesday. I am required to take it easy on Monday. However, I meet an old friend on Monday and one drink leads to more than another. What should we say about what I ought to do on Tuesday? What is the right thing for me to do on Tuesday? The puzzle is that it is so hard to answer this question satisfactorily.

Suppose we say that what I ought to do on Tuesday is fly. Is it flying with a hangover or flying without a hangover that I ought to do? Obviously, flying without a hangover. Flying with a hangover is the last thing that I should do. But I cannot fly without a hangover on Tuesday; for on Tuesday my Monday drinking is past history, and I cannot change the past. True, I could have refrained from drinking on Monday, and so

I could on Tuesday have flown hangover-free. But that only shows that *had* I behaved differently on Monday, it *would* have been the case that I ought to fly on Tuesday, not that it *is* the case that I ought to fly on Tuesday. Put it this way. It is surely uncontroversial that *if* I drink heavily on the day before I am due to fly, then I ought not fly on the day I am due to fly. But I do drink heavily on Monday, hence, by *modus ponens*, I ought not fly on Tuesday. Moreover, surely it is simply obvious that I ought to resign on Tuesday: the right thing for me to do on that day is to resign. That's incompatible with flying, so it cannot be true that I ought to be flying on Tuesday.

This, in outline, is the case for saying that I ought not fly on Tuesday. I submit that it is a pretty powerful case. Unfortunately, there is also a powerful case for the opposite answer that I ought to fly on Tuesday.

There is all the difference in the world between our case where I freely, foolishly and wrongly drink all day on Monday, and a variant case in which the alcohol is forced down my throat. In the variant case I am not at fault; it would be wrong to blame me; but in our case I am at fault. But why, exactly, am I at fault? Not, presumably, for the drinking itself. We may suppose that there is nothing intrinsically wrong with spending Monday drinking. I am at fault because I ought to fly on Tuesday, and drinking on Monday prevents me from doing this safely. But if I am at fault because I ought to fly on Tuesday, then it must be the case that I ought to fly on Tuesday: '*P* because *Q*' entails *Q*. In any case, if anything is obvious about our example, it is that what I really ought to do is be abstemious on Monday and fly on Tuesday – that is the right course of action over those two days. But this evidently right course of action requires me, as far as Tuesday goes, to fly; and if an evidently right programme calls for flying on Tuesday, then I ought to fly on Tuesday.

The force of the case for saying that I ought to fly on Tuesday is precisely the same as that for saying that certain examples similar to ours refute the letter, though perhaps not the spirit, of the Kantian dictum that 'ought' implies 'can'.

The wedding example Pat has promised to marry on Tuesday, but intentionally catches a jet to a distant country on Monday and so is unable to marry on Tuesday.[11] Those who think that this example refutes 'ought implies can' take it as obvious that Pat ought to marry on Tuesday despite his inability to do so, and the person left at the church may well agree. (Though they may add that the example does not refute the spirit of the Kantian dictum, as it is crucial to the example being a counter-example that Pat catches the jet *freely*.) Their thought is that Pat's failure to walk up the aisle on Tuesday is clearly blameworthy, and that can only be so if Pat *ought* to marry on Tuesday. Those who, on the other hand, deny that the wedding example refutes even the letter of 'ought implies can' retort that it is obvious that what Pat ought to be doing on Tuesday is arranging to fly back home in order to get married on Wednesday. But arranging to fly home is different from, and incompatible with, getting married, so if the former is what Pat ought to be doing on Tuesday, it cannot be right that Pat ought to be getting married on Tuesday. He should instead have his hands full arranging to fly home as quickly as possible.

The puzzle about time and obligation is that in the pilot case there is both a strong case for and a strong case against holding that I ought to fly on Tuesday; and similarly, there is a strong case for and a strong case against holding that Pat ought to marry on Tuesday in the marriage case.

The solution to the puzzle about time and obligation that I wish to advance draws on the familiar view that temporally extended objects may be viewed as aggregates of their temporal parts.[12] I am not going to defend this view here, other than to remark that its ability to found a solution to a tricky puzzle is a point in its favour.

According to this view, I am an aggregate of my various temporal parts, including the Monday-of-our-pilot-example-part and the Tuesday-of-our-pilot-example-part. Hence, the relationship between my actions and the actions of my Monday and Tuesday temporal parts is broadly similar to the relationship between what you and I do together and what you do and what I do. The way we made sense of the road intersection example will serve as a model for making sense of the pilot example. In the intersection example I said that what you and I together ought to do is make it the case that you give way and I drive on: what you ought to do is give way, and what I ought to do is stop. In the pilot example I say that what my Monday part together with my Tuesday part ought to do is bring it about that the Monday part abstains and the Tuesday part flies: what my Monday part ought to do is abstain, and what my Tuesday part ought to do is resign, not fly.

It is now clear why it was so hard to answer the queston 'What ought I to do on Tuesday?' The question is ambiguous. It can be read as a question about my Tuesday temporal part, what ought it to do, and, as just noted, the answer is that my Tuesday temporal part ought to resign. After all, my Tuesday part has no control over Monday part's behaviour. The drinking my Monday part indulged in is in the past, out of the Tuesday part's control. Hence, there is no question but that the Tuesday part ought to resign, for its only alternative is to fly with a hangover, and it is non-controversial that that ought not be done.

On the other hand, 'What ought I to do on Tuesday?' can be read as asking what I – the aggregate of, *inter alia*, my Monday and Tuesday parts – ought to be doing on Tuesday, to which the answer is that, as far

as Tuesday goes, I ought to fly. For what I ought to do is abstain on
Monday and fly on Tuesday, and the Tuesday section of that programme
is to fly.

In general the point is this. We must distinguish what actions a
temporally extended person ought to do, from what actions various
temporal parts of that person ought to do, just as we distinguished what
group action ought to be done from what constituent individual actions
ought to be done. And the question as to what a person ought to be
doing at t may be understood as asking what the t-temporal part of that
person ought to do, or as asking, concerning the temporally extended
action that temporally extended person ought to do, what the t-section of
that extended action is.[13]

I emphasized earlier that there was no great mystery about how, for
instance, it can be that in the intersection case what you and I ought to
do together is make it the case that you give way and I drive straight on,
yet what I ought to do is stop. My options are different from our options.
The same explanation applies to the pilot case. The options available to
me include abstaining on Monday and flying on Tuesday: that's the
better of those available to me, hence, that's what I ought to do, and that
requires flying on Tuesday. However, the options available to my
Tuesday temporal part are limited to flying with a hangover or resigning,
and resigning is the better of those two; hence, my Tuesday part ought
to resign.

Matters arising

I have been advertising the importance of distinguishing the question of
the moral status of group acts from the question of the status of their
constituent acts. The group acts may involve a number of different
individuals, the constituent acts then being acts by these individuals, or
they may be individual acts themselves – acts by some temporally
extended individual – the constituent acts then being acts by temporal
parts of the individual, or no doubt we might have a mixture of the two
sorts of case. Suppose you accept the importance of this distinction –
without it nothing satisfactory can be said about our puzzle concerning
the difference principle, or about our puzzle concerning time and
obligation – what matters then arise?

Three matters seem to me to be particularly pressing. First, how to co-
ordinate what we have said about the rightness or wrongness of group
actions and individual actions with questions of praise and blame for
individuals and groups? For instance, can a group action be praiseworthy
without any of its constituent individual actions being praiseworthy? And

what is it to praise or blame a group, as opposed to its members, anyway?

Second, we have seen that initially plausible-sounding principles like 'If a group act is wrong, at least one of its constituent individual acts is wrong,' fail. But it is surely unbelievable that there are *no* valid principles linking the moral status of group acts with the moral status of constituent individual acts. What, then, would be an example of a valid principle?

Third, ethical theories historically have focused on giving an account of the morality of individual acts, not of group acts. Indeed, often they focus on the morality of an individual act of a relatively small temporal part of an individual. They tell us how to decide what we ought to do in the immediate future. For some ethical theories it is easy to see, in outline at least, how to extend them to group acts. Group acts just as much as individual acts make a difference to how much pleasure there is in the world. Hence, pleasure utilitarianism takes the topic of group morality in its stride. But the whole question is much less clear for some other ethical theories. The third pressing question is thus how, if at all, one might extend the account those ethical theories offer of what makes individual acts right or wrong to group acts.

In the final section of this chapter I am going to pursue these last two questions, particularly as they arise for the self-interest theory of morality. It will emerge that a version of this theory of morality is self-refuting. It may be that our argument to this effect is at bottom close to one of Parfit's, but I make no promises.[14]

We have seen that a group act may be right when each of its constituents acts is wrong. Everyone together driving at 60 kilometres per hour may be right, but it still be wrong for any individual to drive at 60. However, the example we gave to illustrate this was one where the right group act was not in fact performed. Everyone did not together drive at 60. They in fact all drove at 80. I know of no counter-example to the following principle:

(P) If a group act is right, *and it is in fact performed*, then each individual constituent act is right.

In addition to having no counter-examples, (P) has a general argument in its support. Suppose G is a group act with constituent individual acts $i_1, \ldots i_n$, and that G is right and actually performed. Then each i_x is actually performed. A group act is performed if and only if its constituent acts are performed. But then each i_x must be the best that the relevant agent can achieve, for if $i^\star_x$ were better for that agent, G would, contrary to hypothesis, not be the right group act. For there would then be a group act $G^\star$ with at least $i^\star_x$ for i_x, which was better than G.[15]

Accordingly, I recommend (P) to you. We will now see how (P) can trouble S, the self-interest theory of morality. S is a good example of a theory for which, unlike pleasure utilitarianism, it is obscure how to extend its account of rightness and wrongness for individual acts to rightness and wrongness for group acts. This is simply because in assessing rightness and wrongness for an individual act, S gives a special role to the agent's relationship to the possible outcomes – only those which benefit the agent count – and this leaves it unclear what to say of a group action that involves a number of agents.

One response to this difficulty would be for an advocate of S to refuse to answer the question, to maintain that S only tells us for each individual agent and each individual action whether or not the agent ought to perform the action. S is silent about which group actions ought to be done. But then, by our earlier arguments, S is impoverished as a *moral* theory, whatever its merits may be as a description of human behaviour.

The obvious approach for an S theorist to take towards the moral assessment of group acts is to average benefits and costs across the relevant agents. In assessing what I ought to do, we entertain a bias totally in favour of me, for you we bias in favour of you, but for what you and I together ought to do, we eliminate preferential treatment between us, though presumably we still favour us as opposed to others. Let's call this theory 'S-with-averaging-for-group-acts'. It is this theory I hold is in deep trouble. It inevitably violates (P).

Consider the following prisoner's dilemma type of situation.

| | | you | |
		A	B
me	A	3rd best for me 3rd best for you	best for me 4th best for you
	B	best for you 4th best for me	2nd best for me 2nd best for you

According to S with (or without) averaging, I ought to do A and you ought to do A. For doing A benefits each of us regardless of what the other does. Now, what about what you and I together ought to do: which group act is right for us? Obviously, it cannot be our both doing A, because something else – our both doing B – is better for *both*, so that S with averaging must rank the latter above the former. Moreover, and consistently with this, on any reasonable way of averaging, we can choose the benefits so that second-best for both comes out ahead of best for one combined with fourth-best for the other. The conclusion is that S with averaging can make our both doing B the right group act at the same time as making my doing A and your doing A the right individual actions. The violation of (P) is now patent. Suppose we in fact both do B. We do the right group act. Hence, by (P), the constituent individual acts should also both be right. It should also be true that my doing B and your doing B are the right individual acts. But, by S, even if we both do B, it is still the case that the right thing for me to do is A, and for you to do is A. S with averaging runs foul of the highly plausible (P).[16]

Notes

1   It does not matter for what follows whether this should be spelt out further in terms of *identity* or in terms of a relation of *constitution* between a group action and its individual actions not analysable in terms of identity.

2   I take the distinction between subjective rightness and wrongness and objective rightness and wrongness to be non-controversial, though precisely how to draw it is not, see, for example, Richard Brandt, *Ethical Theory*, Prentice Hall, Englewood Cliffs, N.J., 1959, ch. 14. In my discussion of some of Derek Parfit's views in *Reasons and Persons*, Oxford, Oxford University Press, 1986, later in this paper, I have interpreted him in terms of objective rightness and wrongness. I think that this is the correct (or correctable, without damage to the points at issue) way to interpret these views. But I should point out that early in *Reasons and Persons* (p. 25) he says 'In most of what follows, I shall use *right, ought, good*, and *bad* in the objective sense. But *wrong* will usually mean *subjectively* wrong, or *blameworthy*.'

3   Or perhaps 'our opening all the wine *actually* on the table' does the trick.

4   Parfit, *Reasons and Persons*, p. 68.

5   Slightly modified from Parfit, *Reasons and Persons*, p. 70.

6   Parfit, *Reasons and Persons*, p. 70. Parfit is, of course, aware that he needs to give an account of the relevant notion of a *collection*, see pp. 71–2, but my discussion is independent of his account.

7   Slightly modified from Jonathan Glover, 'It makes no difference whether or not I do it', *Aristotelian Society Supplementary Volume* XLIX (1975), pp. 171–90. Parfit acknowledges the example's influence on his thought in *Reasons and Persons*, p. 511n. Glover does not use the example to discredit the difference principle as such. He uses the example to discredit ignoring very small – perhaps unnoticeable – differences. Parfit, though, gives the example – or rather certain variants on it – both roles. See his discussion in *Reasons and Persons*, p. 80. I say nothing here about how to handle the ethics of making very small differences.

8   More precisely, this is what Parfit should and, I take it, would say about the case given what he says about the variants on it.

9   I should point out that, judging by his discussion of the second case, *Reasons and Persons*, pp.70–1, Parfit would not regard this result as disastrous.

10 For a good deal more on this kind of case and associated issues, see Frank Jackson, 'On the semantics and logic of obligation', *Mind*, XCIV, 274, pp. 177–96 (1985), and Frank Jackson and Robert Pargetter, 'Oughts, options, and actualism', *Philosophical Review*, XCV, 2, pp. 233–55 (1986).

11 This kind of example is discussed in Michael Stocker, '"Ought" and "can"', *Australasian Journal of Philosophy*, 49, 3, pp. 303–16 (1971), and Robert Young, *Freedom, Responsibility and God*, London, Macmillan, 1975, ch. 2.

12 Made familiar through the work of J. J. C. Smart in particular, see for example *Philosophy and Scientific Realism*, London, Routledge and Kegan Paul, ch. vii.

13 This treatment also illuminates certain tricky cases where an action only leads to the best if it is appropriately followed up, and although it *could* be so followed up, it *would not* be. Professor Procrastinate receives an invitation in January to review a book. What is best is for him to say yes and complete the review in time, which he could do. But in fact were he to say yes, he would not complete the review in time. As a result, it would be better for him to say no to the inviation so that the book could be sent straight to Dr Efficiency. What ought Procrastinate to do in January? This question is most naturally read as asking what Procrastinate's January part ought to do, to which the answer is to decline the invitation. But it can also be read as asking what the January part of the extended programme that the temporally extended Procrastinate ought to follow is, in which case the answer is accept the invitation. (This treatment is consonant with, but clearer than, our treatment of the case of Procrastinate; see Jackson and Pargetter, 'Oughts, options, and actualism'.)

14 Parfit, *Reasons and Persons*, ch. 5. One obvious difference is that I hold that the argument to follow refutes the relevant version of the self-interest theory. As I will be using the term, to show that a theory is self-refuting is *ipso facto* to refute it.

15 The force of this argument depends on your being at least sympathetic to identifying what ought to be done with the best available action. Also, for simplicity, I have assumed that we don't have ties.

16 Earlier versions of parts of this chapter were read at seminars at Monash, Otago, ANU, Wollongong, and to the AAP conference at Monash in 1986. On each occasion the discussion led me to make a number of significant changes, too many to acknowledge, or indeed remember, fully, but I must mention John Burnheim, Richard Campbell, Lanning Sowden, Kim Sterelny, and most especially Lloyd Humberstone and David Lewis. It will, I trust, be obvious how indebted I am to the stimulation of, and the stimulation of disagreeing with, the relevant parts of Parfit's *Reasons and Persons*.

7

The Singularly Affecting Facts of Causation

D. H. Mellor

I

Few now agree with Bertrand Russell that modern science can do without the notion of cause.[1] It may tell us that causes need only make their effects more probable, not determine them, but that just extends the notion. That there are causes is a hypothesis science still has need of, if only to make sense of the experiments by which it is tested and the technologies in which it is applied.

Physicalists like Jack Smart will thus seek a physical basis, such as energy transfer, for causation itself.[2] The basis may in turn need causes, but that need be no problem. Energy transfers, for example, could always be linked by other energy transfers to their causes and effects. Or the basis could vary from case to case, as the molecular basis of solubility and other dispositions does. Causation can always have a basis without always having the same basis.

But what basis? That looks like an empirical question, as it does for dispositions: finding out what makes salt soluble is a job for scientists, not philosophers. Before seeking bases for dispositions, however, we must ask if they need them, and if so of what kind. Those are philosophical questions, whose answers turn on what dispositions are. Broad's dispositions need microstructural bases;[3] Ryle's need nothing;[4] and Goodman's need events.[5] The bases, if any, we ascribe to dispositions depend on how we conceive them.[6]

Similarly with causation. The search for its bases, if any, must be guided by a conception of it, and may be misguided by a misconception. One such misconception is Davidson's influential thesis that singular causation relates events rather than facts.[7] Suppose for example Don's climbing rope breaks half way up a cliff, he falls 200 metres on to rocks, and dies instantly as a result. Davidson would say that the causes and effects here are the events, Don's fall and his death, not the facts, that Don fell and that he died. I say that is wrong. Don's fall did cause his death, but only because Don died because he fell. Causation relates those events only because it relates those facts; and most causation relates facts without relating events at all. Why that is so, why it matters, and how it affects what causation is and what its bases may be, are what this chapter is about.

II

First the questions need clarifying. For a start, they only concern singular cases of causation like the one above, not, for example, the claim that falls like Don's are a general cause of death. Whatever singular causes and effects are, their general counterparts (falling, dying) will be the same: neither events nor facts but properties.[8] So we need not discuss general causation, and by 'causation' hereafter I mean the singular kind.

Next I must say what I take events and facts to be. 'Event' especially is now a term of art, and different artists use it differently. I, like Davidson, take events like Don's fall and his death to be particulars: entities picked out by names, definite descriptions or other singular terms. In that respect they are just like people and things – like Don himself, for example, and his hat.

Facts by contrast make whole sentences, statements, thoughts or propositions true. This is not, I should say, a correspondence theory of truth: facts are defined in terms of truth, not vice versa. Facts might perhaps be further analysed, but not here. All that matters here is that facts are not events, because they are not particulars of any kind.

Facts and particulars are, I believe, causation's only relata. They certainly encompass their obvious rivals. States of affairs, for example, like Don's falling and his dying, must obtain in order to be causes and effects: that is, the corresponding propositions, that Don falls and that he dies, must be true. In other words, those states of affairs must be facts.[9] So, *pace* Sanford,[10] must 'event aspects', for example those emphasized in 'Don's falling *fast* caused him to die *instantly*', which says that Don's death was instant because his fall was fast (see VII below). This indeed differs from saying that Don died because he fell, but the cause and effect are still facts: that Don fell fast, and that he died instantly. Aspects of events, which are properties if they are general, are facts if they are singular. And so, I submit, are all causes and effects that are not particulars: what else could they be?

But events, I agree, are particulars. The events – Don's fall and his death – differ from the facts that he fell and that he died. So it is a real question which causation links, and if both, how the links are related. That in turn will depend on how such facts and such events are related, a relation that I agree with Davidson[11] Ramsey rightly stated:

> 'That Caesar died' is really an existential proposition, asserting the existence of an event of a certain sort, thus resembling 'Italy has a king', which asserts the existence of a man of a certain sort. The event which is of that sort is called the death of Caesar, and should no more be confused with the fact that Caesar died than the King of Italy should be confused with the fact that Italy has a king.[12]

Having thus prevented both confusions, we can return to our question, which is not whether causation relates events as opposed to people and other things, but whether it relates particulars of either kind. It is put in terms of events only because there are too few things like Don and his hat to go round. Causes and effects can all be particulars only if events like Don's fall and his death are also particulars, and some would deny Davidson's thesis by denying that. But not I: I deny only that such particulars supply the primary relata of causation; and thinking that they do is by no means the only reason for believing in them.[13]

I believe causes and effects include both facts and particular events. But causes and effects are, confusingly, also called events by some authors for whom they are really facts.[14] Now these in themselves are just rival uses of 'event' which I could simply disclaim. But backing them are identity criteria, for causally related entities like Don's fall and his death, that make them facts, and which need rebutting; not because better ones make them particulars, but because such entities, whether facts or events, neither have nor need any special criterion of identity. However, since Davidson, Kim and many others think they do, I must digress to say why they don't.[15]

In denying particular events a special identity criterion I am not saying they are just like things, still less that both are 'individuated to perfection by spatiotemporal coextensiveness'.[16] Nor do I agree with Davidson that they differ from things merely in grammar.[17] The grammatical distinction has a basis in reality: events, when extended in time, have temporal parts, and things do not.[18] That is what lets events be changes in things,[19] and thus be the actions[20] and the other happenings that we associate with verbs.

But this does not make events 'a fundamental ontological category'.[21] Fundamental to grammar it may be, but not to ontology. Maybe (*pace* Ramsey[22]) particulars and universals form two fundamental categories, and maybe concrete particulars and abstract ones like numbers and sets form two more. But not concrete particulars with and without temporal parts. At any rate, the 'category' of events needs no criterion of identity to defend it. How could it, when the paradigm 'category' of things has none? Things after all range from quarks, through molecules, cells, organisms, societies, mountains and planets, to clusters of galaxies. There is no one way to individuate particular things of all these kinds: each kind has its own criterion. And so do the equally multifarious kinds of particular events, ranging from quantum events, through molecular and cellular interactions, births, wars and avalanches, to explosions of supernovae. And as Quine says, events like explosions are as well individuated by their criteria as things like mountains are by theirs: one cannot deny particularity to events on that score without also denying it to things.[23]

There are criteria of identity for events of all kinds, but they are not all the same. And they do not distinguish events collectively from things. What does distinguish events – their having temporal parts – is not a criterion of identity. Nor is Davidson's thesis that events are distinct (i) when, and (ii) only when, some of their causes or effects are – a thesis that does not even distinguish events from facts.[24] For (i) is just the 'diversity of discernibles': entities of any kind that differ in some cause or effect are distinct, because all entities are distinct that differ in any way. And (ii) is as likely to be true of things and facts with causes and effects as it is of events: how, after all, would we distinguish causal entities of any kind that do not differ in cause or effect, when we only perceive anything *via* its effects?

Davidson's 'criterion' in short is as trite, and as ineffective as it is needless. But some of its rivals are all too effective, because they stop events being particulars at all. Thus Kim, who calls causes and effects 'events', defines an event as a thing having a property at a time.[25] But that cannot individuate *particular* events, because it makes events facts, by making them make sentences true: namely, those ascribing properties to things at times. Hence Kim's variant use of 'event' for a kind of fact. His use is not of course improper, 'event' being as it is a term of art. But it is misleading, because the word has also long meant a kind of particular, not only in Davidson but way back, long before my 1927 Ramsey quotation above. And for authors now to apply 'event' with both connotations to causes and effects, while disputing whether they are particulars or facts, makes the word seriously ambiguous. But not hopeless, provided each of us says what he means by it. And what I mean by it is what Davidson means: my events, like his, are all particulars.

III

I will take it then that Don's fall and his death are particular events, if only to give Davidson a run for his money. The question is whether causation relates those events, or the facts that Don fell and then he died. But how do we decide? English usage is no guide: 'Don's fall caused his death' and 'Don died because he fell' are equally idiomatic. Most statements of causation sound as well in either form:

(1) '*c* causes *e*'

which represents cause and effect as events, referred to by the singular terms '*c*' and '*e*'; *or*

(2) '*E* because *C*'

in which sentences '*C*' and '*E*' state the cause and effect – and state them as *facts*, since '*E* because *C*' always entails both of them. (Everyone will agree that Don cannot have died because he fell unless it is a fact that he fell and a fact that he died.)

For the present (1) and (2) will be my canonical forms of causal statement, representing causal relata respectively as events and facts. But before using them in my argument I must defend them, (2) especially, against some common but misplaced objections. The obvious objection is that many causal statements are not of either form, like the example in section II above: 'Don's falling fast caused him to die instantly.' But we can always recast them to fit, as we saw in that case, simply to show what we take their relata to be: events or facts. We must just see that the fit is not too procrustean, that the recasting begs no relevant questions.

Some recasting must be in order. For example, since we see causation – like everything else – only when it is past, we habitually report it as past: 'Don's fall *caused* his death'; 'Don *died* because he *fell*'. But we are considering causation at all times, not just past ones. So in (1) and (2) I assume an atemporal present tense: the canonical forms of our examples will be:

(3) 'Don's fall *causes* his death'

(4) 'Don *dies* because he *falls*'

These forms beg no questions about causation's temporal implications: it remains an open question, for example, whether (1) and (2) respectively entail '*c* precedes *e*' and '*E* after *C*' (see VIII below).

But I go further, as I did in II. I count as type (2) many statements seemingly of mixed type, like 'Don's falling caused him to die', or of type (1), like 'Don's fast fall caused his instant death.' In such cases even

Davidson[26] agrees with Vendler[27] that the singular terms are really 'occurrences of verb-nominalizations that are fact-like or propositional', and admits that 'caused' is being used as a connective. But when it is being used like that, that is what it is. These statements really *are* type (2): trivial variants of 'Don dies because he falls' and 'Don dies instantly because he falls fast'.

Some recasting I do resist, especially of my type (2) into Davidson's[28]

(5) 'The fact that C caused it to be the case that E'

(5) is not only turgid, it misrepresents the thesis that causation relates facts. The thesis is not that causation relates entities referred to by singular terms like 'the fact that C': that makes facts look like a kind of particular, which is what is being denied. It is that causes and effects are reported by sentences like 'C' and 'E', and – as is undeniable – that for (2) or (5) to be true, 'C' and 'E' must be true. The facts that (2) or (5) say are related are whatever make 'C' and 'E' true; and any account of facts that accounts for truth will account for them. Causal facts need no special criterion of identity, such as Kim's in II, to justify (5)'s gratuitous reference to them. Why should they, when (as we saw in II) events have none, and none is needed, either for events or for causal facts, to make them identical just when their causes and effects are?

The only appeal of (5) is that it reports nothing but causation, whereas statements of type (2) are also used to report proofs (for example, 'there is no greater prime number, because if there were there would be a greater one, because . . . ') and generally to give explanations, not all of which are causal. 'Because' is not an exclusively causal connective.

Why should it be? We are not trying to define a causal connective, only to say whether causation is reported by *a* connective. And if it is, 'because' is the obvious one. It clearly has a causal use, some of whose rules are easy enough to state: for instance, that in a causal 'E because C', as opposed to a proof, 'C' and 'E' must be logically independent and thus contingent. No doubt there is more to it, but we need not say what. All we need is the fact that 'because' has a distinctive causal use. Given that, we can restrict type (2) statements to causal ones by fiat: which I hereby do. And that, given (5)'s other defects, makes (2) the incontestably canonical way to report causal relations between facts.

IV

However, statements of type (2) cannot be used to report causal relations between facts if, as Davidson says, there are none to report. What else might they be used for? Davidson says they are used to give causal *explanations*: the causal connective 'is best expressed by the words "causally explains"'.[29] That is, his type (5) is really:

(6) 'The fact that *C* causally explains the fact that *E*'

Facts are the relata, not of causation, but of causal explanation.

Now we may all distinguish causation from causal explanation; but to explain away causal statements of type (2), Davidson needs more than a distinction: he needs a dichotomy. His causal *explanantia* can neither be nor correspond to causes, nor his causal *explananda* to effects. This is hard to believe. That causes generally explain their effects is a strong connotation of causation, which explains why we use the explanatory connective 'because' to report it, and why (5), while differing from (6), can still entail

(7) 'The fact that *C* explains the fact that *E*'

Denying that causal explanations report causal relations makes a mystery of all this; and that counts against Davidson's thesis.

There is worse to come. Let us ask what makes (6) differ from non-causal instances of (7), that is, what makes (6) a *causal* explanation? Davidson cannot appeal to the causal relation (which I claim (6) reports) between the fact that *C* and the fact that *E*. For him, the causation must come from a causal relation between particulars *c* and *e* that are somehow suitably related to these facts.

In our example, the particulars, and their relation to the explanatory facts, are obvious enough. If Don dies [*E*] because Don falls [*C*], that explanation can be made causal by Don's fall [*c*] causing his death [*e*]. '*C*' here is related to *c*, and '*E*' to *e*, as 'an existential proposition asserting the existence of an event of a certain sort' is related to 'the event which is of that sort',[30] the sorts being respectively falls by Don and deaths of Don. The causation linking *c* and *e*, which by being of these sorts verify the existential '*C*' and '*E*', is what for Davidson makes '*E* because *C*' a causal explanation.

So far, so good. But '*C*' and '*E*' need not assert the existence of events. They may deny it. Suppose Don managed to hang on when his rope broke, and so did *not* die, because he did not fall. That would be as causal an explanation as 'Don dies because he falls'. But '*C*' and '*E*' now assert that no falls by Don or deaths of Don exist. They are negative existential statements, verified by the *non*-existence of such events, and *a fortiori* of causally related ones. Where is the relation between events that Davidson needs to make this explanation causal?

We could of course recast the explanation to remove the negation in it, for example:

(8) 'Don survives because he hangs on'

This seems to generate causally related events: Don's hanging on and his surviving. But these are really negative events, existing only by definition, when real events do not, to be the particular relata of causation that Davidson needs and would otherwise lack. Don's survival is simply his non-death; his hanging on, his non-fall.

And, negative events cannot be particulars, because there *are* no negative particulars. Although the non-existence of negative people and things is well recognized,[31] that of events is less so – doubtless because, as we saw in II, many so-called 'events' are not particulars at all. But Davidson's are, and he can no more have negative events than negative people, as I will show using Ramsey's comparison from II.

First, people: the existential statement 'Italy has a married King' entails 'Italy has a King', because no one can be both a King of Italy and married without being a King of Italy. However, the entailments of negative existential statements go the other way: 'Italy has no King' entails 'Italy has no married King' – and 'Italy has no unmarried King'. The reason is obvious: if no particular person is King of Italy, no married one is, and no unmarried one is. But now suppose 'Italy has no King' is made true by a single 'negative person', the 'non-King' of Italy, who exists just when Italy has no King. To make 'Italy has no King' entail both 'Italy has no married King' and 'Italy has no unmarried King', the non-King will have to be both married and unmarried. But he cannot be both: so he does not exist.

Similarly for events. The existential statement 'Don dies instantly' entails 'Don dies', because no event can be both a death of Don and instant without being a death of Don.[32] But here too the entailments of negative existential statements go the other way: 'Don does not die' entails both 'Don does not die instantly' – and 'Don does not die slowly'. Again, the reason is obvious: if no particular event is Don's death, then no instant one is, and no slow one is. But now suppose 'Don does not die' is made true by a single 'negative event', Don's non-death, which exists just when Don is not dying. To make 'Don does not die' entail both 'Don does not die instantly' and 'Don does not die slowly', Don's non-death will have to be both instant and slow; but it cannot be both, so it does not exist.

In short, if deaths and falls are particulars, non-deaths and non-falls are not. One could of course debate which the particulars are – deaths and falls, or survivings and hangings on – but it would not help. For either way only one of the explanations,

(4) 'Don dies because he falls'

(8) 'Don survives because he hangs on'

can be made causal by a causal relation between particular events. Yet each looks as causal as the other. It is most implausible to say that if (4) is a causal statement, (8) cannot be, and vice versa. But that is the inevitable consequence of limiting causes and effects to events.

The causal parity evident in many pairs of cases like (4) and (8) has elicited many of the literature's rival relata, including those referred to in II. Thus Kim can easily let both (4) and (8) be causal.[33] Dying and surviving are both properties Don can have, so his having either at a time counts for Kim as a causal event. But then, as we saw, Kim's 'events' are really facts, not particulars, and so are Sanford's 'event aspects'.[34] And that is what lets them cope with (4) and (8).

Both (4) and (8) can report causal relations between facts because 'negative facts' are still facts. Whenever 'C' and 'E', entailed by a causal

(2) 'E because 'C'

are false, '$\sim C$' and '$\sim E$' are true; and the facts they state may then be causally related:

(2') '$\sim E$ because $\sim C$'

may be true.

It cannot of course be the case that (2) and (2') are true together, but only because '$C\&E$' and '$\sim C\ \&\ \sim E$' cannot be. Nothing stops (2) being true when 'C' and 'E' are true, and (2') being true when they are false. In our example, though (4) and (8) cannot both be true, (4) may well be true if Don dies and falls, and (8) if he hangs on and survives: and both can be *causal*; that is, made true, when they are, by causal relations between the facts they entail. It makes no odds which of those facts is 'positive' and which 'negative'. Whether (4) or (8) is the instance of (2) (or there is no fact of that matter), the causation will be the same. As a type of causal statement, (2') is no different from (2).

The ability of (2) to make (4) and (8) equally causal strongly suggests that causation relates facts as well as events. But a notorious argument of Davidson's purports to prove that it cannot. We must now see what is wrong with it.[35]

V

Davidson's proof starts from a truism, that 'E because C' cannot be a complete truth function of 'E' and 'C'. It is a partial truth function, we know: false whenever 'C' or 'E' is false. But when 'C' and 'E' are true, it is neither always true nor always false. If it were, either all facts would be causally related or none would be, and no one who thinks causation relates some facts thinks it relates them all. 'E because C' must be true for some true 'C' and 'E' and false for others, the real problem of causation being to say for which. But, Davidson argues, a *causal* 'E because C' would *have* to be a complete truth-function of 'C' and 'E';[36] but it cannot be. So there is no such thing: 'E because C' is not the 'logical form' of causal statements.

Davidson's argument fails to show that a causal 'E because C' must be truth-functional, because at least one of its two assumptions is false. These are that a true causal 'E because C' would never be falsified by replacing either (i) 'C' or 'E' by logically equivalent statements, or (ii) singular terms by others referring to the same particulars. And Davidson also assumes that since (i) and (ii) concern only the logical form of causal statements, they are independent of how causation itself is analysed.[37]

That is his first mistake. It is a logician's conceit that causation's logical form can be fixed without analysis. How could it be? How, if not by analysis, can the logic of a concept be uncovered? In particular, consider how probabilistic analyses of causation may affect Davidson's assumption (i). Many of us now appeal to probability to say for which true 'C' and 'E' 'E because C' is true,[38] and I think a necessary condition is this: (P) 'E' must be more probable (that is, more probably true) than it would be in the circumstances if 'C' were false. I shall not try to prove (P), but it at least shows what an analysis of causation can yield; and if it is true, (i) will be true only if logical equivalents never differ in probability. But that will depend on whether the probability is subjective or objective. I dare say the objective probabilities of logical equivalents never differ. But subjective ones do, because subjective probability measures the strength of our beliefs; and unless I *believe* that two statements are equivalent, I may well believe one more strongly than the other.

So the truth of (i) may well turn on the kind of probability (if any) that causes give their effects, and that depends on the analysis of causation and probability. Many analysts[39] argue, like Hume, for subjective analyses that would make (i) false. I disagree. I think causation needs objective probabilities for several reasons (I give one in VII), and that (i) may well be true. But it is not just a question of logical form.

However, (ii) is false, even as a matter of form, whatever kind of probability causation needs. Davidson's only argument for it is that in two cases replacing one singular term by another referring to the same particular does not falsify a causal statement, but that hardly shows it *never* does. And, as Timothy Smiley has made me see, when 'C' or 'E' in 'E because C' is a contingent identity statement, of the form (say) 'the F = the G', it must do. For since 'E because C' entails 'C' and 'E', it entails here that 'the F' and 'the G' refer to the same particular. So if (ii) were true, replacing either by the other in a true 'E because C' would not falsify it. But it would, by generating (for instance) 'the F = the F because C', which is false, since 'the F = the F' is a necessary truth, and necessary facts have neither causes nor effects.

But do real causal statements ever take this form? Well, suppose in our example that several climbers fall, but that Don falls first because his rope is the weakest. That is,

(9) 'Don's fall is the first fall because Don's rope is the weakest rope'

is true. It follows that Don's is indeed the first fall, and that his rope is the weakest. So 'Don's fall' and 'the first fall' refer to the same event, and 'Don's rope' and 'the weakest rope' refer to the same thing. So if (ii) were true, all the following would be true:

(10) 'Don's fall is Don's fall because his rope is the weakest'

(11) 'The first fall is the first fall because Don's rope is the weakest'

(12) 'Don falls first because his rope is his rope'

(13) 'Don falls first because the weakest rope is the weakest rope'

Yet (10) to (13) are clearly false.

I cannot believe that (9) and many other such cases, which the reader can easily think of, are not causal. Nor could Davidson account for them by calling them causal explanations. For they, like (8), cannot be made causal by a causal relation between particulars. Indeed (9) does, unlike (8), refer to particulars, but we still cannot get from it a relevant truth of type (1). In

'Don's rope being the weakest caused his fall to be the first'

for example, 'Don's rope being the weakest' is a nominalized sentence, not a singular term. It does more than refer to Don's rope: it asserts in the context that his rope is the weakest. And so it must, for what (9) says is that each of two particulars satisfies two given descriptions – and that one does so because the other does. That is why this causal claim depends for its truth on how these particulars are referred to, which a report of a relation between them would not do.

All this, incidentally, is explained by my probability condition (P), since the opacity of (9) is a feature of subjective and objective probabilities alike. (P) says that, if (9) is true, the probability of Don's falling first must be greater than it would be in the circumstances if his was not the weakest rope; and that is doubtless true. But the probability of Don's fall being Don's fall, and of the first fall being the first fall, will be 1 whether Don's is the weakest rope or not: (10) and (11) fail condition (P). And so do (12) and (13), because (P) makes their truth depend on the probability p of Don's falling first if (say) his rope were *not* his rope, being less than it actually is (say 0.9). Now the status of such counterfactuals, with logically impossible antecedents, is debatable: they may be true for all values of p,[40] or false, or have no truth value. But anyway p will have no unique value, or range of values, less than 0.9 or even than 1.

The opacity of (9), and (P)'s explanation of it, do more than refute Davidson's assumption (ii). They show where and how his argument for the truth-functionality of 'E because C' fails. The argument is this: (i) 'E because C' entails any statement got by replacing 'E' (or 'C') by any logical equivalent. But 'E' is logically equivalent to '$\{x:x=x\&E\} = \{x:x=x\}$', because '$\{x:x=x\&E\}$' refers to the set of everything, $(x:x=x)$, just when 'E' is true. So 'E because C' entails '$\{x:x=x\&E\} = \{x:x=x\}$ because C'; but (ii) this entails any statement got from it by replacing a singular term by another referring to the same particular. But for any statement 'T' sharing 'E''s truth value, '$\{x:x=x\&T\}$' and '$\{x:x=x\&E\}$' refer to the same particular, namely the set of everything if 'E' is true, and the null set if not. So 'E because C' entails '$\{x:x=x\&T\} = \{x:x=x\}$ because C' and hence, applying (i) again, 'T because C'. And since the argument applies equally to replacements for 'C', 'E because C' entails 'T because S' for all 'T' and 'S' that share 'E''s and 'C''s truth values. So a causal 'because' would be a complete truth function – which it cannot be.

The falsity of (ii) here, and thus the argument's invalidity, is made obvious by the analogue of (9). Even if (i) is true, and 'E because C' entails '$\{x:x=x\&E\} = \{x:x=x\}$ because C', that no more entails '$\{x:x=x\} = \{x:x=x\}$ because C' than (9) entails (11). The fact that the set of everything = the set of everything no more has a cause (or effect) than do the facts that Don's fall = his fall and his rope = his rope – and for the same probabilistic reasons.

The falsity of (ii) also lets many contingently true replacements for 'E' and 'C' falsify a true '$\{x:x=x\&E\} = \{x:x=x\}$ because C' or 'E because $\{x:x=x\&C\} = \{x:x=x\}$', and again (P) explains why. Probabilities are not truth functions – truths are not all equally probable, even if logical equivalents are – and nor are counterfactuals. A contingent 'T' may share 'E''s truth and still differ from 'E' by being no more probable than it would be if 'C' were false. But then replacing 'E' by 'T' in 'E because C' and '$\{x:x=x\&E\} = \{x:x=E\}$ because C' will make them fail condition (P). Likewise, a contingent 'S' may share 'C''s truth and still differ from it in that 'E' would be no less probable if 'S' were false. Again, replacing 'C' by 'S' in 'E because C' and 'E because $\{x:x=x\&C\} = \{x:x=x\}$' will make them fail condition (P). And this, I submit, is why replacing 'Don dies' or 'Don falls' by most other truths in a true 'Don dies because Don falls' only generates falsehoods, like 'Kim lives because Don falls' or 'Don dies because Kim doesn't fall.' The reason is that 'Kim lives' would be no less probable if Don didn't fall, and 'Don dies' no less probable if Kim did.

All these cases are grist to a probabilist's mill. And every argument for causation needing some kind of probability reinforces type (2)'s claim to be the primary form of causal statements. Probability of any kind is probability of truth, which means it can attach to facts, but not to particulars. Bearers of probability, like a tossed coin landing heads up, are admittedly often called 'events', but they are not particulars, any more than Kim's 'events' in II were. They correspond not to singular terms but to sentences ('the coin lands heads up') that when true state facts. If effects are to have probabilities, causation not only may be reported by type (2) statements: it must be.

However, I need not argue that case here. Even if nothing like (P) is true, the falsity of (ii), evident in Davidson's own argument, refutes him by showing that a causal 'E because C' need not be the complete truth function we know it cannot be. Then (9) unites with (8) to show, regardless of probability, that facts can be causally related when particular events are not. Not all the relata of causation are events.

VI

But some are. There are truths of type (1), 'c causes e', as well as of type (2), and when the two go together, as in (3) and (4), they are not independent. It is no coincidence that causation links Don's fall to his death just when it links the fact that he falls to the fact that he dies. If (4)'s causation does not reduce to (3)'s, (3)'s must reduce to (4)'s; but how? How can relations between events reduce to relations between facts? We saw in V that some type (2) statements are opaque: their truth depends on how they refer to their particulars. But type (1) statements cannot be opaque. A relation between particulars must hold however its relata are described, or it would not relate them. So the statement that it holds must be transparent, that is, true whatever terms are used to refer to its relata. And that is true of type (1) statements: 'c causes e' is not made false by replacing 'c' or 'e' by other terms referring to c or e. If Don's fall causes his death and he is the oldest and fattest climber, then the oldest climber's fall causes the fattest one's death. Thus (3) is transparent, because it reports a relation between particulars.

How then could (3) follow from (4)? The problem here is not the argument disposed of in V. That could not apply to (3), which has no constituent statements of whose truth its own could be a function. Transparency is not a problem in type (1) statements; it just makes it hard for them to follow from statements of type (2), and mostly they do not follow: most type (2) truths, like (8) and (9), generate no truths of type (1). However, some do: those, like (4), whose constituents 'C' and 'E' are existential statements about events. That makes their opacity harmless, because despite entailing the existence of events of certain sorts, they do not refer to them; and that lets transparent truths of type (1), about those events, follow.

To see how this works, consider (4), 'Don dies because Don falls'. 'Don falls' and 'Don dies' do not refer to the events, Don's fall and his death, which (3) says are related as cause to effect. So (4) cannot be made false by replacing terms referring to these events – because there are no such terms. What (4) entails is merely that events of specific sorts – falls by Don [F] and deaths of Don [G] – exist, and we may take it that there is only one of each sort: one fall by Don and one death of Don. Call these unique F and G events 'f' and 'g'. Then the following are true:

(14) 'There is a G event because there is an F event'

(15) 'f = the F event'

(16) 'g = the G event'

And I claim that (14)–(16) entail

(17) 'f causes g'

But not of course conversely: (17) does not entail (14)–(16). What (17) entails (and is entailed by) is the existence of *some* sorts of events X and Y for which the following are all true:

(18) 'f is the X event'

(19) 'g is the Y event'

(20) 'There is a Y event because there is an X event'

F and G are in fact the sorts of event that make (20) and hence (17) true, but they need not be. Any X and Y that make (18)–(20) true (and are essential to the existence of f and g – see VI below) will do.

These entailments, as Jeremy Butterfield has pointed out, entail (17)'s transparency. If 'j' and 'k' are any singular terms referring respectively to f and g, (17) entails the existence of a suitable X and Y for which not only (18) and (19) are true, but also

(18') 'j is the X event',

(19') '*k* is the *Y* event',

With (20) this would entail

(17') '*j* causes *k*'

This shows how the transparent (3) follows from (4). It also shows how causation here really relates the facts, not the events; *f* and *g* only supply the relata of causation (by making it true that there are *F* and *G* events), not the relation itself. These existential facts need not be related as cause to effect; and if they are, it is not because *f* and *g* are. It is the other way round: the events just inherit the causal relation of the facts they supply. It does not even matter that *they* supply those facts: any *F* and *G* events could make (14) true. They need not be *f* and *g*, since being *F* and *G* does not fix their identity: they will have other properties on which their identity may depend. Don's fall and his death could easily differ sufficiently (from his actual fall and death) to be different events, without falsifying (14).

Like any other such sort *X* or *Y*, *F* and *G* (being a fall by Don and a death of Don) have of course to conjoin general properties with some limitation to get the uniqueness (18) and (19) need. The limitation may be explicit '(*Don* dies') or assumed. We assume, for example, that 'Don dies' suffices, because most people only die once (contrast 'Dracula died *last time* because . . . '). Similarly, we assume, Don dies of only one fall, for example, his fall in June 1970, on Mont Blanc.

The real question about *X* and *Y* is what general properties they may include: those, I assume, that figure in natural laws. In (17), for example, *f* and *g* should at least instantiate statistical laws to satisfy condition (P), that is, to ensure that in the circumstances (200 metres up a cliff) the probability of a death would be greater with a fall than without one. In short, I think Davidson is right[42] to claim that though statements of type (1), '*c* causes *e*', 'entail no law . . . they entail there is a law,' if only a statistical one.

VII

So much for (1), '*c* causes *e*'; but there are other transparent types of causal statement. There is the neglected

(21) '*c* affects *e*'

and even, as we shall see, a transparent species of type (2), '*E* because *C*'.

The difference of (1) from (21) involves the existence of the events *c* and *e*; implying, as (21) does not, that the existence of *c* causes *e* to exist as well. And (14)–(16) entail an instance of (1) because, though F and G do not fix the identity of the F and the G events, those events still need those properties. If Don did not fall and die, f and g would not exist. That is why their causal relation involves their existence, so that Don's death is not merely affected, but is caused, by his fall.

Causal properties need not be essential properties, however. Take this statement:

(22) 'Don dies instantly [I] because he falls fast [H]'

That is,

(23) 'There is a G & I event because there is an F & H event'

Again assuming one F and one G event, this implies:

(24) 'The F event is H'

(25) 'The G event is I'

And (23)–(25) I say entail

(26) 'The G event is I because the F event is H'

which asserts that Don's death is instant because his fall is fast.

Being H and I are not essential properties of F and G events. Don's fall and his death could each be less swift and still be the same event. (22)'s causation does not involve their existence, only their being H and I – what Sanford[42] calls 'aspects' of them (see II). Which is why (26) entails not (3), 'Don's fall causes his death', but only

(27) 'Don's fall affects his death'

In short, causing is done by essential properties, affecting by inessential ones. When X and Y in (2) are essential to the X and Y events c and e, c causes e; and when they aren't, it affects it – with something like (26) saying what the effect is. So in general (20) only entails, of whatever c and e are the X and Y events,

(28) 'c causes *or* affects e'

Whether in a given case (1) or (21) makes (28) true (or there is no fact of that matter) is not a question of causation, and so not relevant to the present point – though, as we shall see in VIII, it bears on the relation between events and times.

What is to the present point is that (27), like other instances of (21), is as transparent as (3). And so is (26), despite being of type (2). Replacing its singular terms by others referring to the same events will not falsify it. It even entails

(29) 'Don's instant death is instant because his fall is fast'

which is not false, as the assertion from V is false:

(10) 'Don's fall is his fall because his rope is the weakest'

precisely because instantaneity is inessential to Don's death. 'Don's instant death is instant,' unlike 'Don's fall is his fall', might have been false. So it can, as (29) claims, be true in fact because Don's fall is fast.

The evident transparency of statements like (26) is what makes many, like Davidson, think that all type (2) statements are transparent. But (26) is a special case; like (17), it is only transparent because the statement, (23), that makes it causal does not refer to its events. They are referred to only in (24) and (25), whose transparency lets (26) be transparent as follows. To be transparent, (26) must entail

(30) 'k is I because j is H'

where 'j' and 'k' are any singular terms referring respectively to the F and the G event. But (26) and (30) are of type (2), 'E because C', which entails 'C' and 'E'. So (26) entails (24), 'the F event is H', and (25), 'the G event is I', and (30) entails:

(31) 'j is H'

(32) 'k is I'

To entail (30), (26) must therefore also entail (31) and (32), which it does by entailing (24) and (25), since their transparency makes them in turn respectively entail (31) and (32).

This account of (26)'s transparency should dispel the illusion that it shows a general transparency in type (2) statements. It should also, incidentally, dispel the illusion mentioned in V that the probabilities causation needs can be subjective. They cannot, at least not if condition (P) holds, because subjective probabilities make opaque the following:

(33) 'The probability that the G event is $I = p$'

For example, unless I know that the G event $= k$, I may believe 'k is I' much less strongly than 'the G event is I'; so much less that (26) would meet condition (P) and (30) fail it. But that would make (26) opaque, which it is not. For (P) to hold, (33) must be as transparent as (26): so its probabilities must be objective.

VIII

The above, I believe, exhausts the ways in which causation relates events. They all stem from causal relations between facts – and from a mere fraction of them. Much of the world's causation, like Don surviving because he hangs on, or his falling first because he has the weakest rope, relates facts without relating events at all, as we have seen.

But a kindred relation – temporal order – always relates particulars, namely particular times, as well as facts; and Davidson[43] says that kinship shows that causation always relates events. What it really shows, however, as we shall now see, is that times are not events.

The kinship between temporal and causal order is shown in the temporal analogues of (1)–(4) – which I believe (1)–(4) entail,[44] though I shall not argue the point here:

(1T) 'c precedes e'

(2T) 'E after C'

(3T) 'Don's fall precedes his death'

(4T) 'Don dies after he falls'

The statement (4T) and others of the type (2T) report relations between facts, just as type (2) statements do. For (2T), like (2), always entails 'C' and 'E' (Don cannot die after he falls unless he both falls and dies). So it too is a partial truth function of 'C' and 'E'. But again, not a complete one. '$C\&E$' no more entails 'E after C' than it entails 'E because C' – if only because, if it did, it would also entail the incompatible 'C after E', that is, 'E before C'.

Yet, as Davidson notes, his argument to show that 'E because C' must be a complete truth function has a parallel for 'E after C'. And the temporal argument's transparency assumption (ii) is more arguable than in the causal original. Take the analogue of (9):

(9T) 'Don's fall is the first fall after Don's rope is the weakest rope'

This reads oddly, but will be true if (9) is, since if Don falls first beause he has the weakest rope, it must be the weakest before he falls, and a fortiori before he falls first. But whereas (9) is undeniably opaque, (9T) arguably is not. For one thing, the probability condition (P) need not apply, to engender opacity in (9T) as it does in (9). And the analogues of (10)–(13), for example:

(10T) Don's fall is Don's fall after his rope is the weakest'

are not as self-evidently false as their causal counterparts.

I still think (10T)–(13T) are false: it is hard to credit necessary facts, like the fact that Don's fall is his fall, with temporal location. Even if they are true, Davidson's argument must still fail somewhere. It cannot show that statements of type (2T) are complete truth functions: we know they are not. Nor can it show that 'after', and its converse 'before', are not really connectives. How could it? Since they are used as connectives, that is what they are.

However, we need not settle the question of (2T)'s opacity. Provided '*C*' and '*E*' state existential facts, even opaque truths of type (2T) can yield transparent ones of type (1T) and even (2T), analogous to those that type (2) truths yield. Both (4) and (4T) report relations between the existential facts that there is an *F* event (a fall by Don) and a *G* event (a death of Don). So if f = the *F* event and g = the *G* event, I say (14)'s temporal analogue

(14T) 'There is a *G* event after there is an *F* event'

yields a transparent

(17T) 'f precedes g'

just as (14) yields the transparent (17) 'f causes g'. And the temporal analogue of (22)

(22T) 'Don dies instantly [*I*] after he falls fast [*H*]'

likewise yields a transparent

(26T) 'The *G* event is *I* after the *F* event is *H*'

which says that Don's death is instant after his fall is fast. Temporal and causal relations between existential facts about events yield corresponding relations between events in the very same way.

But what about the temporal analogue of (8),

(8T) 'Don survives after he hangs on'

We saw in IV that if 'Don falls' and 'Don dies' are existential statements about events, 'Don hangs on' and 'Don survives' are not. They, and hence (8) and (8T) which entail them, are negative existential statements. They only *deny* the existence of events, and *a fortiori* of events related either causally or temporally. The truth of (8T) can yield no temporal relation between events, but it can yield a relation between times. Whether Don falls or hangs on, dies or survives, there are times at which he does so. 'Don falls', 'Don dies', 'Don hangs on' and 'Don survives' are all existential statements about times. Abbreviating them by '*DF*', '*DD*' '*DH*' and '*DS*', (4T) and (8T) entail respectively:

(4Tt) 'There is a time when DD after there is a time when DF'

(8Tt) 'There is a time when DS after there is a time when DH'

So if Don falls or hangs on at t_1 and dies or survives at t_2, (4T) and (8T) can both entail a transparent 't_1 precedes t_2'. These times will not of course be instants of time. The fastest of falls takes time, and so does even an instant death. For t_1 and t_2 to be *the* times when Don falls (or hangs on) and dies (or survives), they must be intervals of time. The sub-intervals (and ultimately the instants) they comprise will be defined in turn by the temporal order of related facts about, for example, Don passing various points on the cliff as he falls. All these times, like events, get their temporal order from that of the facts located at them – not vice versa, as Davidson says.[45]

Times may likewise be defined by all temporally ordered facts. Indeed, I suppose that is what times are. (Given relativity, it is really space–time zones that are defined, by spatio-temporal relations between facts. But that is no problem, provided spatial relations also hold between facts, which they do: for instance, Don dies *where* he lands, and *200 metres below where* he starts to fall. But since the extension to space–time is trivial, I will stick to time.) So 'E after C' always entails

(2Tt) 'There is a time when E after there is a time when C'

which, if t_C = the time when C and t_E = time when E, entails

(1Tt) 't_C precedes t_E

That is, 'E after C' turns 'C' and 'E' into existential statements about times, whether or not they are also existential statements about events. And since they often aren't, times cannot always be events: there are not enough events to go round.

Even when 'C' and 'E' are existential statements about both times and events, we still cannot equate them as Davidson does.[46] Don's fall f and death g have of course the same temporal order as the times, t_F and t_G, when Don falls and dies, namely, the temporal order of those two facts. But that does not make those times the same as those events, since they differ causally: f causes g, but t_F does not cause t_G.

This causal difference between times (or space–time zones) and events is not just a matter of stipulation, though it could be. If space–time had to be causally inert, it could be made so by not extending the inference scheme in VII, from

(20) 'There is a Y event [e] *because there is an X event* [c]'

to

(28) 'c causes or affects e'

'to cover times. However, general relativity arguably shows that space–time is not inert: its local structure interacts causally with the matter it contains.[47] So this inference scheme may have to cover times; but f and g will still differ causally from t_F and t_G. Being when Don falls and when he dies are not essential properties of t_F and t_G. Even if these times are identified by their places in a temporal order derived from that of such facts, they are the location of too many other facts for their identity to depend on what Don does in them. They would have been the same times if Don had hung on and survived. So even if causation does *involve* them, it will not involve their *existence*. Thus t_F may *affect* t_G, since t_G is a time when Don dies, because t_F is a time when he falls; but it will not cause it, as f causes g.

IX·

I have said why and how causation relates facts, and how as a result it can relate events and perhaps times. It remains to say why all this matters, and how it affects what causation is, and what physical basis, if any, it needs.

Some ways in which it matters have emerged already. One is that effects must be facts in order to have the probabilities I think the analysis of causation demands. Another is all the causation that is left out if it is limited to events: all the causation, for example, in which nothing happens – as when things have properties (colour, shape, temperature, mass, and so on) at a time because they had them earlier and nothing has happened since to change them.

Since causation needs no particulars, it could even act on a *Tractatus* world that really was a 'totality of facts, not of things',[48] with no particulars at all. It would indeed make that world more than a 'totality of existent atomic facts',[49] since 'E because C' is a partial but not complete truth function of 'C' and 'E'. But it need not generate events. The laws needed to give effects probabilities may need particulars to distinguish their instances:[50] without particular constituents, like a in Fa, facts would not be collectable into laws like '$(x)(Fx{\rightarrow}Gx)$'. But the particulars need not be things or events. If, as I argue, causal order entails temporal order, causation would make a *Tractatus* world temporal; then the entailments in VIII would give it times – and, if its facts were also spatially related, zones and hence points of space–time. And that ontology, as Carnap[51] and Field[52] have indicated, might do for its physics.

But not for its metaphysics. Facts in a causal world cannot all consist of particulars having properties or being related to each other: it cannot just be a Tarski world[53] of particulars satisfying sentential functions, for instance such predicates as '...dies' and '...causes...'. For, as I remarked in VI, a relation can hold (that is, particulars can satisfy a predicate ascribing it) only if it does so however the particulars it relates are referred to. Statements that relations hold must be transparent, but we have seen that many causal truths are opaque. They depend on how particulars are described, as well as on their properties and relations. So a causal world must contain more than particulars and universals. It not only *can* be a 'totality of facts, not of things': in so far as it is causal, it *must* be.

This is not to deny the reality of things and events. Ours is more than a *Tractatus* world made temporal by causation; its particulars are not just space–time zones picked out by the facts located at them. They might be if they were all events: extended events, with temporal as well as spatial parts, could be identified with space–time zones. But there are also things, able to change, and agents, able also to act and to be responsible; and these things and agents must be particulars that extend in time without having temporal parts.[54] That, I maintain, makes them – us – irreducible to events, and *a fortiori* to space–time zones, though I cannot argue that thesis here. However, reducible or not, changeable and interacting things and agents are features of the world that accounts of causation must allow, as mine does: particulars of any kind that supply causally related facts can thereby be causally related too.

So much for the relata of causation. What of causation itself? It is not a relation, in the sense of a universal, different in kind from the particular causes and effects which it relates. When Don dies because he falls, that is just another fact, like the fact that he dies and the fact that he falls. It does not reduce to them: Don can fall and die without dying because he falls. But it is still only a fact, as they are; and it too may have causes and effects. Don may, for example, die because he falls because he wears no helmet – which his dying because he falls may well cause later climbers to wear.

This kind of iterated causation shows moreover how causation can be perceived. Perception is a causal process: we see things, events and facts by their so affecting our senses that we are caused to believe in them. So anything we see must have effects, which causation itself cannot have if all causes are particulars. Hence a specious problem about how it can be detected,[55] which then casts doubt on its objectivity, and hence on that of perceptual knowledge. But if causes are facts the problem goes, and with it goes much Humean scepticism. For now the fact that one fact causes another can itself make us perceive it, by so affecting our senses that we are caused to believe in it. Of course we cannot perceive every kind of causation, any more than we can perceive every kind of cause. Perhaps we cannot see that Don dies because he falls, though I think we can; but there is plenty of causation we can perceive. For example, to see by white light that a thing is red is to see how the light changes colour *because* the thing reflects it as it does.

We rely on causation so much that any account of it must say how we detect it. The ease with which this account does so is yet another reason to believe it, but the very feature that makes causation visible raises a question about its physical basis. If it is not a relation between particulars, and *a fortiori* not a physical one, what is it? What kind of physical fact, beyond the fact that C and the fact that E, makes statements of type (2) 'E because C', true?

Consider the probability condition (P): that 'E' be more probable than it would be in the circumstances if 'C' were false. I admit (P) is debatable, and it certainly does not suffice to entail (with 'C' and 'E') 'E because C'. But it does explain, as we saw in V, the falsity of many causal claims; and to make it sufficient might only need more of the same, for instance contiguity or density, to provide causal intermediaries between causally related facts separated in space–time. If so, causation will neither have nor need the physical basis (or bases) adumbrated in I. For (P) demands only actual and counterfactual probabilities, which is not a physical basis like energy transfer. Probability – like truth – is no subject matter for a science, since it is always the probability (or truth) *of* something which is the real subject matter. Any contingent proposition, about any subject, may be true; and it may also be more probable if some other proposition is true than if that proposition is false. If that, or anything like it, suffices for causation, causation can no more be the province of one science, such as physics, than truth or probability can be.

This is not to deny physicalism. Perhaps all truths of the form 'E because C' are made true by physical facts. The fact that C, the fact that E, and the further facts that make 'E because C' true, can all be physical. But these further facts of causation may still be quite as heterogeneous as the facts they link. Indeed they will be, being apt as we have seen to have causes and effects of their own. So physical facts are not linked causally by a distinct causal kind of physical fact, and it is futile to look for such a kind. Physics, *pace* Russell, has indeed never 'ceased to look for causes', let alone because 'there are no such things.'[56] There *are* such things, and physics should look for them, and also case by case for the causal facts that link them to their effects; but not for causation itself.

Notes

This chapter expands part of my 'Fixed past, unfixed future' (1986), written in 1983. It has been developed in lectures and seminars given at Cambridge, London (Bedford, University and King's Colleges), Essex, Tübingen, Nottingham, New York (Columbia), Michigan, Auckland, Wellington, Dunedin, Christchurch, Monash, Melbourne, Adelaide, and Canberra; and I am much indebted to comments made then, and in many private discussions, especially by Jeremy Butterfield, and also by David Papineau, Timothy Smiley, Gennadiy Sirkin, Nancy Cartwright, David Lewis, Jaegwon Kim, David Sanford, Tom Baldwin, Edward Craig, Frank Jackson, Barry Taylor, Henry Krips, Elliott Sober and Dorothy Emmet.

1   B. Russell, 'On the notion of cause', *Proceedings of the Aristotelian Society* new series 13 (1912), pp. 1–26.

2   H. N. Castañeda, 'Causes, causality and energy', *Midwest Studies in Philosophy* 9 (1984), pp. 17–27.

3   C. D. Broad, *The Mind and Its Place in Nature*, London, Routledge and Kegan Paul, 1925, ch. 2.

4   G. Ryle, *The Concept of Mind*, London, Hutchinson, 1949, ch. 5.

5   N. Goodman, *Fact, Fiction and Forecast*, London, Athlone Press, 1954, ch. 2.

6   D. H. Mellor, 'In defense of dispositions', *Philosophical Review* 83 (1974), pp. 157–81.

7   D. Davidson, 'Causal relations', in his *Essays on Actions and Events*, Oxford, Clarendon Press, 1980, pp. 149–62.

8   See E. Sober, 'Causal factors, causal inference, causal explanation (I)', *Aristotelian Society Supplementary Volume* 60 (1986), pp. 97–115, and D. Papineau, 'Causal factors, causal inference causal explanation (II)', *Aristotelian Society Supplementary Volume* 60 (1986), pp. 116–36.

9   B. Taylor, *Modes of Occurrence*, Oxford, Basil Blackwell, 1985, ch. 2.

10 D. H. Sanford, 'Causal relata', in E. LePore and B. P. McLaughlin (eds), *Actions and Events*, Oxford, Basil Blackwell, 1985 pp. 282–93. See p. 290.

11 D. Davidson, 'Criticism, comment and defence', in his *Essays on Actions and Events*, pp. 122–48. See p. 135. The chapter refers to Davidson's 1967 paper 'The logical form of action sentences', which also appears in this collection, pp. 105–22.

12 F. P. Ramsey, *Foundations*, 'Facts and propositions', D. H. Mellor (ed.), London, Routledge and Kegan Paul, 1978, pp 40–57.

13 See Davidson, 'The logical form of action sentences', and D. H. Mellor, *Real Time*, Cambridge, Cambridge University Press, 1981, ch. 8.

14 For example, J. Kim, 'Causation, nomic subsumption, and the concept of event', *Journal of Philosophy* 70 (1973), pp. 217–36, and Taylor, *Modes of Occurrence*.

15 D. Davidson, 'The individuation of events', in his *Essays on Actions and Events*, pp. 163–80; Kim, 'Causation, nomic subsumption and the concept of event'.

16 W. V. O. Quine, 'Events and reification', in LePore and McLaughlin (eds), *Actions and Events*, pp. 162–71. See p. 168.

17 'Reply to Quine on events', in LePore and McLaughlin (eds), *Actions and Events*, pp. 172–76. See p. 176.

18 See D. H. Mellor, 'Things and causes in spacetime', *British Journal for the Philosophy of Science* 31, (1980) pp. 282–8, and Mellor, *Real Time*, ch. 7.

19 See Davidson, 'Events as particulars', in his *Essays on Actions and Events*, pp. 181–7, and his 'Reply to Quine on events'.

20 Davidson, 'The logical form of action sentences'.

21 Davidson, 'The individuation of events', p. 180.

22 Ramsey, 'Universals', in his *Foundations*, pp. 17–39.

23 Quine, 'Events and reification', p. 168.

24 Davidson, 'The individuation of events', p. 179.

25 Kim, 'Causation, nomic subsumption, and the concept of event'.

26 Davidson, 'Causal relations', p. 162n.

27 Z. Vendler, 'Effects, results and consequences', in R. J. Butler (ed.) *Analytical Philosophy*, Oxford, Basil Blackwell, 1962, pp. 1–15.

28 Davidson, 'Causal relations', p. 151.

29 Ibid., p. 162.

30 Ramsey, 'Facts and propositions'.

31 See Ramsey, 'Universals', and M. Dummett, *Frege: Philosophy of Language*, London, Duckworth, 1973, ch. 4.

32 Davidson, 'The logical form of action sentences'.

33 Kim, 'Causation, nomic subsumption, and the concept of event'.

34 Sanford, 'Causal relata'.

35 Davidson, 'Causal relations', pp. 152–3.

36 Ibid., pp. 152–3.

37 Ibid., p. 149.

38 See N. Cartwright, 'Causal laws and effective strategies', *Nous* 13 (1979), pp. 419–37; B. Skyrms, *Causal Necessity*, New Haven, Conn., Yale University Press, 1980; P. Suppes, *Probabalistic Metaphysics*, Oxford, Basil Blackwell, 1984; W. C. Salmon, *Scientific Explanation and the Causal Structure of the World*, Princeton, N.J., Princeton University Press, 1984; Sober, 'Causal factors, causal inference, causal explanation(1)'; Papineau, 'Causal factors, causal inference, causal explanation (11)'; and D. H. Mellor, 'Fixed past, unfixed future', in B. Taylor (ed.), *Contributions to Philosophy: Michael Dummett*, The Hague, Nijhoff, 1986.

39 Ramsey, 'General propositions and causality', in his *Foundations*, pp. 133–51; S. Blackburn, 'Opinions and chances', in D. H. Mellor (ed.), *Prospects for Pragmatism*, Cambridge, Cambridge University Press, 1980, pp. 175–96.

40 D. Lewis, *Counterfactuals*, Oxford, Basil Blackwell, 1973, p. 16.

41 Davidson, 'Causal relations', p. 160.

42 Sanford, 'Causal relata'.

43 Davidson, 'Causal relations', p. 154.

44 Mellor, *Real Time*, chs. 9–10.

45 Davidson, 'Causal relations', p. 154.

46 Ibid., p. 154.

47   Mellor, 'Things and causes in spacetime'.
48   L. Wittgenstein, *Tractatus Logico-Philosophicus*, London, Routledge and Kegan Paul, 1922, 1.1.
49   Wittgenstein, *Tractatus*, 2.04.
50   Ramsey, 'Universals'.
51   R. Carnap, 'Testability and meaning', in H. Feigl and M. Brodbeck (eds), *Readings in the Philosophy of Science*, New York, Appleton-Century-Crofts, 1953, pp. 47–92.
52   H. H. Field, *Science Without Numbers*, Oxford, Basil Blackwell, 1980.
53   A. Tarski, 'The semantic conception of truth', in H. Feigl and W. Sellars (eds), *Readings in Philosophical Analysis*, New York, Appleton-Century-Crofts, 1949, pp. 52–84.
54   See section II in this chapter and Mellor, 'Things and causes in spacetime'.
55   See D. Hume, *A Treatise of Human Nature*, L. A. Selby-Bigge (ed.), Oxford, Clarendon Press, 1888, Bk 1, Pt 111, section II.
56   Russell, 'On the notion of cause', p. 1.

8

The Diversity of the Sciences: Global versus Local Methodological Approaches

Hilary Putnam

When he wrote *Philosophy and Scientific Realism*,[1] Jack Smart said a good deal about the conceptual scheme of modern science, but he did not much use the word 'science' itself. The word does not appear in the index, nor (as far as I remember) did Jack avail himself even once of the shibboleth of 'The Scientific Method'. In this chapter, I should like to say why I think this was an extraordinarily wise course for him to take!

Philosophers of science as different as Popper, Lakatos, Carnap and, to name more recent figures, Wolfgang Stegmüller and Dudley Shapere, have proposed models of theory acceptance which are supposed to fit all of science. Sometimes these models are also supposed to 'demarcate' the scientific from the non-scientific, or to 'account for the growth of knowledge'. I think it is generally recognized that none of these models fits scientific theories perfectly, but that is not, after all, surprising. Even if philosophy *were* a science, one would not expect to be able to *perfectly* model as complex a phenomenon as theory acceptance, even in a single case; and philosophy – dare one say? – is very far from being a science in any sense of 'science' which does not border on vacuity. But what I want to call attention to is something that goes beyond the fact of life just mentioned, the fact that our pictures and models fall short of their target in various ways. I believe that, in fact, each of the 'global' models just mentioned does have a suggestive kind of 'fit' to *some* theories (the ones that suggested the model in the first place), while fitting other theories very badly. I want to point out that certain theories tend, in this sense, to be *extreme cases* for philosophies of science. Among them are Darwin's Theory of Natural Selection, Relativity Theory and Quantum Mechanics. What I shall undertake in in this chapter is not the huge project of trying to elucidate the structure of these theories, nor shall I address any of the usual controversies connected with them (for example, the controversy, in which I have participated, concerning the issue of conventionalism in the case of Relativity Theory), but to point out the features which make them extreme cases for one or another global approach to philosophy of science. By doing this, I hope to suggest something about the nature of the activity of philosophizing about science, and to suggest a way in which philosophers of science may begin to come closer to the actual methodology of science.

Background

In *Reason, Truth and History*,[2] I discussed the question 'if the scientific method is an evolving one, is there some sense in which it gets better and better other than a purely technological one?' In connection with this, I touched on a large 'budget of problems', the 'main items' being: (1) the interconnectedness of theory appraisal in natural science and theory appraisal in epistemology and metaphysics; (2) the connection between theory appraisal in physical science and theory appraisal in social science; and (3) the question of the existence of an objective notion of rationality and of 'convergence' in natural science. I claimed that a formalized scientific method is an unrealistic aim, while defending the idea that rationality is something objective (even if our conceptions of it are always imperfect and historically conditioned in various ways). I argued further that scientific inquiry is by its very nature value-loaded in a number of ways, and used this point to try to show that Max Weber's celebrated argument for a sharp fact/value dichotomy is not well founded. Finally, I connected these questions about theory acceptance with questions about realism.

The argument of the book was necessarily abstract, and dealt rather sweepingly with large areas of our culture – scientific theories, historical and social studies, ideological disputes and 'value judgements'. In the present discussion, I shall focus more narrowly on scientific methodology, in order to see what difference such an outlook makes to philosophy of science in a narrower sense.

Inductive logic is not formal

In *Reason, Truth and History* I argued, following Goodman,[3] that a purely formal method cannot be hoped for in inductive logic. Goodman has shown that inferences of the same logical form can differ with respect to inductive validity/invalidity, no matter how finely we analyse logical form. The suggestion Carnap[4] made to deal with this problem was to postulate that some properties are in themselves 'purely qualitative', and to require that the primitive predicates in the languages to which formalized inductive logic is applied be of this sort. This represents an intrusion of metaphysics into inductive logic – an intrusion, moreover, of the sort of metaphysics which Carnap himself combated in other areas, the sort that throws us back on intuitions of an inexplicable kind.

Goodman's own suggestion was to consider logical form *plus* the history of prior projection of the predicates involved in the inference, as well as certain related matters (for example, 'entrenchment' and 'overriding').

The problem of a criterion of projectibility is extremely robust; it appears in Bayesian theories of confirmation as an aspect of the problem of the choice of a 'prior'. Bayes's own solution resembles Goodman's, in spirit if not in detail: Bayes thought the 'prior' comes from previous experience. This leads to an obvious regress. The regress may be accepted as unavoidable; but then we give up hope of a global, unchanging formalization.

Goodman's solution is worked out only for very simple cases of inductive inference. Even here it has consequences which I find unacceptable; for example, on Goodman's proposal it would follow that a culture which had *always* projected such 'crazy' predicates as his celebrated 'grue' would now be perfectly justified in doing so – their inferences would now be 'inductively valid'! Let me hasten to say that what I disagree with is not Goodman's claim that fit with past practice is important in induction. While I agree with *that*, Goodman's present system cannot, I think, be regarded as more than a first approximation. It too blatantly neglects the fact that we have other epistemic priorities – call them 'prejudices' if you like, but they are part of our notion of reasonableness.

Popper and the theory of evolution

One of the main approaches I would classify as 'informal' (in spite of the pretensions it sometimes had to being a formal treatment) is Sir Karl Popper's. I criticized this approach in 'The "corroboration" of theories', where I argued that Popper's ideas do not well fit *the* paradigm example of a physical theory: Newton's Theory of Gravitation.[5] Moreover, there is a major theory outside physics that it does not fit even to the extent that it fits physical theories, and that is Darwin's Theory of Evolution by Natural Selection.

Popper accepts and even appeals to Darwinian ideas – not, however, as 'science', but as a 'successful metaphysical research programme'.[6] This move shows that even Popper is aware he cannot stretch his schema to cover *this* theory – and most of us would consider it to be one of the central examples of a 'scientific theory'. What is Popper's difficulty?

It might be useful to begin by making some distinctions which Popper surprisingly fails to draw. The idea of evolution in a non-specific sense (that is, the idea of evolution *minus the causal mechanism*) is pre-Darwinian. This is well known, but perhaps still worth saying because even today (for example in our current replays of the Scopes trial) the suggestion is sometimes encountered that the gradual appearance of more complicated species of organisms – let me refer to this as the *fact of evolution* – depends for its credibility *entirely* on Darwinian theory, as if the discovery that there was something wrong with our present ideas about the *mechanism* of evolution, if it should occur, would suddenly make it an open question whether the geological layers came into existence five thousand seven hundred and forty six years ago, or whenever. Even the fact of evolution is not 'falsifiable' in Popper's narrow sense – the statement that the species came into existence in a certain order, starting with, say, viruses, and were not all created in a seven day period does not, by itself, imply a 'basic sentence' – but it *is* falsifiable in precisely the sense which Newton's Theory of Universal Gravitation is falsifiable: *in combination with auxiliary statments which are appropriate in the various contexts of geology, palaeontology, etc., in which it is applied*, it leads to testable predictions. (Note that 'falsifiability' in *this* sense is not sharply distinguished from *confirmability* – nor should it be.)[7]

The reason I speak of the *fact* of evolution is that this bit of the natural history of our planet is as well established as any scientific fact *can* be, and has, I think, somewhat the same relation to the Theory of Evolution by Natural Selection that phenomenological thermodynamics bears to ergodic theory. Like phenomenological thermodynamics, it can be corrected in detail by the more fundamental theory, but its correctness in broad outline is not dependent upon the confirmation of the more fundamental theory.

When we come to the more fundamental theory – Darwin's Theory of Evolution by Natural Selection – there are again epistemological distinctions to be drawn. At the advancing edge of the theory – and this is where I feel most unsure of myself – it becomes, in places, highly mathematical. Hearing a talk by Richard Lewontin a few years ago,[8] I was struck by the extent to which the kind of modelling he was doing looked, in broad outline if not in mathematical detail, like a kind of stochastic mechanics. At still other points on the advancing edge, we get controversies – Stephen Gould[9] is involved in a number of these – which resemble controversies in history rather than in mathematical physics.

And, it goes without saying, there are now rich areas of overlap with genetics and molecular biology. But this is not what I want to talk about. The claim that Darwin made – the one that is responsible for the 'cosmological' excitement generated by the theory – was not a mathematical claim, not a claim about Mandelian genetics (which Darwin did not know of), nor even a claim of the kind that Gould is so concerned to argue, about gradualism and continuity versus 'leaps', but rather a vastly important claim about the Origin of the Species. Darwin said that the species – *all the species except the primordial one* – came into existence by 'natural selection'.

This is simultaneously a universal statement and a causal explanation. And it is *this* statement that gives Popper trouble. Why it gives him trouble is easy to see. Even if, under suitable conditions, we could observe the mechanisms that Lewontin is modelling in operation and 'corroborate' his theory, this would hardly test Darwin's great causal–cosmological claim.

The question that exercises philosophers is, of course, 'what could test Darwin's causal–cosmological claim?' The simplest position would be that we can just make an induction. If the evidence supports the propositions that (1) natural selection is operating now as evolutionary biologists claim it is, and (2) no other mechanism capable of producing species is now operating (apart from a limited amount of deliberate human intervention of various kinds, which certainly could not have been responsible for producing species in the first place), then we should, barring contrary evidence, just make the induction that natural selection always operated and that no other mechanism (with the insignificant exception noted) ever operated to produce species. But this is not just too simple for an anti-inductionist like Sir Karl; I suspect it is too simple for *any* philosopher of science to take seriously.

Even when philosophers agree that something is wrong (or 'too simple') they rarely agree on *why* it is wrong, and this case is no exception. Let me, therefore, give my own reasons for thinking that it is too simple, and not pretend to speak for the mythical philosophical community. The first thing worth noticing about the 'induction' proposed is that it ignores entirely the way in which our willingness to make inductive projections depends on our estimate of the *lawlikeness* of the proposition being projected. We are sure that all life here on earth contains DNA; yet I suspect that science fiction readers among us are not willing on that basis alone to accept 'all life everywhere in the Universe contains DNA' as a law; not because we want a larger sample size, or even because our sample is not drawn from 100 or 1000 different planets rather than from one (although that would surely help), but because we are not able to see why it should be *physically necessary* that all life contain DNA. Indeed, in *Philosophy and Scientific Realism*, Jack Smart expressed the view that *no* biological generalization is physically necessary,[10] and he may well be right. On the other hand, it may be that experts can think of reasons why it should be physically necessary that life contain DNA. If so, I would not be surprised to find that they *were* willing to accept this statement as a law. But that is not surprising: our estimate of the *lawlikeness of a statement* generally depends on knowledge quite remote from the 'direct' evidential support for the statement, and can even be non-experimental. Even a person who thought that the first of the two propositions above was sufficiently lawlike to justify extrapolating it back a billion years or two might have the opinion that the corresponding extrapolation of the second proposition ('there was never any other mechanism that operated') is not a law but just a contingent historical claim. And such a person would regard the induction I mentioned as fishy – as analogous to, say, an attempt to conclude that people always knew how to read and write from the fact that the people we now observe know how to read and write. (Notice that this latter would be a bad induction even in the absence of direct knowledge of a time at which people did not know how to read and write; we have too much 'cross inductive' evidence that technological devices, methods, and so on, are the sorts of things that tend to be discovered at a time and then persist.)

What of 'simplicity'? We might argue that the other mechanisms for producing speciation that have actually been proposed – Lamarckian evolution and Special Creation – involve a genetic theory which has been refuted, in the first case, and the postulate of an Intelligent Being who was in existence prior to all forms of life studied by biology (but is inaccessible to scientific investigation), in the second. This latter postulate is not only unscientific, but would be considered anthropomorphism by many religious people: in my view, it makes God into a Super-Humanoid in the world, while appealing to the fact that it is God who is being invoked as an efficient cause, and not, say, Martians, to insulate the theory of Special Creation from scientific objections.

This line of thought is one I find convincing. But let us examine it a little. It depends on the principle (which, I have argued,[11] underlies even our mundane belief in the existence of a material world), that an important reason – and a *good* reason – for accepting an idea is the absence of any serious alternative, as well as the maxim 'don't postulate in-principle-unobservables.' Positivists (and I count Sir Karl as a Neopositivist) apply the first principle tacitly when they accept certain theoretical statements which have never withstood any Popperian test because there was never any 'rival hypothesis' (for instance, 'space has three dimensions'). But they are uncomfortable with this sort of argument when the question is a historical one, and it seems clear that the Theory of Evolution by Natural Selection does contain elements which resemble historical reconstruction more than they do the statement of universal laws and the derivation of predictions from them. This may, of course, change. In 100 years (give or take) textbook presentations of evolutionary theory *might* look like textbook presentations of mathematical physics (I doubt that the theory as a whole will ever be reduced to such a form, but it *might be*), and then, presumably, even Sir Karl would grant that the theory has made the transition from pre-science to science. But, in its present form, it depends heavily – the causal–cosmological claim which is the heart of the theory depends heavily – on one's acceptance of the methodological maxims just mentioned.

But doesn't the acceptance of physical theories depend on the same methodological maxims? Of course it does; but it would be wrong to dismiss the intuition that there is a significant difference between physical theories and the Darwinian theory of speciation. I suspect that the heart of the issue has to do with the – admittedly difficult or impossible to explicate, but still vitally important – notion of 'lawlikeness'. As I mentioned, lawlikeness is connected with 'physical necessity'. A lawlike statement puts forward a putative physical necessity, or at least something which is physically necessary under idealized circumstances. (Dudley Shapere has done a good deal of work on the different sorts of 'laws' and 'lawlike statements' we find in science, emphasizing in particular the different kinds of descriptive and idealizing functions such statements play.)[12] Now, one of our ways of deciding the lawlikeness of a statement is simply to ask ourselves the question 'is this the sort of statement that I would expect, if true anywhere, to be true *everywhere*?' Newton's inverse square law for gravitation is not *exactly* true anywhere, but it is the sort of statement that, if true in one region of (flat) space–time, we would expect to be true in every region. So, as long as we did not even consider the possibility of curved space–time, let alone space–time of variable curvature, this is a paradigm case of a lawlike statement. Of course, *how we know* that this statement couldn't be true for, say, a trillion miles from Terra, and false everywhere else, is an interesting philosophical question. It certainly isn't analytic that this couldn't be the case: one could imagine a science fiction story (say by Robert Sheckley) in which it turned out that we were in a little bubble of space–time which obeyed peculiar laws made up by some extraterrestial. But in that case there would be a *reason* why those laws obtained only in this little (cosmologically speaking) region. It may be that it is part of the way our minds work that we demand of certain sorts of statements that they should hold everywhere or nowhere, not in the sense of being a Kantian synthetic a priori, but in the sense of being what Saul Kripke[13] calls a basic 'prejudice'. Prejudices in Kripke's sense are not irrational beliefs; rather, they are epistemological ultimates which we conform to unless the price is too high. (Some such idea – the idea of a defeasible synthetic a priori – is suggested in some of Reichenbach's early writings.)[14]

An example of a *non*-lawlike statement may help. We are willing to believe that it may be true in some places and not others that people speak English. If asked why, we can give a reason – say, that English evolved from Anglo Saxon, and Anglo Saxon was not spoken everywhere, but this, of course, just pushes the question back to the similar question 'why was Anglo Saxon not spoken everywhere?' We just aren't bothered by the fact that such things are true in some places and not others in the way we would be if (in a flat space–time) the Law of Universal Gravitation held in a particular region (shaped, let us suppose, like a chilliagon, in its spatial cross-section), and not anywhere else. We don't expect *certain* sorts of regularities to just obtain by accident. That's one of our ultimate Kripkean 'prejudices'.

But we don't have any similar defeasible 'prejudice' to the effect that natural selection must either be the sole cause of speciation at every time or be the sole cause at no time.[15] If there *were* mechanisms other than natural selection capable of producing speciation, why shouldn't they depend on conditions which obtained in the past (or might obtain in the future) but which do not obtain now?

In short, I am suggesting that the reason we don't think that the generalization 'only natural selection produces species' *must* be true at every time or at no time (even apart from the problem of what produced the first living material) is that it doesn't quite look 'lawlike', or, at any rate, it isn't one of our present day 'prejudices' that this statement is lawlike.

What of the argument that the other mechanisms which have actually been suggested – Special Creation and Lamarckian Evolution – are either hopelessly unscientific or refuted? Isn't this an argument for the lawlikeness of 'only natural selection is *capable of* producing species?' Well, yes; but notice the idea that Special Creation is 'hopelessly unscientific' turns on the acceptance of a huge cultural and ideological change that took place in the West starting around the year 1500 and only reached unstoppable momentum in the seventeenth century. The acceptance of this idea – let us admit it – does have something 'metaphysical' about it (though not, I think, in a bad sense).

Am I then agreeing with Popper? Is natural selection (including the causal–cosmological claim) a 'metaphysical research programme' and not science? Well, why can't it be *both* a metaphysical research programme *and* science?

Here we come to the nub of the issue. If we limit 'science' to the formulation of 'laws', and we take these to be statements which, like the familiar differential equations of fundamental physics, we expect to hold true in every region or in no region (at least assuming the fundamental idealizations of the branch of physics in question); if we think the epistemology of science can be reduced to pretending that all scientists do is write down systems of such 'laws' and derive 'basic statements' from these systems, or these systems plus 'co-ordinating definitions' (Reichenbach), 'initial conditions' (Popper), or whatever; then we should not be surprised if practically nothing but physics turns out to be 'science'. This model doesn't fit the epistemology of evolutionary theory. But in a less tendentious sense of the term 'science', *of course* evolutionary theory is science. I have to ask why on earth we should expect the sciences to have more than a family resemblance to one another? They all share a common heritage, in that they owe allegiance to a minimum of empiricism (they 'put questions to Nature'; they are conducted in a fallibilistic spirit, and so on); they frequently depend on very careful observation and/or experimentation (think of the amount of data that evolutionary biologists have collected!); and they interact strongly with other disciplines recognized to be 'sciences'. But there is no set of 'essential' properties that all the sciences have in common.

If evolutionary theory does not, taken as a whole, fit Popperian (or more broadly positivistic) accounts of science, there are other models it does fit. 'Inference to the best explanation' accounts would not be disturbed by the way in which facts quite remote from the 'subject at hand' enter into our acceptance of evolutionary theory, or even by the way in which general methodological convictions enter. It was the aim of these accounts to allow such things to come into theory acceptance. I shall discuss cases which are 'extreme' for 'inference to the best explanation' accounts in a moment. But first I want to discuss yet another way of dealing with evolutionary theory.

Lakatosian 'research programs'

The very important work of Imre Lakatos[16] is, perhaps, *the* vehicle by which neo-Popperian ideas have become part of mainstream philosophy of science (as, for all their popular appeal, Popper's never did). If I do not think they help with the problems discussed in this chapter, that is not because they are devoid of interest or significance. It is because they do not, by themselves, give us any guidance in epistemology.

Lakatos thought that the unit of scientific research is not the 'theory' (the particular organized set of statements about some set of phenomena), but the evolving sequence of theories and related activities he called a 'research programme'. This idea was put forward much earlier in a different terminology by Stephen Toulmin in *The Philosophy of Science: An Introduction*[17], but it was re-invented and successfully marketed for the first time by Lakatos. Lakatos also thought that successive theories which belong to the same research programme share a common set of assumptions, a 'theory core' which can be identified in advance. (Here I demur: I believe, with Hardin and Rohrlich,[18] that we can only tell what is 'core' and what is 'protective belt' after a theory has been superseded, or rather, after it has become a 'limiting case' of a superseding theory which belongs to a later 'research programme'. One could not say *in advance* that the 'core' of Newtonian physics is what it has to say about speeds low relative to the light speed or about phenomena involving large numbers of quanta. Certainly, there is something important about the idea of the research programme, as well as about the notions of theory core and protective belt – these notions have already shown themselves to be 'robust', that is, capable of surviving transplantation into a number of different philosophies of science. They do not tell us anything about when we should *accept* theories, however, and they do not say anything about epistemology.

It is when he gets to epistemology that Lakatos shows his Popperian heritage. Like Popper, he believes falsifiability – which he construes more reasonably than Popper, in that he allows auxiliary hypotheses to play an important role – is vitally important. But he does not believe that good theories are always falsifiable. (He and I independently made very similar criticisms of Popper on this score in our papers in the Popper volume.)[19] Lakatos resolves the tension between his desire to keep 'making risky predictions', the one-and-only *sine qua non* of science, and his recognition that we must allow a research programme to have periods in which it is *not* making such risky predictions, by saying that the unit of epistemological assessment is the whole research programme and not the theory or statement. (Like the Popperians, Lakatos is totally contemptuous of what we actually *say* about theories and statements – pointing out that we often speak of theories and statements as 'well confirmed', 'implausible', 'well established' and so on, which in 'ordinary language philosophy' is an intellectual sin beneath contempt.)

A theory that leads to risky predictions over the long run is called 'progressive', in Lakatosian jargon. Now, no knowledgeable person would deny that evolutionary biology taken as a whole is a 'progressive research programme' in Lakatos's sense. Many successful predictions (which satisfy the Popper–Lakatos criterion of 'riskiness', in that they were not probable already on the basis of background knowledge) have been made in a number of different areas which share the general

Darwinian–Mendelian paradigm. It is when we inquire about the *epistemological* significance of this that our problems begin.

Does the progressiveness of a research programme really account for, or explicate, the *rationality* of accepting the current incarnation of that research programme? Here Lakatos is surprisingly coy. He wants, it seems to me, to save the idea that science is a uniquely rational activity *without* giving the working scientist any substantive advice at all – and while one can understand both desires, they are obviously hard to reconcile.

If a theory or a research programme is *supported* by evidence to the extent that it is currently 'progressive'; if 'coherence,' 'simplicity,' and other traditional 'inductivist' parameters do not have to be considered at all; then we are going to get very strange results. It may be that, for all I know, Velikovsky's theories are *well-supported* by such a criterion; he certainly has been lucky with some risky predictions. Even if we cannot find an actual contemporary example, it is certainly possible that a theory including assumptions which are wildly off the mark leads to a 'progressive' research programme: just imagine that those particular assumptions don't get tested (perhaps because they are difficult to test), and it is only *part* of the 'theory core' that is responsible for the successful predictions. (Historical examples are easy to find; Ptolemaic astronomy was, for a long time, a progressive research programme, but the assumption that, in addition to the heavenly bodies and their orbits, there are invisible 'spheres' in which the bodies are embedded had nothing to do with the success of the predictions Ptolemaic astronomers made – indeed, their own theory of 'epicycles' required planets to pass *through* the spheres that were supposed to 'carry' them.)

One way to meet this problem would be to require that a progressive research programme make predictions which test *all* of the *core assumptions* of the theory. This would require some way of telling what *are* the 'core' assumptions without relying on hindsight. It would also require a way of telling when the 'protective belt' has been 'adjusted' too often. It seems to me that this leads back to precisely the kind of traditional epistemological problem that Lakatos wants to abandon.

At any rate, the question of whether the predictions evolutionary biologists have made really test the causal–cosmological claim which fundamentalist and other opponents of the theory of evolution attack, is, as we have seen, a difficult one for a Popperian, and I do not see how it is any easier for a neo-Popperian like Lakatos. If the only criterion for being part of a research programme is a sociological one, if the *sociological* unity of the community of evolutionary biologists is enough to justify considering all of evolutionary biology one research programme, and the 'progressive' character of this programme justifies accepting *all* of it, then we are, perhaps, justified in accepting evolutionary theory on Lakatosian grounds. But then, by parity of reasoning, we were once justified in accepting the idea of 'spheres', even though that idea had nothing to do with the success of science in any period. Such a view gives too much to the idea that only predictive success matters in science, in my opinion. If, on the other hand, we have to show that a 'crucial experiment' directly testing the causal–cosmological claim has been performed, or that a 'risky prediction' whose success *directly* supports that claim has been made, then, if we become Lakatosians, we shall have as much trouble fitting the acceptance of the real 'core' of evolutionary theory, the causal–cosmological claim which is its very heart and soul, into our picture of 'scientific rationality' as Popper does. The idea that all there is to rational procedure is making novel predictions still haunts philosophy of science.

Inference to the best explanation

The view that Bayes himself held seems to have been revived recently, at least in a qualitative form, by Richard Boyd.[20] The idea of a basically Bayesian picture of theory acceptance (with the 'prior' coming from background knowledge about 'likely sorts of mechanism') fits a good deal of what Kuhn has called 'normal science'; but I would argue that it does not fit some of the major scientific revolutions (the quantum mechanical revolution in particular) without undue 'schema stretching'.

Boyd's approach is an instance of what has been called inference to the Best Explanation epistemology. This approach has not been very much elaborated (in spite of the fact that many philosophers refer to it approvingly). I want to examine it briefly with a special eye to the case of quantum mechanics.

Someone who learned about quantum mechanics only by reading recent articles in *Philosophy of Science* might well think that all the conceptual problems were connected with Bell's Theorem. This is, perhaps, a comment on the peculiarity of the relationship between the philosophy of any science and the science. To be sure, Bell's theorem is important because it puts 'hidden variable' theories at a severe disadvantage (it shows, so to speak, how high the price is for taking the hidden variable approach); but the physical community had almost no interest at all in hidden variable theories even before Bell proved his theorem. The discussion in the literature of philosophy of quantum mechanics has for a long time been remarkably indifferent to the way physics is going.

I obviously do not have space for a technical discussion at this point, but I have to say a few words about the history of the problem of 'interpreting' quantum mechanics. The problem is as old as the discovery of the phenomenon of quantum mechanical interference (of which the most famous illustration is the celebrated two-slit experiment). That phenomenon already convinced physicists that the squared norm of the state vector is not a 'classical probability'; or, to put the same point in a different way, it convinced them that the peculiar transition from probability to actuality we witness in quantum mechanical experiments is not a mere conditionalization of a previously valid probability to additional evidence. While a few physicists (Bohm, De Broglie) attempted to find classical models for the 'reduction of the wave packet' (models involving 'pilot waves' in the case of De Broglie and a special force in the case of Bohm's theory), the overwhelming majority of all physicists – and not, by any means, only the operationalists – followed Bohr's advice to simply stop trying to think of quantum mechanical reality in classical terms. That is to say, they took the advice to accept the theory (which has, remember, a higher level of accuracy and a greater quantity of direct experimental evidence in its favour than any previous theory in the history of physical science), *even though there is no 'likely sort of mechanism' which we know of which could account for the phenomena the theory postulates*. The problem isn't just that the 'prior probability' of the kind of phenomena that quantum mechanics postulates would seem to be as close to zero as empirical probabilities ever get, if prior probabilities are really calculated from background knowledge about 'likely sorts of mechanism'; the problem is that we don't even know that a 'mechanism' *is* what accounts for those phenomena. Certainly, no one has been able to suggest a mechanism that would not violate constraints that working physicists are not willing to give up. This does not appear to be a case in which we have to look for an *unlikely* mechanism because we have discovered unlikely phenomena; it looks more like a case in which *thinking in terms of 'mechanism' is not what is called for*.

What I have just said is not the opinion of very many philosophers of physics. Almost every philosopher of physics has their own 'realistic' interpretation of quantum mechanics. This is a game which I know very well – played it myself for years! What I want to urge is not that we stop playing this game – it *is* a fun game, and some interesting theorems get proved – but that we attach greater importance to the fact that physics goes on quite well without any visible success in this game.

Indeed, even to say that what we are dealing with in quantum mechanics is 'unlikely sorts of phenomena' may be making the situation in quantum mechanics look too Bayesian. A Bayesian might say, after all, that what is relevant is not the prior probability of the phenomena we witness in quantum mechanics (provided it isn't actually zero), but the result of conditionalizing that prior probability to the very unlikely observations that we have made – although how that conditional probability is to be determined if our prior probabilities really come from previous experience, Bayesianism does not tell us. What I have in mind is this: if we suppose that there *are* 'phenomena' in the standard sense in quantum mechanics, events describable in the language of 'pre-theories', to use the terminology employed by a number of authors, which quantum mechanics must simply *explain*, then we are assuming that quantum mechanics is compatible with the existence of a global truth about all phenomena (that all phenomena statements 'commute', in other words), and not simply with the existence of a true description of the phenomena that *each* observer can conceivably measure. But no way of rendering this assumption compatible with quantum mechanics is known except 'brute force', for example, just assuming that all macro-observables commute, whether simultaneously measurable or not. The radical nature of quantum mechanics is shown by the fact that at least one famous thought experiment (Schrödinger's Cat) challenges even *this* assumption.

In any case, the Bayesian story cannot account for the fact that Einstein's Special Theory of Relativity was accepted by a number of famous physicists (Planck, Lorentz) *before* the realistic 'space–time' interpretation of that theory had been proposed by Minkowski. What these physicists – let me add Einstein himself to the list – accepted was *not* just the existence of some 'phenomena', some events 'describable in the language of pre-theories', which had a low 'prior probability', they accepted the statement that *there is no objective two-term bivalent relation of simultaneity between distant events*. If the notion of 'prior probability' applies to such statements at all, statements which would have been treated as a priori false since the beginning of conceptual thought about these matters, it would seem that this statement had prior probability *zero*. Even if one somehow argues (perhaps on Quinean grounds) that no statement ever has probability exactly *one* or exactly *zero*, why the principles Einstein appealed to (principles of formal symmetry and of rejecting in-principle-unobservables) – should have had more weight than the existence of objective simultaneity, when a priori they would seem likely to have exceptions, is not explained by 'inference to the best explanation' epistemology at all.

Extreme cases for philosophy of science

Briefly (and too simply) put, my position is that quantum mechanics and 1905 Relativity fit positivist stories fairly well, but don't fit 'inference to the best explanation' accounts (at least without more clarification than we have yet received of what 'best' means when a theory doesn't have a generally accepted interpretation, clashes with statements which are 'a priori relative to background knowledge', and soon). Darwinian Evolution seems to fit Inference to the Best Explanation accounts, but doesn't fit positivist or Popperian accounts. In this sense, certain theories are extreme cases for certain philosophies of science. I am suggesting that one should stop hoping for a single pattern which fits all theories. Perhaps one can still say some things about scientific procedure in general, but the time has come to recognize that scientific theories are of different 'types' and that informative philosophizing has to descend to a more 'local' and less 'global' level.

Notes

1 J. J. C. Smart, *Philosophy and Scientific Realism*, London, Routledge and Kegan Paul, 1963.
2 H. Putnam, *Reason, Truth and History*, Cambridge, Cambridge University Press, 1974.
3 N. Goodman, *Fact, Fiction and Forecast*, Cambridge, Mass., Harvard University Press, 1955.
4 R. Carnap, *The Nature and Application of Inductive Logic*, Chicago, Chicago University Press, 1951; *The Continuum of Inductive Methods*, Chicago, Chicago University Press, 1952.
5 H. Putnam, 'The "corroboration" of theories', in P. A. Schlipp (ed.), *The Philosophy of Karl Popper, Book 1*, pp. 221–40, reprinted in H. Putnam, *Mathematics, Matter and Method: Philosophical Papers Volume 1*, Cambridge, Cambridge University Press, 1975.
6 Popper has at various times made a number of different claims about evolutionary theory. Thus, in 'Natural selection and the emergence of mind', *Dialectica* 32 (1978), pp. 339–55, he writes 'I still believe that natural selection works this way as a [metaphysical] research programme. Nevertheless, I have changed my mind about the testability and the logical status of the theory of natural selection; and I am glad to have the opportunity to make a recantation' (p. 345). What is Popper's 'recantation'? It turns out that Natural Selection, far from being unfalsifiable, is actually falsified! ('it is not only testable, but it turns out not to be strictly universally true'). Why is natural selection falsified? Because '*not* everything that evolves is useful' (p. 346). Two comments: (1) that anyone would take a theory of evolution to *assert* 'everything that evolves is useful' is amazing; (2) anyway, Popper *still* thinks that what Ernst Mayr, Stephen Gould, et al. call 'the theory of evolution' – which, of course, does *not* assert that everything that evolves is an *adaptation* – is a 'most successful metaphysical research programme'. In his autobiography, *Unended Quest: An Intellectual Autobiography*, La Salle,

Ill., Open Court, 1982, Popper takes the same line: 'Darwinism' is 'not a testable scientific theory, but a metaphysical research programme'. To the extent that it creates the impression that an 'ultimate explanation' has been found, it is 'not so much better than the theistic view of adaption'. However, 'it suggests the existence of a mechanism of adaption, and it allows us even to study in detail the mechanism at work. And it is the only theory which allows us to do all that.'

7 See Putnam, 'The corroboration of theories', and Putnam, 'A critic replies to his philosopher', in M. Burnyeat and T. Honderich (eds), *Philosophy As It Is*, Harmondsworth, Middx., Penguin (in reply to Popper's 'Putnam on "auxiliary sentences", called by me "initial conditions"', in *The Philosophy of Karl Popper*.

8 R. Lewontin, *The Genetic Basis of Evolutionary Change*, New York, Columbia University Press, 1974.

9 S. Gould, *The Panda's Thumb*, New York, Norton, 1980; *The Flamingo's Smile*, New York, Norton, 1985.

10 Smart, *Philosophy and Scientific Realism*, p. 52.

11 See H. Putnam, 'Language and philosophy', *Mind, Language and Reality: Philosophical Papers Volume 2*, Cambridge, Cambridge University Press, 1975, pp. 1–32.

12 D. Shapere, *Reason and the Search for Knowledge*, Dordrecht, Reidel, 1979.

13 The notion that we have a series of ultimate epistemological 'prejudices', which are not unrevisable, but which guide us in theory acceptance, was used by Kripke in his (unpublished) lectures on time and identity at Cornell University in 1978.

14 H. Reichenbach, *The Theory of Relativity and A Priori Knowledge*, Berkeley, University of California Press, 1965.

15 When I read an earlier version of this chapter to the Philosophy of Science Association, Jerry Fodor suggested that this is explained by the fact that biology is a 'special science' (in his terminology) and special sciences don't have strict laws. This is just Smart's view on the status of biology; I find the view plausible, but it would not have been so at any time prior to Galileo. Galileo and Newton could not assume physics was a 'fundamental science' to justify their inductions; they had to rely on the (unstated) 'prejudice' described above. Moreover, even the acceptance of Newtonian physics does not, by itself, rule out the existence of exceptionless biological 'laws'; Smart's (and Fodor's) reasoning depends on the acceptance of a Newtonian (or post-Newtonian) *world view* and not just the acceptance of Newtonian (or post-Newtonian) *equations*. Given such a world view, the distinction between 'fundamental' and special sciences looks reasonable; but the acceptance of a world view is not the sort of thing Positivist and Neo-positivist accounts (such as Popper's) can give an account of. And that's my point.

16 I. Lakatos, *The Methodology of Scientific Research Programmes: Philosophical Papers Volume 1*, Cambridge, Cambridge University Press, 1978.

17 S. E. Toulmin, *The Philosophy of Science: an Introduction*, London, Hutchinson, 1953.

18 L. Hardin and F. Rohrlich, 'Established theories', *Philosophy of Science* 50 (1983), pp. 603–17.
19 Schlipp (ed.), *The Philosophy of Karl Popper*.
20 R. Boyd, 'Scientific realism and naturalistic epistemology', in *PSA 1980*, Philosophy of Science Association, 1981, pp. 1–50.

9

'Life's Uncertain Voyage'

Peter Singer

Introduction

In a previously published work, Helga Kuhse and I have discussed the ethical issues raised by the birth of severely handicapped infants.[1] In that work, we rejected the view that all human life is of equal worth, a view sometimes referred to as the 'doctrine of the sanctity of human life'. In this chapter I take the rejection of this view for granted. Because the view that all human life is of equal worth has had the support of the Judaeo-Christian tradition, and until quite recently was scarcely questioned by any Western thinker (with the exception of racists, who excluded 'inferior races'), there have been few attempts to work out an alternative basis for valuing life. Although a number of recent writers have made some efforts in this direction, many crucial questions have been left untouched.[2] For instance, much of the debate has been about *when* a human life begins, or as may be better put, when a human being acquires the moral standing which makes its death a bad thing. This appears to assume that a human life has little or no value up to some specific point, and thereafter has some fixed value for the remainder of the time that the being is alive. But why should we assume this? Is it not possible that the value of a person's life varies as the person develops?

Some economists certainly believe that it does. They have been assigned the unenviable task of estimating the value of human lives, so that governments can calculate how much should be spent on building safer roads, or how much it is reasonable to require the construction and mining industries to spend on safety measures. Some of these economists seek to answer this question by measuring the value of the 'human capital' lost by an accidental death. They try to find the value of the loss of expected net future earnings caused by death. In calculating these *net* earnings for a child, the costs of rearing, education and training must be deducted from the gross earnings the child can be expected to receive. On this approach, the value of a human life is at its highest when our education or training has just been completed, and it declines gradually thereafter.[3]

But, you will no doubt be saying to yourselves, this calculates only the narrowly economic value of a life, and has nothing to do with the value which makes death a tragedy. Some other economists, working in the health care field, are well aware of this objection. In their attempts to compare the value of different forms of medical treatment, they have developed the idea of a quality-adjusted life-year, or QALY.[4] This, as its name suggests, is a year of life, adjusted for its quality. Suppose you have severe angina. Your life expectancy without surgery is ten years, but the angina so reduces the quality of your life that you are indifferent between the prospect of ten years of life with angina, and four years of life without angina. Then a year *with* angina is worth only 0.4 of a QALY to you. Accordingly, a coronary artery by-pass operation which carries a ten per cent chance of killing you, but will, if you survive it, get rid of your angina without altering your life-expectancy, looks like a good bet. For those who calculate QALYs, our lives are worth most at birth, because then we can expect to have the greatest number of QALYs ahead of us. (It is not entirely clear, however, why these health economists do not begin counting QALYs *before* birth – for instance, in calculations of the benefits of pre-natal diagnosis for defects like Down's syndrome, economists balance the costs of preventing such births against the gains in terms of saving expenditure on children born with the condition. Nothing is said about the life-years which would be gained by *not* preventing the births of these children.)[5] After birth, if the advocates of QALYs are to be believed, the value of our life begins its steady and persistent decline.

So here are two different models, already in use, of deciding on the value of a human life, and neither of them holds that all lives are of constant value irrespective of the stage a person's life has reached. Of course, the truth might lie somewhere else altogether. We could appeal to the analogy of athletic prowess, and hold that the value of life peaks as our bodies begin to decline when we are in our 20s and early 30s. Then again, maybe the value of a life is more like the accumulation of experience, constantly increasing as we get older; or perhaps it is like that subject so close to academic hearts, superannuation, growing steadily year by year until we retire, from which point we begin to draw on our accumulated reserves.

If none of these models seems quite correct, they at least question the assumption that from some specific point onwards, a life has a constant value. I shall explore this question using a different analogy.

The journey

Suppose that I have long been fascinated by mountains, and by walking in high country with vistas of snowy peaks. As an Australian, however, my opportunities for doing so are limited; our mountains have their own special interest, but by world standards they are not spectacular. As an avid reader of travel books and the *National Geographic*, I learn that the grandest of all mountains are the Himalayas, and my most cherished ambition becomes a trek in Nepal, to the Thyangboche monastery from where one looks up to a panorama of stupendous peaks, including of course Everest itself. So I go to a travel agent and make enquiries about plane tickets to Nepal. Unfortunately the cost is far more than I can afford, but I am not daunted. I find a freighter that, in return for my doing routine chores, will take me to Calcutta. The ocean voyage is far worse than I expected; I am seasick, my 'cabin' is a stinking hole which becomes unbearably hot as we near the tropics, and I am given the most unpleasant tasks on the ship. At last, however, we reach Calcutta and I can disembark. Now, since I have little money, I must walk or hitch-hike to Nepal. The country through which I pass is hot and dusty, and I am unable to take any pleasure in the exotic nature of my surroundings. I must sleep rough, and eat sparingly to husband my savings. Several times I fall ill with the usual forms of diarrhoea and related complaints, but eventually I make it to Kathmandu. Here the Himalayan trek begins, and although it is still very hard work, my spirits begin to rise, for the sparkling Himalayan peaks are now beckoning in the distance. Some three weeks after leaving Kathmandu, I emerge from the forest into a clearing and there stands the monastery. It is everything I had hoped for; and the hardships of the journey now all seem to have been worthwhile.

That is the first version of the story. Now consider some variations on the theme. In the second version, everything goes as in the previous story, up to the point at which I am trekking in to Thyangboche. After several days' hard walking, with just tantalizing glimpses of the scenic splendour to come, I begin to feel weak and ill once again, but this time it is no minor infection; a local health worker diagnoses hepatitis B, and I have to be evacuated back to Kathmandu. I recover, but I am in no fit state to resume the trek. My strength and determination is at an end, and all I can do is return, dejectedly, to Australia.

The third version runs parallel to the first only up to the point at which I make my first visit to the travel agent and discover that the trip will cost more than I can afford. In this version, my enquiries about working my way over on a freighter are met with a discouraging response. So I give up the whole idea of the journey and my disappointment gradually fades, until I cease to dream of distant snowy peaks.

In the fourth version, if indeed it can be called a 'version' at all, I never had any interest in seeing the Himalayas. I continue to lead the same life as, in other versions, I had lived before I became interested in going to Nepal.

If we imagine ourselves leading the life of the central figure in each of these versions of the story, how would we rank them? Which would we most prefer to live through, and which would we least prefer? I think the answer is clear: I would most prefer the first version, in which my cherished ambition is satisfied, and I would least prefer the second version, in which all the hard work and sacrifice were in vain. The third version, in which the journey was abandoned in the early planning stages, is to be preferred to the second, and the fourth version, in which there were no plans for a trip at all, is better than the second version, although obviously still nowhere near as good as the first. I hope that this ordering will be generally shared, and in what follows, I shall presume that it is.

Now to the point of all this travel writing. We may look at the life of a person as a kind of journey. This is scarcely a new idea: Dante wrote of 'the journey of our life' in *The Divine Comedy*,[6] and Shakespeare was especially fond of the metaphor. The title of this paper comes from *Timon of Athens*, and the same metaphor can be found in *Othello* and in *Julius Caesar*.[7] The parallel may be a useful device for exploring some ideas about the value of life.

Granted, a human life is in many ways very different from a journey, and particularly different from the kind of journey I have just described – that is, a journey with a single, culminating goal. Although Solon may have said 'Call no man happy until he is dead,'[8] and Aeschylus put it in even more explicitly goal-directed terms ('Only when man's life comes to its end in prosperity can one call that man happy'[9]), others have taken a contrary view. Leonard Woolf entitled the final volume of his autobiography 'The Journey, Not the Arrival Matters', a title which appears to be a variation on Robert Louis Stevenson's 'To travel hopefully is a better thing than to arrive.'[10] Some will even say that a closer metaphor for most human lives would be not a purposive journey at all, but the meanderings of a beggar drifting from one spot to another according to where the pickings seem best.

As far as the purposes of this chapter are concerned, though, it will be

enough if we acknowledge that the first part of our lives is a preparation
for the remainder, and that this preparation involves a considerable effort
by both the child and the parents. Think, here, of the discomfort and
inconvenience of pregnancy, and the pain of childbirth; of all the care
that is needed to ensure that an infant survives, the feeding, cleaning,
and keeping warm, dry and safe. Think, too, of the restrictions involved
in having to be with, or arrange for someone else to be with, a young
child every hour of the day and night. Then there is the cost of food and
clothing and, whether the costs are met privately or by the community,
of the education that every child must receive in order to become an
acceptable member of society. I am not denying that childhood, and the
time when we bring up our own children, can be wonderful periods of
our lives. Planning for a journey can also be enjoyable. Here, as with the
pleasure that we get from bringing up children, much of the enjoyment
derives from the fact that this is a forward-looking activity, and we are
savouring the pleasures of anticipation. Whatever the balance of
pleasures and pains of being a parent, much of the positive value we
derive comes from the fact that all this activity is goal-directed, and the
goal is to rear a child to maturity. Once the children themselves
understand that they will grow to be adults, they too will join in this
purposive activity, and share in its goal.

We might put this by talking of 'investment in a life'. The expression
is open to misinterpretation; I do not want to suggest anything
mercenary, or even self-seeking, about this investment. I intend the term
in its broadest sense, to refer not especially to the investment of money
(though I do not exclude this) but also, and usually in this context much
more importantly, to emotional investment. When one cares for a child,
one invests one's time and energy with that child; and when one loves a
child, one invests one's feelings in the child, so that one cannot but
suffer if something bad should happen to the child. In this sense, parents
usually invest in the life of their child even before birth. The investment
generally grows sharply after birth, reaching its peak – or, perhaps
better, reaching a high plateau – only some years later. Others apart
from the parents will also invest in the lives of children: grandparents
and siblings often quite soon after birth, more distant relatives and
friends often only much later. The child, too, begins to invest from quite
an early age, not eating sweets now in order to avoid tooth decay later, or
practicing tedious piano pieces so that she can later reach a level of
playing which is more enjoyable and more satisfying.

The starting point

If life is a journey, when does it begin? Here is a list of possibilities, from the earliest onwards:

1 when your parents decided to have a child (assuming that there was such a decision);
2 when you were conceived;
3 when you first become conscious;
4 when you were born;
5 when you first became aware of yourself as a being existing over time, and understood that you had a future and a past; in other words, when the journey became inwardly as well as outwardly a journey, or, as Michael Tooley puts it, at the point at which different desires existing at different times can be correctly attributed to a single continuing subject of consciousness.[11]

Those who have followed the recent debates over the moral status of embryos, foetuses and infants will have no difficulty in recognizing these possible starting points. Can the metaphor of the journey help us to make progress in this debate? I think it can. First, as I have already said, it has often been assumed that we are looking for one crucial point, before which there is nothing wrong with ending a life, and after which there is as much wrong with ending it as there is with ending the lives of people like you and me. But is there one crucial point in a journey, before which abandoning it does not matter, and after which it matters as much as abandoning the journey at any stage could matter? No; in the third version of the story, our hero could not proceed beyond the initial inquiries. This was a pity, but it was not nearly so great a loss as having to abandon the journey just when it had almost reached its goal. A journey develops in stages, from the earliest desire to go somewhere, through the planning and making of arrangements, to the actual departure and the travel before the destination is reached. If we can assume, for the moment, that the point of the journey is to reach the destination, then the more one has put into the journey, the worse it is to have to give it up before its purpose has been realized.

So if a life is at all like a journey, we should not expect there to be any crucial point, before which abandoning it does not matter, and after which it matters as much as abandoning it at any stage could matter. But we still need to ask when the journey begins, that is, when life begins to take on *some* value, even if not as much as it may later have. Here it is important to remember that if life is a journey, it is a journey from more than one perspective. The perspective of the child is not the only one; we have already seen that the parents, and other relatives and friends, may invest heavily in the life. So we must consider both the *inward* perspective, that of the other person leading the journey, and the *outward* perspective, that of the others who have invested in it.

The earliest stage of a journey is the desire to go somewhere, and the planning that follows from it. But so far as the *inward* perspective is concerned, even in a planned pregnancy, the planning is not that of the embryo or future child. The journey that begins with the desire to have a child, and the arrangements consequent upon that desire, such as ceasing to use contraceptives, is of course planning by the parents. So it is only from the *outward* perspective that the journey begins here. If the pregnancy is not planned, the journey cannot begin, even from this outward perspective, until the fact of the pregnancy is known to the mother, at least. Perhaps it would be better, however, to speak of the journey from the parents' perspective as beginning with the *acceptance* of pregnancy and the wanting of the child. In a planned pregnancy this may pre-date the pregnancy itself; in an unplanned pregnancy it often comes soon after the pregnancy becomes known. In some cases there may be a period of indecision about the pregnancy, and an abortion may be contemplated. That decision can, like the decision about ceasing to use contraceptives, be seen as a decision whether or not to go on a particular journey.

Assuming that the decision to embark on the journey of creating a life is made, the effort needed at this stage is usually minimal. This effort increases, at least for the mother-to-be, throughout pregnancy and labour. Thereafter, both the effort and the emotional investment in the new life normally continue to grow for both parents, although this may vary greatly in some circumstances. If a journey begins so badly that the prospect of getting anywhere worthwhile seems slight, it may be better to abandon it, and hope to make another journey in more favourable circumstances. This parallels the birth of a severely disabled infant, where the parents may, if the infant dies, have another, healthy child.[12] Another example, indicating the same attitude even when the child is healthy, comes from a newspaper story of a Texas hairdresser who was 'somewhat upset' when her pet Rottweiler killed and ate her four-week-old daughter; but she 'wept hysterically' when told that the dog would have to be put down: 'I can always have another baby', she said, 'but I can't replace my dog Byron.'[13] At first the comment strikes us as incomprehensible; but when understood in terms of emotional investment, it starts to become less crazy, even if the woman's priorities remain peculiar.

Of course, the parallel with a journey which may be tried again under more auspicious circumstances holds only so far as the outward perspective is concerned. There is no parallel here with the inward perspective of the infant, since if the disabled infant dies it will not be that infant, but another, who makes the journey. But we have yet to consider this inward perspective, and it is to it that I now turn. Seen from the inside, as it were, the earliest stage of life's uncertain voyage cannot be the planning for the pregnancy, for the voyager is then not even in existence. Nor can it be conception, for while the traveller does then begin to exist, an entity without consciousness cannot have experienced the start of anything, and has had neither pleasure nor pain in its existence. So the journey cannot have begun, from the internal, or subjective, standpoint of the traveller. Admittedly, survival of this period before consciousness is a condition without which no subsequent journey could occur. And the same is true, of course, of the act of conception itself. If my parents had not ceased to use contraceptives when they did, my journey would never have begun. But for the life-traveller, such thoughts can only be retrospective. They are like the thoughts of the conventional traveller, who says 'if my uncle had not left me $5000 when he died five years ago, I would never have been able to afford this journey.' The inheritance from the uncle may have been a condition without which the journey could not have gone ahead, but it is not itself a stage in my journey.

Should we regard the first conscious moments as the start of the journey? In favour of such a starting point is the fact that from then on, the living being does have to suffer the hardships of the journey, and can take pleasure and comfort from the periods when it goes well. But there are powerful arguments against this too.

This first argument is that a being that is conscious, but has no sense of its own existence over time, must lack the desires necessary to set the plans for the journey in motion. So no *purposive* journey can have begun at this stage. But does the journey *have* to be purposive? It may be objected that to say this is to set the standard far too high. Many journeys are a series of wanderings, from one short-term objective to the next, and only in retrospect can we throw a cloak of unity and coherence over them. If this is true of real journeys, it is even more true of lives, when viewed as journeys. Life is not a journey in the sense of being a venture on which we deliberately embark with a purpose; and if in time many of us acquire overall goals or objectives which guide our lives, there are probably even more of us who do not. So the 'lack of purpose' objection to consciousness as the starting point is not conclusive.

But there is a further, more powerful objection to regarding the beginning of consciousness as the beginning of the journey, when we consider the matter from the perspective of the life-traveller. The best way to put this objection is to ask *who* is making the journey. When there is consciousness, but no sense of self, there is no continuing mental entity who persists throughout the experiences which make up the life. So it can be argued, as Michael Tooley has suggested, that what we need is *continuity of mental substance* – that is, some mental connections between the different experiences stretching over time which make up a life.[14] These might be forward-looking connections, such as desires or anticipation of my future states; or they can be backward-looking connections, memories of former states. But in either case, the conscious being must possess, at some time, the concept of a continuing self. If we have two stages of a physical organism which are not linked in either of these ways, then they cannot be parts of the same person's journey. Thus the stage of infancy is not linked to later stages of our lives in the necessary way. As an infant, I could not anticipate or desire future states of my own existence, for I lacked the conception of myself as a baby with a future; and as a later child and adult, I cannot remember being a newborn infant. So the first month of life (at least) of the baby from which I developed was not, in the relevant sense, a part of *my* life's journey. It was, like the gestation *in utero* of that baby, and like the decision my parents (I believe) took to have a child at that particular time, a necessary condition of my journey, but it was not the journey itself.

The end

A similar point may apply to the permanent loss of self-awareness. In his recent book *The End of Life*, James Rachels has used the distinction between a *biological* life and a *biographical* life to make a similar point. He illustrates it by reference to people who suffered accidents as a result of which they went into long-term coma, and then died without recovering consciousness. Miguel Martinez was a Spanish soccer player who became comatose as a result of a injury; when he died, eight years after the accident, his family said 'Miguel died at the age of 34, after having lived 26 years.'[15]

It is relatively easy to accept that for Martinez, life's voyage ended when he went into a coma, not when he died. But what of a case in which consciousness remains, though all mental continuity is lost? If Martinez, instead of going into a coma, had been reduced to a state of infantile idiocy in which he showed no ability to remember the past or desire any future state, we might also say that his life's journey was over. If we still think life is or is not in the interests of Martinez, we are invoking the same sense of interests employed when we ask whether we can harm a person's interests after that person is dead.[16]

Rachels has supplied an even more intriguing example, drawn from the work of the neurologist Oliver Sacks, to illustrate this point. Sacks has a patient, called Jimmie R., who suffers from Korsakov's syndrome, a result of alcohol-induced brain damage. Jimmie can remember his life only up to the time he was 19. Since then – and that was many years ago – he has had no long-term memory. On first meeting, he seems quite rational, but two minutes later he will not remember having met you, and the conversation will start again. This lack of memory prevents him from holding a job, or even being able to live outside an institution; and as Rachels points out, it 'deprives him of a life in a deeper sense'. Sacks professes his own bafflement about 'whether, indeed, one [can] speak of an "existence" given so absolute a privation of memory or continuity'. Rachels points out that 'existence' is the wrong word: Jimmie undoubtedly exists; what is doubtful is whether he has a *life*, in the biographical rather than the biological sense.[17]

We are now in a position to suggest some tentative conclusions about the relative tragedy of death at different stages of life. The beginnings of mental continuity can be regarded as the first stages of the journey. So to die before mental continuity has developed is to die before the journey has even begun, and is not – or at least not for the being who dies – a loss. It is like the fourth version of the tale of the Himalayan trekker, in which there is no trek, and not even a plan for a trek. To die soon after the development of mental continuity (say as a child of about one or two years old) is a loss comparable to having to abandon the journey in its earliest stages, as in the third version. The tragedy of death at a later stage will vary in accordance with how much of the journey has been undertaken, how much of the goal has been achieved, and how much more might have been achieved. Thus, to use once again some apt examples provided by Rachels, the death of Bertrand Russell at the age of 97 was not tragic, for he had travelled as far, and as successfully, as anyone could reasonably expect. Moreover, his journey was already beginning to go less well; there was little more that was likely to be accomplished. The death of F. P. Ramsey, a gifted young philosopher who died at the age of 26, on the other hand, was a tragedy: here was a journey that had begun well, was full of promise, and was cut off just at the point at which the promise was beginning to be fulfilled. If Russell's life is analogous to the first tale of the Himalayan trekker, Ramsey's life resembles the second one, in which I undertake all the preparations, but fail to reach my goal. (Ramsey certainly achieved quite a bit before he died, so the preparations were not entirely in vain: it is only in comparison with what he might have achieved, had he lived a normal lifespan, that his life resembles the second tale.) We can also understand why, to take a death nearer to us, we may feel that the recent death of Stanley Benn was rendered a little less tragic than it might otherwise have been by the fact that he was able, shortly before his death, to complete a book which is the culmination of much of his work over recent years. Unlike Russell, Benn would no doubt have achieved more if he had lived longer; but unlike Ramsey, he had perhaps, with the final book, accomplished the greatest part of what he could have been expected to achieve.

It may be objected that the view I have outlined cannot be accepted because it is so radically at odds with widely held beliefs about the value of human life. In particular, if we take seriously the idea of life as a journey, the value of every life will vary according to the stage of the journey that the person has reached. So the wrongness of killing will be highly variable, and it will be right to spend much more on medical treatment for some than for others.

It is of course true, as pointed out at the beginning of this chapter, that the view I am advancing is very different from traditional Judaeo-Christian ideas about the value of life. That is not in itself an objection. But can we live with the consequences? At first glance it does seem wrong to vary the seriousness of a murder according to some judgement of the value of the life of the murdered person. But viewing life as a journey does not compel us to do this. We can quite easily distinguish such practical matters as the criminal law from the philosophical views we hold about the value of life. An analogy here is religious toleration. In those pluralistic Western societies which do not have an established religion, the official view of government is that all religions are equally acceptable, and their adherents are equally entitled to worship as they choose. Philosophically, it would be very difficult to defend the view that each religion had an equal claim to be regarded as true; but as a matter of practical politics, religious toleration is desirable. Therefore, in deciding on matters affecting religion, governments treat all religions as if they were equally valid. We could take the same attitude in regard to the value of life: for certain purposes we could treat everyone's life as being of equal value, even though we know that this is not really the case. In fact, however, it is not necessary to go so far, because we already operate with an attitude to human life which is somewhere between the 'official' view that all life is of equal value, and a view like the one I have put forward. For example, we do not generally think the same efforts should be put into keeping seriously ill people alive irrespective of their age. We make greater efforts to keep alive people in their 20s than we would to keep alive those who, because of their age, would clearly be near the end of life's journey even if they did recover from their present illness.

Replaceability

Seeing life as a journey gives us an account of how each biographical life gains in value as it gets under way, and as more goes into making the journey. It indicates why taking some kinds of lives can be worse than taking other kinds of lives. In some cases we are interrupting a journey, and in others we are not. With embryos, foetuses, infants, the severely mentally retarded, and some non-human animals, we presumably are not interrupting a journey, at least not a journey which has an inward perspective. So the death of such a being will not be tragic, in the sense that a person's death is often tragic. But we must remember that extrinsic factors can be of great importance here. The life of a being may represent a journey for others – for instance the parents – even if it is not a journey from the internal perspective of that being itself. But can the metaphor help us with the most baffling problems utilitarians face about life and birth and death: replacement and the problem of deciding on an optimum population?

The problem of replacement arises from an argument against vegetarianism, first raised, to the best of my knowledge, by Leslie Stephen, who wrote 'Of all the arguments for Vegetarianism, none is so weak as the argument from humanity. The pig has a stronger interest than anyone in the demand for bacon. If all the world were Jewish, there would be no pigs at all.'[18] This argument assumes that pigs reared to be made into bacon lead lives which they would want to lead, if they had the choice, and that the loss caused to one pig by killing it can be made up for by the benefit brought to another pig who is then brought into being for a while, to be killed in its turn. The assumption about the quality of porcine life is highly dubious in the modern world of factory farming, but we cannot blame Stephen for that, and for present purposes we can put our doubts aside. The interesting philosophical question is whether pigs are *replaceable* in the manner Stephen's argument suggests. The idea of replaceability is not just a handy way of escaping the ethical obligation to be a vegetarian, provided we grant some factual assumptions. It also raises a more general problem for utilitarians. If pigs are replaceable, why not people too? Of course, there may be practical difficulties with killing people in such a way as not to cause general fear and terror, but is this really the *only* objection to regarding people simply as receptacles for happy experiences? If, in some extraordinary circumstances, we really could slightly increase the total happiness by painlessly killing one person and creating another, would this be the right thing to do?

In *Practical Ethics* I suggested that the best answer the utilitarian could give to this problem was to move from classical, or hedonistic, utilitarianism to preference utilitarianism.[19] A preference utilitarian, I said, could explain why replaceability might hold for those animals not capable of desiring to continue to live, but would not hold for *persons*, who have a conception of themselves over time and would normally have a preference for continued life. But the objection was soon raised, for instance by H. L. A. Hart in his review of *Practical Ethics*, that on a preference utilitarian account, the preference for living of the person brought into existence – which we will be able to satisfy – should be able to make up for thwarting the preference of the person killed.[20]

For a time I was confident that I had an adequate reply to this objection. My underlying thought was that since preferences exist, it is good to satisfy them – but that this does not mean there is any value in first *creating* a preference, and then satisfying it. I suggested that we might regard bringing a preference into existence, and then satisfying it, as akin to going into debt, and then paying the debt. So the creating and satisfying of a new preference adds up, not to some positive utility score, but to zero; hence it cannot outweigh the utility lost by thwarting an existing preference. But I now think that Michael Lockwood is right when he says that this view is a form of negative utilitarianism, and is vulnerable to the same objections which sink that position.[21] For instance, the 'debit' view of preferences would mean that it would be wrong to bring a child into the world if we can anticipate that the child will have just one unfulfilled desire, no matter how many fulfilled desires the child may have. The one unfulfilled desire can never be outweighed by all the other fulfilled desires. This cannot be right, and the approach which leads us to it must be rejected. The objection made by Hart to the preference model could also be strengthened by pointing out that *every* preference for continued life will eventually be thwarted (unless we tire of life before we die) so that it does not really matter, so far as the total sum of thwarted desires is concerned, whether our preference for continued life is thwarted sooner or later.

The metaphor of the journey suggests a better answer. Think again of the Himalayan trekker in the second version of the story, in which I fall ill only a day or two away from my destination. I will scarcely be consoled by the thought that I can start all over again – taking the trip on the freighter, then all the discomforts and hazards of making my way across India, and so on. This kind of replacement does not recover what has been lost; and the more that has been invested in the journey, the less adequate 'replacement' will be. So if we see life as a journey, we have an intuitive feel for why replacement will not work. We should note, too, that the traveller in the second version of the journey would be *less* consoled still by the thought that *someone else* will be able to make the journey. And even if we take, not the self-interested point of view of the traveller, but some impartial or objective standpoint – Sidgwick's 'point of view of the universe', if you like – the replacement of the disappointed traveller by another does not compensate for the loss, because all the time and effort will have to be invested once again before the pay-off takes place. There will be the hardships of *two* journeys, and the rewards of only one. Metaphor can be helpful, but in the end we need to cash out the metaphor in terms of an overall ethical theory, with a satisfactory notion of value. Can this be done with the metaphor of life as a journey? In keeping with my general views in ethics, I shall seek to do so within a framework that is broadly utilitarian.

At first it might seem that any consequentialist theory will be unable to take account of the idea that life is a kind of journey. For consequentialist theories – unlike theories based on justice or desert – are necessarily forward-looking. The thought that a death is worse if it takes place after a long journey, and just prior to achieving the goals of that journey, seems to be backward-looking: that is, the loss is judged to be worse because of all the effort that has gone before. For a consequentialist, however, the effort is all water under the bridge; it is past, and no matter how much of a disvalue it may have been, it cannot be undone. The only consideration that matters is *how much* loss of *future* value a death will cause.

Yet if we see the initial stages of a person's life as a period in which sacrifices are made for the sake of a future benefit, we have an account of when death is worst which is compatible with even the most straightforward form of consequentialism, hedonistic utilitarianism. Death will be worst when, had death not occurred, the net expected utility would have been greatest. At an early stage of the journey, most of the sacrifices are still to be made and the success of the enterprise is uncertain. The expected utility is therefore low. At a later stage, when almost all the sacrifices have been made and the prize is within reach, the expected utility is high. This calculation of costs and benefits must include not only those of the person whose death is in contemplation, but also of the family and friends of that person, and these will reinforce the tendency towards holding that the more that has been invested, both emotionally and materially, in a person's life, where the returns on the investment are still to be realized, the greater the tragedy of death.

So hedonism is not without ways of accounting for the aspects in which a biographical life resembles a journey. Nevertheless, those who are not committed hedonistic utilitarians may feel that this leaves too much out. In particular, it leaves out of account the wants and strivings that have gone into reaching a certain point on the journey; and what of the sense that an entire life, full of striving and hard work, can be rendered pointless if it leads to nothing? To many this will seem not *just* a matter of the pleasure or happiness which might have been gained. Is there a more sophisticated version of consequentialism which can make sense of this?

Preference utilitarianism differs from the classical version in that the consequences to be maximized are not sensations such as pleasure, but the satisfaction of preferences. The term 'satisfaction' here can be misleading, for most preference utilitarians are not seeking to maximize a mental state of satisfaction, but rather to bring about whatever it is that is preferred.[22] Such a theory can come closer than hedonistic utilitarianism to making sense of the view just described. It must be a form of preference utilitarianism, however, which does not judge preferences simply by the intensity with which they are felt at a given time. How preferences are to be weighed is, of course, a problem for any form of preference utilitarianism. It would be nonsense always to give priority to the most intensely felt preference at any given time; we all recognize in our own prudential calculations that that is not a wise thing to do. So somehow the preference utilitarian must give preferences a weighting which is independent of present intensity. The restriction usually suggested, following Butler's classic account of prudence, refers to reflection 'in a cool hour', based on an accurate knowledge of the relevant facts.[23] If we build enough into this notion of full information, careful thought, and so on, we shall end up identifying preferences and interests. We shall then have a form of utilitarianism which seeks to maximize that special subset of prefrences we call our interests. Among our interests, we would certainly give priority to long-standing, overarching preferences which (irrespective of how intensely they may be felt at a particular time) must be presupposed to make sense of the whole range of a person's activities. Interests are the kind of thing you can accumulate, or build up. It is true to say of interests that the longer I have been striving towards something, the greater the interest I have in achieving it; but that would sound odd if we substituted 'preference' for 'interest'. If I have been planning my Himalayan trek for three years, with all the sacrifices that involves, I have a greater interest in going than someone else who has just suddenly thought how much fun it would be to go, even if the psychological intensity of our desires does not differ (perhaps the other person is the kind who is easily caught up with sudden enthusiasms).

On this view, then, the consequences of the death of a person at the stage of life equivalent to my disappointed Himalayan trekker are worse than death at the equivalent of either an earlier stage of the journey, or after the journey has achieved its major goal or goals. The reason is that such a death causes a more significant interest to go unfulfilled. The interest is constituted not just from the preferences actually held at the moment of death, but also from those which guided so many of the person's activities during the earlier stages of the journey.[24] It seems plausible to hold that this value, the value that is lost by a person's death after years of effort and striving towards a goal, is not going to be replaced by bringing a new person into existence, for then, as with the hedonistic version, there will be two lots of strivings for only one lot of fulfilment. Even if we do hold that there is some positive value in bringing into the world a being whose preferences will be satisfied, we can plausibly deny that the positive value of bringing a new being into the world is ever going to make up for such a loss. I shall say more about *why* this is plausible in the concluding section of this chapter, to which I shall come in just a moment. Note, too, that this account is immune to the objection, so powerful against the account I offered in *Practical Ethics*, that all our preferences for continued life are going to be thwarted someday, so it doesn't matter when they get thwarted. On the present account, we can answer that it does matter, because premature death will prevent us from fulfilling our interest in achieving goals which, given a normal lifespan, we can hope to reach.

Population policy

Finally, then, what about population policy? Since Derek Parfit focused our attention more sharply on a choice first noticed by Henry Sidgwick,[25] utilitarians have had great difficulty in resting comfortably either with the *total* view – that the optimum population is that which leads to the greatest total amount of happiness – or with the *average* view – that the optimum population is that which leads to the highest average level of happiness. As Parfit has put it, we find the first view repugnant because it implies that for any well-populated world of very happy people, there is some other world (Parfit calls it 'Z') of far more people, all just marginally above the level at which the value of life ceases to be positive, which is a *better* world because it contains a greater total amount of happiness. But if this is repugnant, the second view seems plainly absurd, because it tells us that if we have a world of, say, one billion extremely happy people, and we have the option of bringing into existence an additional four billion people who would all be happy to be alive, and whose existence would actually *add* marginally to the happiness of the previously existing billion people, this would be a *bad* thing to do, just because the resulting world would have a lower average happiness, even though the people who would have existed anyway will be better off, and the other people who will come into existence will be very glad to be alive.

The journey metaphor seems not to help with the fundamental issue. We are choosing between many trips to some rather dull nearby beach resort, as against a few trips to Nepal. If the beach resort is worth visiting at all, there may be *some* very large numbers of trips there for which it would be worth sacrificing a small number of trips to Nepal. So this suggests that the total view may be right after all, and we should accept the so-called 'repugnant conclusion'.

But while the journey metaphor does not offer any means of avoiding the repugnant conclusion, it may suggest a reason why the conclusion is less repugnant than we might otherwise think. One standard way in which proponents of the total view have sought to reduce the repugnance of Z is by saying that this repugnance is generated by our imagining that the lives of those living in Z are *much* worse than our own lives. But this assumes that our own lives are *far* above the point at which life ceases to be worth living. If we take a more pessimistic view of our own lives, the average life in Z might be only a *little* worse than our own lives – and what is so repugnant about believing that a large number of lives a little worse than our own could be better than a small number of lives much better than our own?

The problems with this way of reducing the repugnance of Z is that it seems to imply that if the quality of our own lives should fall only a small amount – just fractionally below the level of lives in Z – we would be better off dead. This we are understandably reluctant to accept. But seeing life as a journey explains why we can hold that the quality of our own lives is only a little above the level at which life ceases to be worth living, and yet deny that if the quality of our own lives were to fall, we would be better off dead. The point depends on distinguishing the value of our lives, *taken as a whole* from the value of our lives, given that we have already reached a certain stage in life's journey. The net expected value of our lives, taken as a whole, may well be such that if it were to fall a little, it would be better if we had never lived; and at the same time, the value of our lives, given the stage of the journey we have already reached, may be such that it would have to fall a great deal for the *remainder* of our lives not to be worth completing.

This somewhat pessimistic view of the worth of our lives, taken as a whole, also explains the point I made just before starting on the issue of population policy. Perhaps one reason why replaceability is so unattractive is that, since life is an uncertain voyage, it is dubious whether it is wise to embark at all; but if we nevertheless find ourselves on the journey and survive its initial perils and ordeals, we do eventually reach a point at which it is definitely worthwhile to keep going.

Notes

1 See especially Helga Kuhse and Peter Singer, *Should the Baby Live?*, Oxford, Oxford University Press, 1985.

2 See, for example, Joseph Fletcher, 'Indicators of humanhood', *Hastings Center Report* 2, (November 1972), pp. 1–4; Mary Anne Warren, 'On the moral and legal status of abortion', *The Monist* (1973), pp. 43–61; Jonathan Glover, *Causing Death and Saving Lives*, Harmondsworth, Middx., Penguin, 1977; Michael Tooley, *Abortion and Infanticide*, Oxford, Clarendon Press, 1983; John Harris, *The Value of Life*, London, Routledge and Kegan Paul, 1985; and James Rachels, *The End of Life*, Oxford, Oxford University Press, 1986.

3 For a critical discussion of this approach, see E. J. Mishan, 'Evaluation of life and limb: a theoretical approach', *Journal of Political Economy* 79 (1971), pp. 687–706.

4 See R. Zeckhauser and D. Shepard, 'Where now for saving lives?', *Law and Contemporary Problems* 40 (1976), pp. 5–45.

5 See the review of such calculations in R. L. Lakehurst and S. Holterman, 'Application of cost-benefit analysis to programmes for the prevention of mental handicap', in the 1977 Ciba Foundation London Symposium, *Major Mental Handicap: methods and costs of prevention*, North Holland, Elsevier, Excerpta Medica, 1978.

6 Dante Alighieri, *Inferno*, Canto, 1, 1.

7 William Shakespeare, *Timon of Athens*, V, ii; *Othello*, V, ii; *Julius Caesar*, IV, iii.

8 According to Herodotus, *The Histories*, Bk. 1, ch. 32.

9 Aeschylus, *Agamemnon*, line 928.

10 Robert Louis Stevenson, *Virginibus Puerisque*, VI, 'El Dorado'.

11 Michael Tooley, *Abortion and Infanticide*, Oxford, Clarendon Press, 1983, p. 120.

12 For evidence of this tendency, see Kuhse and Singer, *Should the Baby Live?*, pp. 155–6 and p. 214.

13 'Mother weeps for dog that ate her baby', *Sun*, London, 18 March 1985; cited in James Serpell, *In the Company of Animals*, Oxford, Basil Blackwell, 1986, p. 22.

14 Tooley, *Abortion and Infanticide*.

15 Rachels, *The End of Life*, p. 55.

16 See, for instance, Joel Feinberg, *Harm to Others*, Oxford, Oxford University Press, 1984, pp. 83–95.

17 Rachels, *The End of Life*, pp. 52–3.

18 Leslie Stephen, *Social Rights and Duties*, London, 1896.

19 P. Singer, *Practical Ethics*, Cambridge, Cambridge University Press, 1979, pp. 80–1, 100–3.

20 H. L. A. Hart, 'Death and utility', *New York Review of Books*, May 15, 1980.

21 Michael Lockwood, 'Singer on killing and the preference for life', *Inquiry* 22

(1979), pp. 157–70.

22 This distinction appears to have been made first by W. D. Ross, *The Foundations of Ethics*, Oxford, Clarendon Press, 1939, p. 300; I owe this reference to Roy Perrett's paper 'The fear of death', read at the Australasian Association of Philosophy Conference in Melbourne, 1986. Perrett's paper, which will form a part of his forthcoming book, *Death and Immortality*, The Hague, Nijhoff, 1987, indicates how this distinction can also overcome the ancient Epicurean objections to treating death as an evil.

23 Joseph Butler, *Fifteen Sermons* XI, reprinted in D. D. Raphael (ed.), *British Moralists, 1650–1801*, Oxford, Clarendon Press, 1969, p. 373. See also R. B. Brandt, *A Theory of the Good and the Right*, Oxford, Clarendon Press, 1979, chs VI–VII; and R. M. Hare, *Moral Thinking*, Oxford, Clarendon Press, 1981, pp. 104–6.

24 For a related view of prudence, see Phillip Bricker's discussion of a man whose life was ruled by his desire to win posthumous fame by writing a masterpiece, but who, now that he is dying and the fame he has coveted is within his grasp, changes his mind: 'Prudence', *Journal of Philosophy* 77 (1980), pp. 381–401, esp. pp. 389–90.

25 See H. Sidgwick, *The Methods of Ethics*, 7th edition, London, Macmillan, 1907, pp. 414–16, and D. Parfit, *Reasons and Persons*, Oxford, Clarendon Press, part IV.

10

Replies

J. J. C. Smart

I was much moved by the kindness of Philip, Richard and Jean in thinking of this volume and of undertaking the considerable labour of editing it. It was an act of true friendship.

When the idea was first mooted I judged it tactful to know as little about it as possible. I am naturally delighted with the choice of contributors, and I am very grateful to my friends who have sent in the very fine chapters that make up the book. I should like also to pay tribute to the many other friends who have influenced me philosophically and who are not represented here. In particular I should like to mention two former colleagues of mine at the University of Adelaide in the 1950s. C. B. Martin did much to cure me of the hidden verificationism which sometimes characterized the Oxford approach and the neo-Wittgensteinianism of the time. Charlie Martin also, of course, impressed by his example, as he was, and is, an exceptionally deep and original thinker, who has always gone for the big problems. Martin moved from Adelaide to Sydney, and during his time there he had an immense effect on Australian philosophy generally. Then there is U. T. Place, with whom also I still keep in close touch. (Some of our recent discussions have taken place while walking the Yorkshire moors with his dog Horace.) It is well known that Ullin Place pioneered the so-called Identity Theory of mind, and indeed converted me to it.

I have just spoken of intellectual conversion; there is de-conversion, too. Martin had a lot to do with that, and so did my getting interested in biology. I had continued to be a church-goer for largely emotional reasons, not unconnected with my admiration for my parents and others who were very much committed to Christianity. I think that I tried to reconcile my penchant for a scientific world view with my early attachment to religious belief by means of some sort of neo-Wittgensteinian double talk. I am now ashamed of some of the things I said in two articles I wrote on the philosophy of religion which were printed in a volume edited by Antony Flew and Alasdair MacIntyre.[1] Something of a retraction appeared in 1959 in my note 'Philosophy and religion'.[2]

The 'philistinism' of which Armstrong speaks on the first page of his essay goes with a liking for straight talking with which at this time my religious proclivities sometimes got in the way. As to aesthetic matters, my chief interests are in literature, but prose not poetry. (Hence, perhaps, the remark about Shakespeare, who I admire for his towering intellect and verbal facility, but who I don't find myself reading.) I enjoy very many of the great eighteenth- and nineteenth-century novelists and biographers.[3] Most of them are straightforward writers. (I am baffled by literary critics who actually praise *ambiguity*!) I also enjoy history and talking to historians, even though when I was first at Adelaide I doubtless made myself unpopular by calling history 'academicized gossip'. What I really meant was that it was no good for predicting the future, especially as I was under the influence of Popper's fine critique of 'historicism'. If history is no good for prediction, what is it good for? I do not worry too much about the question now. It broadens the mind, but it is enough for me that much of it is fun and I much enjoy conversation with good historians. The historical higher criticism of the New Testament does have an obvious use, however. If I had in my youth read as much of this as I have in recent years I would have had less difficulty in freeing myself from my religious proclivities.

Reply to Armstrong

I must thank David for his very kind remarks about me. I do not deny the philistinism, about which I have just now said something. David may have given the impression that philistinism goes down well in Australia, and perhaps it does, though my first impression of Australia was very different. Never in Britain had I seen so many boys and girls walking about carrying violin cases as I did in the vicinity of the Adelaide University conservatorium! The question of whether Shakespeare or Mt Lofty (which at the time to which David refers had not been disfigured by its three television masts) does or ought to give the greater aesthetic pleasure raises an interesting quasi-philosophical problem. Shakespeare had the wonderful ability always to choose the right word, with a rarely equalled insight into human character. Contemplating him we feel great awe. Consider, however, the extraordinary interlocking complexities of the structure and biochemical processes of even one cell of one leaf of one gum tree on Mt Lofty. Consider again an outstanding sculpture of a human head. When I contemplate such a sculpture I am naturally impressed, but the impression is mixed up with the reflection that the sculpture has nothing between its ears, whereas my wife's beautiful head (for example) contains 10^{10} neurons (each neuron being of amazing complexity), not to mention blood vessels, glands and other extraordinary organs. It seems to me, therefore, that nature always far outstrips art. I leave it to aestheticians to tell me where I am wrong.

In his paper Armstrong begins by tracing the development of my own thinking about the secondary qualities: criticisms on the part of M. C. Bradley and C. B. Martin and a suggestion by David Lewis have helped me to move from the behaviourist account in my paper 'Colours' (1961)[4] to a position very close to the one to which Armstrong had already moved.[5] According to this later view of mine, colours are physical properties of the surfaces of objects. (I leave out qualifications about rainbows and the like.) My worry was that these properties must be highly disjunctive and idiosyncratic ones. Lewis said 'Disjunctive and idiosyncratic, so what?' Though disjunctive and idiosyncratic (that is, of interest to humans but not, say, to Alpha Centaurians) they could still be perfectly physical properties. To adapt an analogy used by Robert Boyle,[6] the shape of a lock might be of interest only because of a certain shaped key, but the shape of the lock is something perfectly physical – indeed geometrical – which can be described without reference to the key.

By and large I agree with Armstrong's positive theory of the secondary qualities, though I am not sure how far I can accept his theory of universals, and so I shall not comment on this. I do, however, want to comment on Armstrong's long footnote (p. 14), in which he remarks on E. W. Averill's important paper 'Colour and the anthropocentric problem'.[7]

In this note Armstrong quotes a passage, also quoted by Averill, in which I say: 'Colours are the (perhaps highly disjunctive and idiosyncratic) properties of the surfaces of objects that explain the discrimination with respect to colour of normal human percipients, and also the experiences of these percipients.'[8] There is an important syntactical ambiguity here which may have misled Averill in his interpretation of me. (Armstrong has it right.) The words 'and also' are not meant to be governed by 'colours are' but by 'that explain'. However, I do not think that Averill's main arguments are affected by this matter.

In my article 'Colours' I introduce the notion of a normal human percipient, which is that of someone who can make at least as many discriminations as any other. Thus if Jones makes the best discriminations at the red end of the spectrum and McTavish the best at the blue end, the notion of a normal human percipient might be realized by Jones and McTavish acting in concert, or perhaps 'normal human percipient' might express an idealized notion, as does 'the mean sun' in astronomical chronology. I also assume that the discriminations are made in sunlight. I think this accords well with the ordinary use of colour words. However, there are pressures in another direction, to which Averill responds by relaxing the condition that canonical discriminations be made in sunlight, and also by relaxing the notion of a normal percipient by allowing super-discriminating humans who might be produced by genetic engineering, or who might even possess the power of responding to polarized light as bees do. Well, if all sorts of bug-eyed monsters are allowed, we do get away from anthropocentricity. Which is the right analysis of our concept of colours? I began on the slippery slope by allowing that a normal human percipient might be an idealization, or perhaps a syndicate. I am inclined to think that we capture ordinary usage best by sticking to illumination in daylight and not allowing, as Averill does, various special conditions of illumination which might allow discriminations to be made that cannot accord with what I take as ordinary usage. But whether it is he or I that is right about the ordinary use of colour words, or which of two contary pressures to respond to, he does of course end up with a perfectly acceptable physicalist account of colour. I like it because of its rejection of anthropocentricity. With my account of colours the anthropocentricity exists but is as harmless as the key-centeredness of the shape of a lock. (Harmless, that is, so long as it is recognized for what it is. We must not get confused and project this anthropocentricity on to the perceived world.) Thus ontologically I see no need to disagree with Averill. I might say that when he talks of how coloured surfaces appear to percipients, I would rather talk about how these percipients discriminate (with respect to colour) various shapes on surfaces. I think that Averill could consistently be interpreted in this way. I should also like to remind the reader that, for me, 'discriminate with respect to colour' is a simpler notion than that of 'colour', just as in set theory 'equinumerous' is a simpler (or more fundamental) notion than that of number.

Reply to Cohen

Though I was a graduate student at the Queen's College, Oxford, of which Jonathan has since become a Fellow, somehow our paths did not cross until much later. We were fortunate to have him as a visitor to the

Research School of Social Sciences at the Australian National University; we have met at overseas conferences, and I have enjoyed his hospitality at Oxford, not to mention walks in the Cotswolds and in the Australian bush.

As Jonathan says, I am an extensionalist. Indeed, it is hard not to be an extensionalist, in so far as ostensibly intensional constructions can be dealt with extensionally in possible worlds semantics. However, for Quinean and Davidsonian reasons I do not want to go in for possible worlds semantics. I like Davidson's programme of bending ostensibly intensional locutions in natural languages into extensional form, but, be this as it may, I will be mostly content if intensional locutions are not needed either for science or for metaphysics.

Intensionality can often be avoided by going meta-linguistic. I hold that the notion of law of nature should be dealt with in this way. Thus I hold that when Einstein appreciated the Lorentz invariance of Maxwell's electromagnetic equations and consequently sought a Lorentz invariant modification of Newtonian mechanics, he was thinking meta-linguistically. Lorentz invariance *shows* itself (to echo Wittgenstein's *Tractatus*[9]) in the sentences of special relativity, but is *said* in a metalanguage. In this sense I hold that the word 'law' should not occur in the object language of science. Laws of nature, I hold, are statements of cosmic coincidence, not merely local coincidence. (In my paper 'Laws of nature and cosmic coincidences',[10] to which Jonathan refers, I deny that these notions can be formally defined.) I am content to allow that the sentence 'laws of nature are cosmic coincidences' has the air of a paradoxical epigram. For me there are coincidences and coincidences, just as in George Orwell's *Animal Farm* all animals are equal but some are more equal than others. We can think of laws as assertions of cosmic geography, and accidental generalities as merely local. Similarly with counterfactuals. I am attracted to the view that a counterfactual 'if it had been the case that p then it would be the case that q' is assertible just in case q is deducible from p together with contextually agreed background assumptions.[11] Whether we should say that counterfactuals are true or false is debatable, since the view obviously has affinities to the view, held by John Mackie at one time, that such conditionals are condensed arguments, and also to Mackie's later suppositional account.[12] On an explicitly meta-linguistic view they could be said to be 'true (or false) in context C' in the metalanguage. One difficulty about this account is that we may have discussion and disagreement about the truth of a counterfactual, but I think that this may be explained by interpreting a discussion of this sort either as disputing agreement about background assumptions or as disagreement about whether a conclusion really follows from certain premisses.

Counterfactuals, on this account, are a bit fuzzy because of fuzziness of agreement on background assumptions, and of compliance with the co-tenability of such assumptions. This is all right for an extensionalist like me: why should I claim that counterfactual locutions are sharply characterizable?

The branch of science in which worries about counterfactuals or possible worlds seems to obtrude most is in quantum mechanics. Some expositions interpret the ψ of the wave equation as having to do with frequencies in ensembles of possible systems similar to the actual one under investigation. I think we need to avoid this by interpreting it in terms of objective chance in the actual world, of which actual frequencies may be evidence. But objective chances are queer things. I suppose that they have to be treated as hypothesized entities.

If Jonathan will allow me to go meta-linguistic (though still extensional) in my account of object language intensionality, then our positions come, I *think*, much closer to one another. We are alike in rejecting possible worlds. We both have worries about the Tooley–Dretske–Armstrong account of laws.

On p. 21 Jonathan raises the question of whether I should interpret idealizing generalizations instrumentally. Sometimes I might, but *in general* I prefer to interpret them realistically in terms of the approximate satisfaction of an ideal predicate by a real entity: thus in certain contexts we could treat 'is a Newtonian particle' as approximately satisfied by a real billiard ball or a real satellite. I shall remark further on idealizations in my reply to Ellis.

Jonathan's distinction between ampliative and non-ampliative counter-factuals interested me, though I think that both can be treated in the same way if the sort of account of counterfactuals that I have suggested above is correct. Jonathan's relation of the distinction to the notions of variative and enumerative induction, however, is ingenious.

Reply to Davidson

I first met Donald in early 1958 when I was returning to Australia from a visit to Princeton and I went for a day to Stanford. Since then I have admired him immensely not only (of course) as a philosopher but also as an extraordinarily versatile person. A minor example of his versatility occurred in 1968, when we were lucky enough to have him to give the Gavin David Young lectures at the University of Adelaide, and on the way home to USA he walked up Mt Kilimanjaro, the highest mountain in Africa. Soon after I came to the Australian National University we were fortunate again to have him as a visitor for several months.

The main philosophical influence that Donald has had on me was perhaps to make me understand the importance of semantics and the theory of truth. His continuing research programme was based on the plausible conjecture that under the surface of the apparently intensional language we speak there is an underlying structure whose logic is the familiar first order logic. The programme is also based on the insight that a semantics should be recursive. So Donald made use of Tarski's demonstration of a recursive semantics for languages based on first order logic. In a sense, Donald argues that ordinary language is not really intensional: the appearance of intensionality is a surface phenomenon. Some philosophers are happy to make modal and other locutions intensional by quantifying over possible worlds. Donald's refusal to fall back on to 'possible worlds' talk is congenial to me, and of course I greatly admire his attempts to avoid this sort of thing by various clever expedients, as, for example, in his 'On saying that'.[13]

In the case of adverbs, Davidson avoids possible worlds semantics by quantifying over events (including actions) and this brings me to the topic of his present discussion. As an account of the semantics of action I can only applaud it, except to make the following comment, which is in no sense a criticism. Donald's analysis does not bring out *explicitly* the importance of the mind (the brain) in action. That is, to some readers the talk of arm-raising may look too behaviouristic. However, to think this would be a mistake. Donald's reference to intention indirectly refers us to brain states that (at least tokenly) correspond to beliefs and desires. A neuroscientific theory of action would say a lot about the brain. Consider the rapid computations that must go on in the brain of a batsman when deciding whether to hook a fast and short ball to the boundary, or else to sway his body so as to let the ball go harmlessly by. Again, a brain in a vat (of familiar philsophical fantasy) might believe itself to be raising its non-existent arm to stab a non-existent rival, and we might want to censure it morally for this. So though there is here no action of arm-raising, there is something very like it. There is nothing inconsistent with Donald's chapter in these considerations. He is not at all concerned with neuroscience or with neurological fantasy, nor to deny the importance of the brain.

I enthusiastically agree with Donald's adherence to the 'belief–desire' pattern of explanations of actions. (Here I am using 'desire' very generally to include intentions and pro-attitudes.) It has become fashionable in certain quarters to pour scorn on this, and it is thus greatly reassuring to have someone so eminent as Donald as an ally. As he notes, some philosophers have said that beliefs alone can cause actions. I find this incomprehensible. It is as incomprehensible to me as the notion that a simple imperative sentence such as 'let me go out of the house' should be deducible logically from simple indicative ones, such as 'it is raining'. In suitable circumstances, whether I go out of the house or not will depend on whether or not I quite like getting wet. Two persons with the same beliefs will behave differently in the same circumstances because they want different things in the circumstances. Suppose that you design a robot torpedo (say) that has sensors analogous to eyes and electronics analogous to a nervous system. At any stage of its journey it may have a representation (in some rather abstract sense) that is analogous to a belief. But you need to build in more. You must ensure that it not only has a representation of the target and the route thereto, but you must build in something analogous to desire, so that it goes to the target. Ethics is concerned not with knowledge but with action and decision, so that our ethical principles depend ultimately on what (overridingly) we most *want*.

Is the 'belief–desire' form of explanation mere 'folk psychology' which should be replaced by, or perhaps reduced to, some neuroscientific mode of explanation? Davidson does not take this line, and this is because he thinks that the belief–desire model is connected with normative notions of rationality. I'm not quite convinced that this is what makes the difference. Thus Donald mentions consistency, and yet consistency can be defined non-normatively. So I'll leave this particular matter up in the air. This is where I'm undecided and find myself still doing a bit of fence-sitting. But nevertheless I think I can agree that there is something about this sort of explanation that makes it unsuitable for scientific purposes.

Donald mentions the 'open-system' nature of belief–desire explanation. He notes that you get the same sort of thing in technology (aerodynamics, say) or in such sciences as geology. So this is not the special difference. The difference, he thinks, comes from an ideal of rationality. He says: 'Reason–explanations make others intelligible to us only to the extent that we can recognize something like our own reasoning powers at work' (p. 47). This leads us to considerations about meaning and interpretation, about which Donald has written so much. But I'll dodge the notion of radical interpretation here and try to make the same point in a simpler way, by reference to Quine's criticisms of the analytic–synthetic distinction and consequently of the notion of synonymy, and hence of the notion of 'proposition'.[14] The problem with the belief–desire model is that beliefs and desires are *propositional* attitudes. It is not just that the notions are indeterminate. So are many notions used by science, and they can usually be made more determinate if necessary. (I am not talking about quantum mechanical indeterminism here: the notion of quantum mechanical indeterminism is quite a precise and determinate one.) The problem with the indeterminateness of the notions of the propositional attitudes is that the indeterminateness comes from a higher and semantic level – from the notion of meaning itself.

Nevertheless I cannot help feeling (perhaps I am sitting on the fence again here) that the belief–desire pattern, irremediably indeterminate though it may be, can be used in a way similar to that of many scientific idealizations. The telephone line outside your house is not infinitely long, but the theory of infinite lines may help us to understand it. We are all irrational some of the time, but most people most of the time are rational.

I have argued in the past that there are not strict laws in biology (or at least in the central largely biochemical core of it, as in the theory of the human immune system, say). This is no ontological worry for the physicalist. There are not strict laws in electronics, which applies physics to wiring diagrams. Biologists apply physics and chemistry to terrestrial natural history (often very sophisticated natural history, developed with electron microscopes and other very sophisticated devices). Few biologists are tempted to generalize cosmically, except in their spare time. Such a generalization as 'all life in the universe is carbon based' may possibly be true, but it is highly speculative and dubitable, so I liked Donald's remark about aerodynamics. But I am still a bit puzzled about the full extent to which the problems about the propositional attitudes, radical interpretation and attributions of rationality make psychological explanations so very different in practice from explanations in technology.

Reply to Ellis

When Brian Ellis first came into my lecture room, not long after I had arrived at Adelaide, he was wearing a South Australian hockey blazer, and I knew then that he would become a good philosopher! He was a wonderfully nimble and active goalkeeper who represented the combined Australian Universities, and I had the pleasure of playing against him in South Australian club hockey. Much later, in 1972, I moved to La Trobe University where Brian had previously become its foundation professor of philosophy and had built up an exceptionally big and high quality department. I had been nearly 22 years at Adelaide, a university which I had come to love very much, all the more so because I learnt a great deal of its history from Sir William Mitchell, whom I knew between the ages of 89 and 101. He would tell me about the great men of Adelaide's early days, such as Horace Lamb, W. H. Bragg and J. W. Salmond. He always thought of himself primarily as a philosopher, but he had been for years a very great Vice-Chancellor and later Chancellor. Mitchell would not have approved of the changes that occurred in the university in the aftermath of the student unrest of the early 1970s, and nor did I. In particular I did not wish to be an active participator, as I would have had to be, in bringing about some of these changes in a university that I loved so much. I am academically conservative and it was easier to come to terms with these changes in a different university, especially as at La Trobe I was a Reader and had no administrative responsibilities. I had a happy four and a half years in the philosophically very active department that owed so much to Brian's cheerful leadership.

Brian's contribution to this volume is extremely stimulating. The section of his chapter entitled 'The ontology' is a fine piece of metaphysical speculation with its roots, as is right and proper, in contemporary science. Fields and energy transfers take the prime place, but 'spatio-temporal relationships' also come into it. I agree with Ellis that these spatio-temporal relations cannot be reduced to causal ones.[15] I am not too keen on the concept of causality anyway,[16] though I am happy with it if it is just that of an energy transfer process, as in Ellis's ontology.

A big ontological difference between Ellis and myself (I think) is that I am strongly inclined to an absolute theory of space–time (though not of course of space and time taken separately). This is partly because a relational theory has to talk about actual *and possible* relations, and I want to keep modality (and possible worlds) out of physical theory. In any case, while the question of Mach's principle remains controversial, it is unsafe to assume that physics can do without absolute space–time. Indeed, modern theories of superforce (so I gather) suggest that many-dimensional space with fancy topological properties takes a very central explanatory place in modern cosmology.

At any rate, it seems clear on much simpler grounds that physical explanations are not always causal (or much to do with energy transfers) but can be geometrical. Consider the explanation of gravity in General Relativity, the notion of gravitational force giving way to that of a geodesic. At an even simpler level, consider the resolution of the clock paradox in special relativity. Peter remains at home on earth while Paul is shot off to a distant star and then returned to earth. AB is Peter's world line, and if Paul's on his outward and return journeys are AC and CB respectively, $AC + CB < AB$. (If AB, BC and CB are sides of a triangle in Minkowski space and are all time-like lines, then $AC + CB$ is less than AB, not greater than AB as in the Euclidean case.)

Another locus of slight disagreement between myself and Ellis is on his view (which is also Michael Devitt's)[17] that considerations of truth and reference have nothing to do with ontology. Ellis and Devitt rely on argument to the best explanation, and I agree with this. Now it seems to me that if a physical theory provides the best explanation, then if we believe that the theory is true, we have reason to believe in the entities quantified over in the theory, and if we believe that the theory is *approximately* true then there is a *prima facie* case for believing in the entities of which the predicates of the theory are approximately true. Ellis rightly draws attention to the place of idealizations. Suppose that we are using the theory of Newtonian particle mechanics. We know that there are no Newtonian particles. Nevertheless, in certain contexts we can say that billiard balls or planets approximately satisfy the predicate 'is a Newtonian particle.' (Clearly the notion of approximate satisfaction must be partly a contextual one.) Knowing that there are no Newtonian particles, we *pretend* that there are such. That is, I would say that we pretend to operate a classical Tarski-type semantics, rather than actually operate one, since there are no entities that exactly satisfy the predicates.[18] If we think that electrons will go the way of Newtonian particles (but not of phlogiston) then we still have reason to think that there are entities that approximately satisfy the predicate 'is an electron'.

Reluctantly, I accept numbers and sets into my ontology, for Quine's reasons. Mathematics, including classical analysis, is part of the seamless web of any physical theory that provides the best explanation of phenomena. In this sense the world behaves as if there are sets. We could perhaps imagine a world in which elementary number theory was enough for physics: in this case, the argument to the best explanation would incline us to believe in numbers but not in sets of them.

Brian's most challenging argument is that on my own principles I should believe in properties. Thus in modern physics the behaviour of particles does seem to be partly explained by their possession of properties, charge, mass, spin, and even more exotic ones such as colour and charm. I am attracted to Brian's proposal, for Brian's excellent reasons. I am, however, doubtful how to work it out. If it were just a matter of referring to simple monadic properties of particles there would be no problem. (Indeed also if it were only a matter of *non-quantitative n*-adic properties.) We could modify Quine's canonical notation to allow proper names of properties, and then say (for example) '*x* has mass' instead of 'massy *x*' where 'massy' is a predicate. We would introduce the dyadic predicate 'has'. Mass, charge, spin and so on would be theoretical entities (called 'properties'). This notion of property would have nothing to do with the bad old notion of properties as connected with meanings of words; these properties would have no more to do with meaning or synonymy than would electrons, molecules, or stars.

My problem arises from the necessity of allowing for quantity. We do not just say 'has a mass' but 'has a mass of – grammes'. Better still, we say 'has a mass in grammes of – ' where the blank is to be filled by a name or description of a real number. Here I am availing myself of

Quine's brilliant dodge of avoiding talk of impure numbers.[19] Thus the length in yards of a cricket pitch is identical with the real number 22. Here Quine would employ a dyadic predicate 'has a length in yards of'. The postulation of properties would lead us to use a triadic property *length* but at the expense of having the semantically obscure phrase 'in yards of'. In Quine's theory 'length in yards of' would seem to be without internal structure. Perhaps such phrases could be treated as predicate operators. However, it is not clear how to fit predicate operators into a canonical notation that would suit Quine, since the semantics for predicate modifiers seems to require reference to possible worlds.

I suspect that this semantic obscurity which arises from phrases like 'in yards of', 'in grammes of', 'in centimetres of', 'in spin conventional assignments of', and so on, has been neglected by believers in properties (whose theories work more smoothly for qualitative cases).

If we reject properties is all or much lost? Brian says that sets are not explanatory: it is trivial that if we have the members we have the set. In reply I would say that it is not trivial that a set 'under a certain description' (to use a rather horrible phrase) has such and such members. If we reject properties we can still think of the predicates 'has a spin of ½' or 'has a charge of *e*' as specifying, or partly specifying, certain interesting sets, certain cosmic natural kinds. (I would not count cows or platypuses as constituting natural kinds: they are too complex and terrestrial, insufficiently cosmic.) Description of a Humean world, provided that this world is simple in certain ways, can provide explanation. (Perhaps Brian is a bit Humean too, despite his belief in properties. Causation in the sense of energy transfer involves no idea of necessary connection, such as Hume rejected.)

In short, I am attracted by Brian's suggestion that I admit properties into my ontology, but am not absolutely convinced that argument to the best explanation pushes me this way, and I am unclear how to work the theory out when we have to deal with quantitative properties.[20]

Reply to Hare

Whether or not they are deserved, I am very touched by Dick Hare's kind and friendly remarks in his opening paragraph. In my thinking about ethics I owe a great deal to his work. We are nearer one another in normative ethics than in meta-ethics, but that is due partly to differences in philosophy of logic. Dick is unsurpassed as a writer of elegant and lucid philosophical prose. He writes economically and is generous enough to allow that readers can read between the lines. (Sometimes that faith in the good sense of readers has turned out to be over-optimistic!) As is often the case in mathematical treatises, some things should be left as an exercise to the reader. I suspect that the prolixity and tortuousness of much philosophical writing nowadays comes from the desire to protect oneself against every possible objection that anyone could raise, however foolishly. Dick has more respect for his readers than to fall into this trap.

In 'Why Moral Language?' Dick discusses a chapter of my book *Ethics, Persuasion and Truth*[21] in which I follow M. Zimmerman in arguing for the dispensability of moral language, that is, words such as 'ought', 'right', 'good' and their cognates. I also argue for the dispensability of imperatives. I am not saying that we could *conveniently* do without the moral words and imperatives, but it is illuminating to see how, nevertheless, we could in principle get on in our ethical discussions without them. It needs to be stressed that in this chapter I am talking only about the *pragmatics* of ethical language: I discuss the *semantics* of 'ought' and 'good' in subsequent chapters, and in an earlier chapter I sketch a semantics for imperatives. I have of course always been aware of the possibility of a logic of imperatives ever since reading Dick's pioneering article nearly 30 years ago.[22]

In discussing the pragmatics of ethical language I am discussing the use of ethical language to persuade people to act in certain ways. The argument is that purely factual statements will do the job, in order to canalize certain of the attitudes of the addressee to which we are appealing, and if the addressee does not have such suitable attitudes we are unlikely to 'bulldoze' him or her by using words such as 'ought'. (I seem to remember that John Anderson has used the word 'bulldoze' in this sort of way.) Hare draws attention to J. L. Austin's distinction between 'illocutionary' and 'perlocutionary' acts, and this corresponds very closely to the distinction between semantics and pragmatics. Thus semantics as I understand it has nothing to do with C. L. Stevenson's causal theory of meaning, which is thoroughly confused and neglects the sorts of distinction that Austin had in mind.

Following Quine, let us construe 'I believe that p' as 'I believe-true $\ulcorner p \urcorner$', and 'I desire (or want) that p' as 'I desire-true (or want-true) $\ulcorner p \urcorner$'. Or in the manner of Davidson, just as 'I believe-true that' or 'I desire-true that' where the $\ulcorner p \urcorner$ is separately exhibited as the referent of 'that'. This gets rid of intensionality: 'desire-true', unlike 'desire' is a relational predicate.

Then, to take Hare's example on p. 80, I can say that I predict the judge will come to want-true the proposition that he or she sentences the prisoner. I do not need to analyse this in terms of accepting a prescription, though of course no doubt the judge would accept the prescription.[23] I think that Hare's other examples can be dealt with similarly. Instead of the doctor saying 'take two pills a day' he could say 'taking two pills a day will reduce your blood pressure without bad side effects.' 'Take in the jib sheet' is indeed better than 'taking in the jib sheet will help win the race' – if we are too long-winded we will ensure that we do lose the race. I agree with Hare that in practice the imperative mood is a necessary part of language. Indeed, as I said myself in the chapter under discussion, it saves circumlocution.

Hare offers another good argument on behalf of imperatives. Sometimes we need not mention reasons. Members of a committee may vote for different reasons. Though why shouldn't the committee pass on to a higher committee, say, not a recommendation but a factual statement, for instance 'the majority of members of the committee wanted to reface the Old Library in Clipsham stone'? The chairman could have said 'I desire that you say "aye" if you desire that the Old Library be refaced.' Still, all this is very awkward. It would be odd indeed if imperatives and 'ought' sentences had survived in language if they were not useful in practice. Even if theoretically dispensable (say in a world in which we had so much time that conciseness of expression was not needed and we could always state reasons).

Another interesting thought of Hare's is that acceptance of 'ought' goes with acceptance of universalizability. The question of universalizability is too large a matter to go into here. In *Ethics, Persuasion and Truth* I make use of Bruce Vermazen's semantics for 'ought' sentences.[24] This semantics does not in general imply universalizability. (Nevertheless Vermazen agrees with Hare in building universalizability into the moral 'ought'.)[25] I myself want to take 'moral' as to do with deciding what to do, and the egoist and amoralist's decisions count as moral for me. A person's overriding attitude need not be universalizable in Hare's sense.[26] I concede that even if universalizability is not part of the *logic* of 'ought', there is nevertheless a considerable linguistic pressure to universalize 'ought'. Part of the disagreement between Hare and myself here may be a purely verbal one, about the way we want to use 'moral'.

Moreover, I am in complete agreement that imperatives and words such as 'ought' are needed in moral education, or even to preserve the health and life of children. Children have to learn to internalize prescriptions. If a three-year-old were as intelligent as Zimmerman's judge we could no doubt prevent the child from doing X by asserting the factual proposition 'Daddy loves you very much and consequently wants you not to do X', but of course this will never do with a real three-year-old. Nor even would it do to say 'if you do X (run on to the busy road, say) Daddy will smack you.' 'Don't run on to the road' is more succinct and will do whether smacking or just parental disapproval or whatever is the implied sanction. Children need to learn to internalize universal prescriptions too, before they are competent to know the reasons for them. Even dogs respond to imperative utterances, though this consideration is a bit unfair as they do not *understand* the imperatives.

My disagreements with Hare are relatively domestic ones. Unlike him, I do not accept the notion of analyticity (except in trivial cases) and I do not want to build universalizability into the logic of the moral words. Nevertheless, I am of course in favour of universalizability and acknowledge pressures to use 'ought' in a universalizable way. (I believe that the pressures come partly from some sort of felt analogy with science.) In these short comments I have not been able to do justice to the richness of argument in Dick's contribution. He has never been one to write down his prejudices and then give a false appearance of rationality to them by calling them 'intuitions'. In opposing this sort of moral philosophy we are at one.

Reply to Jackson

When I first came to Australia in 1950 I visited Melbourne almost at once to get to know Douglas Gasking and A. C. Jackson, who already had such a great influence in Melbourne and Australian philosophy. (I also had fruitful and enjoyable visits to Sydney to see John Mackie.) I well remember Jackson's son Frank, then a small boy, playing cricket in Ormond College grounds. Little did I think that one day he would be my successor in the Australian National University. Before that time, Frank and I had twice been departmental colleagues. After he graduated from Melbourne he came to my department at Adelaide as a temporary lecturer; having just got married he preferred not to go abroad for graduate study. This was fortunate for us. Happy were the days when there were such opportunities for the exceptionally gifted young, when the Ph.D. had not become something of a trade union ticket. Frank later collected a Ph.D. while teaching at La Trobe University, but this was in the nature of a work of supererogation – it became a very good book anyway.[27] Then we were together for a time at La Trobe, once again as departmental colleagues.

Though I have important disagreements with some things in the above-mentioned book *Perception*, in nearly all of Frank's recent writings I find myself convinced by his reasoning. The present discussion is no exception. Some readers may be amused by a story about the devastating force of Frank's arguments. While I was at La Trobe I developed a tendency to fall asleep during seminar papers given by colleagues and visitors. This would occur however interesting I was finding the paper: it was the hypnotic voice of someone reading that did it. I got a reputation of being able to engage in the discussions as if I had heard all the paper. I lost it when I fell asleep during one of David Armstrong's papers. In the discussion I made what I thought was an intelligent objection, whereupon David said 'Well, Jack, while you were asleep Frank Jackson considered that objection and refuted it!'

I shall comment on Frank's paper from a utilitarian point of view. Why is it useful to talk of group action? Presumably because it is useful to hold groups responsible, to praise or blame, reward or punish them.

Frank's discussion of Parfit's examples of the beans, the bandits and the villagers leads him to say that in a group each member may do nothing wrong, but the group as a whole may have done wrong. I am inclined to think that the act utilitarian would agree with this but not a co-operative utilitarian, as in Donald Regan's well-known book.[28] (The issue between act and co-operative utilitarianism puzzles me and I still vacillate a bit when I think about it.)

Frank says that he is discussing objective rightness and wrongness. He sometimes tends to equate this with praiseworthiness and blameworthiness; see pp. 104 and 106. If what Pat did was wrong, it does not follow that he ought to be blamed, though no doubt in *this* case he ought to be. I think that the two things should be kept distinct. As Sidgwick said, the utility of an action need not go along with the utility of praise or blame of it.[29] (I think that non-utilitarians too should keep distinct the questions of rightness and wrongness on the one hand, and praiseworthiness and blameworthiness on the other, even though perhaps they may re-establish some sort of connection between them.) However, I do not think that this matter vitiates Frank's main argument.

Besides the practical utility of having a concept of group action, there is also a theoretical one. In thinking about co-operative utilitarianism I am inclined to think of a group of co-operative agents as a single supra-personal agent which acts in act-utilitarian fashion.[30]

One final remark. I applaud Frank's talk of temporal parts of persons performing actions. Some philosophers will say that this is not even good English, but I say that it is good English because it succinctly expresses the right philosophy.[31]

Reply to Mellor

Hugh says that physicalists like me seek a physicalist basis for causation. (Brian Ellis does in his contribution to this volume.) Possibly so, but I have a strong propensity to agree with Russell and say that the concept of causality is not needed in science and metaphysics. I tend to regard 'cause' as a peculiarly inexact word useful for surgeons, physicians, plumbers and technicians. Up to a point I agree that it is useful in discussing experiments, but only from this technical point of view. However, we could say, for instance, 'if this wire is not disconnected then this apparatus works,' and persuade someone to join the wire. Even here causal talk is avoidable, though awkwardly so.

Hugh analyses causal statements in terms of relations between facts. But I do not want facts in my ontology. The reason is Davidson's: in Tarski's theory of truth the basic relation is satisfaction of a predicate by an object, or a sequence of such. It is not correspondence to fact, which goes with a *Tractatus*-like picture and substitutional theory of quantification.[32] I am impressed by Davidson's semantic arguments for causation as relating events and not facts, though here perhaps Hugh could point to Barry Taylor's somewhat Davidsonian treatment of facts.[33]

Suppose we consider the fact that Jim loves Mary. We could take this as the sequence 'Jim, Mary, "loves".' Here a fact seems very like an event, since I construe the event of Jim kissing Mary as the sequence of a temporal stage of the mereological object that is Jim together with Mary and the predicate 'kiss'.[34] I don't think this readily expresses the ordinary language concept, since it does not allow for the sorts of treatments of adverbs and the like that Davidson gives. But I think it will do for scientific theory and metaphysics, if this can be expressed, as I think it can, without adverbs or predicate operators.

Consider Hugh's example 5 on p. 116: 'the fact that C caused it to be the case that E.' Hugh allows that we could say 'E because C', even though 'because' is not an exclusively causal connection, since it can be used to report mathematical proofs and non-causal explanations. However, I want to follow Gilbert Ryle and say that 'because' is never a connective whether causal or otherwise.[35] It works like 'so' and 'therefore'. Why could not Davidson say instead of 'Don dies because he falls', the more canonical '$(\exists x)(x$ is a death of Don) because $(\exists x)(x$ is a fall of Don)'? For 'Don survives because he hangs on' we could have '$\sim(\exists x)(x$ is a death of Don) because $\sim(\exists x)(x$ is a fall of Don)';[36] see p. 118. Remember that in translating into canonical notation we must put the 'not' outside the sentence. Rather similarly, we can avoid Mellor's charge that on Davidson's analysis a non-thing would have to be both married and unmarried. I do not think that 'Don does not die because he does not fall' need be understood as a causal statement, though it is obviously related to such. The essential thing for Davidson is the avoidance of intensionality by quantification over events, and the denial of such obviously fits into the same semantic point of view.

I am unclear as to the semantics that Hugh would prefer for his nominalized sentences. (The problem is to make the semantics recursive, as Davidson rightly requires.)

Here I have contented myself with expressing a disagreement between my approach and Hugh's, and to give some hints as how I might try to rebut or evade his arguments. I was very impressed by many of his semantic considerations, which require far more thought than I have so far been able to give them. In particular I shall be interested to see how others, such as Davidson himself, may respond to them.

Reply to Putnam

As always, Hilary Putnam in his chapter is exciting, stimulating and challenging. I well remember the marvellous and eye-opening experience of conversation with him when I first met him in 1957: we used to drink beer and talk philosophy at the Nassau Inn at Princeton. Hilary had been away visiting Minnesota while I was at Princeton but fortunately had come back for a week or two around the Christmas holiday period. These conversations were one of the great formative influences on my philosophical development, and moreover they were warm-hearted and great fun. Over the years I have continued to learn from Hilary's writings, even though I have tried to argue against his very subtle critique of metaphysical realism. Hilary's present paper is independent of this issue and, as I have so often done in the past, I find myself in the state of being convinced by his arguments.

I am indeed very sympathetic to the general theme of the paper. As Hilary points out, I have myself argued for important differences between the biological and the physical sciences. Explanations in the biochemical core of biology stand to physics and chemistry much as technological explanations of the functioning of electronic or mechanical devices do. Putting it very crudely, just as electronics is physics plus wiring diagrams, so this central core of biology is physics plus natural history. By 'natural history' here I do not mean primarily ornithology and the like, but the descriptions of cells and organs that can be got by optical and electron microscopy, staining techniques, chemical tests and other methods. Because of this natural history component it is wrong to think of biology as deducible from physics and chemistry in the way one physical law may be deduced from another. This is no threat to an ontological physicalism: the case is the same in engineering, as in explaining the working of a television set. (Such an account does not apply to the theory of evolution, ecology, population studies, and so on, for which different treatment is needed.) My physicalism is not a reductionist or translational one. After all, we learn words such as 'star', 'tree', 'iron', 'chromosome' at least partly by means of ostension and with the help of indexical expressions. This does not go to show that trees, stars, bits of iron, or for that matter chromosomes, are not purely physical entities.

In his opening paragraph Hilary commends me for avoiding the expression 'The Scientific Method'. I doubt whether I have always been so careful. In fact, at the time I was reading Hilary's paper I found myself using this very expression in a conference paper I was revising for publication! I hope, however, that in this particular context the generality and inattention to specific differences when I used the phrase 'the scientific method' was harmless. I agree with Hilary that too simple an application of the Popperian use of the notion of a hypothetico-deductive method and of falsifiability will not do.

Hilary points out that assertion of the historical *fact* of evolution is testable by combining it with auxiliary statements of geology, palaeon-tology, and so on. We do not need the Darwinian hypothesis of natural selection in order to establish this historical fact. Hilary goes on to say that the Darwinian theory itself is testable, by using the proposition that we have evidence that natural selection is operating now. (No doubt the rise of drug-resistant strains of bacteria provides some of the most spectacular evidence for this.) Hilary then says that we can also say that if no other mechanism capable of producing new species is to be found (genetic engineering and selective breeding apart) then it is reasonable to make the *induction* that natural selection has always been the operative mechanism and that it explains the fact of evolution we have got from the palaeontological evidence. I would say that both the arguments for the palaeontological fact of evolution and those for a theory of natural selection could be subsumed under a general account of hypothetico-deductive method together with considerations of simplicity (fitting facts and hypotheses into the web of belief in a simple way). This general account of course conceals the differences to which Hilary illuminatingly draws attention.

Hilary's remarks about the philosophy of Quantum Mechanics are both helpful and challenging. He remarks that hidden variable theories are ruled out. The problem for the realist is of course to combine realism with a rejection of hidden variables. Obviously there is no *immediate* inconsistency between realism and the rejection of hidden variables: the problem is to combine the two things in the context of a plausible theory. I must say that I never fail to be made uneasy by the paradox of Schrödinger's cat. (Here I am talking of intellectual uneasiness. As Hilary has remarked elsewhere, one may feel a certain moral qualm about Schrödinger's choice of example.[37]) It does look as though we have to accept a superposition of macro-states. In his *Realism and Reason*[38] Putnam takes this 'heroic course'. Heroic it is, but what less heroic alternative have we? It is worrying.

Hilary remarks on the early history of the Special Theory of Relativity. He thinks that the Bayesian story cannot explain why the Special Theory of Relativity was accepted before Minkowski's realistic 'space–time' theory had been proposed. He thinks that the lack of an 'objective two-term bivalent relation of simultaneity between distant events' (p. 150) would have had zero a priori probability. I am not so sure of this, because reflection on the fact that Maxwell's equations are Lorentz invariant would have given some positive probability to the hypothesis that the true laws of mechanics are invariant too. I concede that Einstein at first presented the special theory in a very positivist idiom, contrasting markedly with his later philosophy. Minkowski came as a blessing. Ideally even a relative notion of simultaneity need not occur in the Theory of Relativity, but only that of space-like versus time-like separations of events. It is Quantum Mechanics that provides worry for realists. Of course I am sure that I am not in any way disagreeing with Hilary here. His 'briefly (and too simply) put' point is that there are theories which fit different ones (but not all) of positivist, Popperian and Best Explanation studies of scientific explanation. I can accept this, I think.

Reply to Singer

Like Jackson, Peter Singer was a colleague of mine when I was at La Trobe University. It was a big loss to the department there when both he and Jackson moved to Monash University. I regard Peter as one of the great moralists, because I suspect that more than anyone he has helped to change the attitudes of very many people to the sufferings of animals. Peter is utilitarian in normative ethics, and a humane attitude to animals is a natural corollary of utilitarianism. Utilitarian concern for animals goes back to Bentham, who, presumably alluding to the Kantians, said that the question was not whether animals can reason, but whether they can suffer.[39] Besides being an outstanding moralist, Singer has of course done outstanding work on meta-ethics and on analytical investigations of moral questions. In the present case he is concerned with what gives life its value and why it is wrong to kill. His form of utilitarianism is 'preference utilitarianism', for which I have some sympathy but in which I also see difficulties. If I prefer *A* simply because it leads to *B* we should not count both as preferences. We should count only intrinsic preferences. This leads us back to something closer to classical utilitarianism, though it cannot be hedonistic, since one might have an intrinsic preference for something to be done after one's death. Singer holds that hedonistic utilitarianism can do much to account for one's feeling of loss if a promising life is cut off even painlessly, but not as much as preference utilitarianism can.

These problems aside, I very much like Singer's illuminating comparison of a life with a journey and the clever way in which he has worked out the details.

Notes

1 'The existence of God', pp. 28–46, and 'Metaphysics, logic and theology', pp. 12–27, in Antony Flew and Alasdair MacIntyre (eds), *New Essays in Philosophical Theology*, London, S.C.M. Press, 1955.

2 J. J. C. Smart, 'Philosophy and religion', *Australasian Journal of Philosophy* 36 (1958), 56–8.

3 I derive great enjoyment from listening to classical music (here again I favour the eighteenth and nineteenth centuries). In Oxford before I came to Australia J. O. Urmson once remarked to me that I had no soul. What he meant was that I didn't go to concerts. Unfortunately I am completely unmusical, and so the difference between a live and a recorded or radio performance is lost on me. I can't sing a note or play an instrument, and have often envied those who can.

4 J. J. C. Smart, 'Colours', *Philosophy*, 36 1961, 128–42.

5 On p. 6 Armstrong follows my use (in 'Sensations and brain processes', *Philosophical Review* 68 (1959), 141–56) of Feigl's expression 'nomological danglers' to refer to dangling entities, not, as Feigl did, to the dangling laws themselves. Subsequently I followed Feigl's usage.

6 Robert Boyle, *Origin of Forms and Qualities*, 1666.

7 E. W. Averill, 'Colour and the anthropocentric problem', *Journal of Philosophy* 72 (1985), 281–304.

8 Ibid.

9 L. Wittgenstein, *Tracatus Logico-Philosophicus*, London, Routledge and Kegan Paul, 1961.

10 J. J. C. Smart, 'Laws of nature and cosmic coincidences', *Philosophical Quarterly*, 35 (1985), pp. 272–80.

11 See W. V. Quine, 'Necessary truth', in *The Ways of Paradox and Other Essays*, New York, Random House, 1966.

12 See J. L. Mackie, *Truth, Probability and Paradox*, Oxford, Clarendon Press, 1973, chapter 3.

13 D. Davidson, 'On saying that', in D. Davidson and J. Hintikka (eds), *Words and Objections*, Dordrecht, D. Reidel, revised edn 1975, pp. 158–74.

14 W. V. Quine, *Word and Object*, Cambridge, Mass., MIT Press, 1960.

15 See J. J. C. Smart, 'The causal theory of time', *Monist* 53 (1969), pp. 385–95, reprinted in J. J. C. Smart, *Essays Metaphysical and Moral*, Oxford, Basil Blackwell, 1987.

16 Cf. my reply to Mellor below.

17 See Michael Devitt, *Realism and Truth*, Princeton, N.J., Princeton University Press, 1984.

18 This approach of course contrasts with that of my colleague Richard Sylvan (né Routley) who holds in Meinongian fashion (or, more properly, Noneist fashion) that we can refer to non-entities. One of the attractions of this approach for those who accept this notion of reference is that one can deal easily with ideal theories in science. See R. Routley, *Exploring Meinong's Jungle and Beyond*, Philosophy Department, Research School of Social Sciences, The Australian National University, 1980, pp. 12, 802–3. For my own view see J. J. C. Smart, 'Difficulties for realism in the philosophy of science', in L. J. Cohen, J. Łos, H. Pfeiffer and K.-P. Podewski (eds), *Logic, Methodology and Philosophy of Science*, Amsterdam, North-Holland, 1982, pp. 363–75, reprinted in J. J. C. Smart, *Essays Metaphysical and Moral*.

19 See W. V. Quine, *Word and Object*, Cambridge, Mass., MIT Press, 1960, section 50.

20 Brian is of course aware that there is a problem here. For some suggestions see Brian Ellis, Robert Pargetter and John Bigelow, 'Forces' (forthcoming), and John Bigelow and Robert Pargetter, 'Quantities' (forthcoming). See also comments on the former paper by Adrian Heathcote in n. 5 of his 'A theory of causality: causality = interaction (as defined by a suitable quantum field theory)' (forthcoming). An ontology of properties cannot altogether supplant set theory. Thus consider Maxwell's equations taken as relating various positions in space and time and values of the electric and magnetic fields. Differential operators are employed, hence mathematical analysis, and hence set theory.

21 J. J. C. Smart, *Ethics, Persuasion and Truth*, London, Routledge and Kegan Paul, 1984, ch. 3.

22 R. M. Hare, 'Imperative sentences', *Mind* 58 (1949), pp. 21–39.

23 Certainly not all wantings or desirings are cases of accepting prescriptions. A dog can desire-true the sentence 'Fido has a bone'. One does not need verbal abilities to desire-true a sentence: talk of desiring-true a sentence is simply used by us to refer to a state of mind (brain-state) of the dog. See Quine, *Word and Object*, p. 213.

24 See Bruce Vermazen, 'The logic of practical "ought"-sentences', *Philosophical Studies* 32 (1977), pp. 1–71.

25 Ibid., p. 35.

26 On this point see D. H. Monro, *Empiricism and Ethics*, Cambridge, Cambridge University Press, 1967, chapters 15–16.

27 F. Jackson, *Perception: A Representative Theory*, Cambridge, Cambridge University Press, 1977.

28 Donald Regan, *Utilitarianism and Co-operation*, Oxford, Clarendon Press, 1980.

29 H. Sidgwick, *Methods of Ethics*, seventh edition reprinted with foreword by John Rawls, Indianapolis, Hackett Publishing Company, 1981, p. 413.

30 See J. J. C. Smart, 'Utilitarianism and its applications', in Joseph P. DeMarco and Richard M. Fox (eds), *New Directions in Ethics*, London,

Routledge and Kegan Paul, 1986, pp. 24–41, especially p. 30.

31   For example, contrast Hugh Mellor's contribution to the present volume, in which he holds that things do not have temporal parts, though processes do.

32   See Donald Davidson, 'True to the facts', in his *Inquiries into Truth and Interpretation*, Oxford, Clarendon Press, 1984, pp. 37–54, as well as J. J. C. Smart, 'How to turn the *Tractatus* Wittgenstein into (almost) Donald Davidson', in E. LePore, *Truth and Interpretation*, Oxford, Basil Blackwell, 1986, pp. 92–100.

33   Barry Taylor, *Modes of Occurrence*, Oxford, Basil Blackwell, 1985.

34   This is very like Jaegwon Kim's account of events. He would not mention temporal stages, but would make the sequence include a time. See J. J. C. Smart, 'Sellars on process', *Monist* 65 (1982), pp. 302–14, reprinted in *Essays Metaphysical and Moral*, and references therein to Jaegwon Kim and R. M. Martin.

35   Gilbert Ryle, 'If, so and because', in Max Black (ed.), *Philosophical Analysis*, Ithaca, Cornell University Press, 1950, pp. 323–40.

36   Someone may quibble that Don has to die at some time, and often falls at various times during his life. So we should really replace 'Don' by a reference to a small temporal stage of Don, or else assume a contextually understood time reference.

37   Hilary Putnam, *Realism and Reason, Philosophical Papers*, vol. 3, Cambridge, Cambridge University Press, 1983, p. 251.

38   Ibid., p. 252.

39   Jeremy Bentham, *Principles of Morals and Legislation*, chapter 17, section 1, sub-section 4,n.

List of Contributors

D. M. Armstrong	Challis Professor of Philosophy, University of Sydney
L. Jonathan Cohen	Fellow and Praelector in Philosophy, The Queens College, Oxford University
Donald Davidson	Professor of Philosophy at the University of California, Berkeley
Brian Ellis	Professor of Philosophy at La Trobe University, Melbourne
R. M. Hare	White's Professor Emeritus of Moral Philosophy at the University of Oxford, now Professor of Philosophy at the University of Florida, Gainesville
Frank Jackson	Professor of Philosophy at the Research School of Social Sciences, Australian National University, Canberra
D. H. Mellor	Professor of Philosophy at the University of Cambridge and Fellow of Darwin College
Jean Norman	Research Assistant in Philosophy at the Research School of Social Sciences, Australian National University, Canberra
Philip Pettit	Professorial Fellow in the Director's Unit at the Research School of Social Sciences, Australian National University, Canberra

Hilary Putnam	Professor of Philosophy at Harvard University
Peter Singer	Professor of Philosophy at Monash University, Melbourne
J. J. C. Smart	Visiting Fellow in the Automated Reasoning Project, Research School of Social Sciences, Australian National University, Canberra
Richard Sylvan	Senior Fellow in Philosophy at the Research School of Social Sciences, Australian National University, Canberra

Bibliography of the Works of J. J. C. Smart, M.A. (Glasgow), B.Phil. (Oxford), Hon.D.Litt. (St Andrews), FAHA

Books

1961   *An Outline of a System of Utilitarian Ethics*, Victoria, Melbourne University Press, 1961. Revised edition in J. J. C. Smart and Bernard Williams, *Utilitarianism: For and Against*, London, Cambridge University Press, 1973; Spanish Translation, *Utilitarismo: Pro y Contra*, Madrid, Editorial Tecnos, 1981; Italian translation, *Utilitarismo: Un Confronto*, Naples, Bibliopolis, 1985.

1963   *Philosophy and Scientific Realism*, London, Routledge and Kegan Paul, 1963.

1968   *Between Science and Philosophy: An Introduction to the Philosophy of Science*, New York, Random House, 1968.

1984   *Ethics, Persuasion and Truth*, London, Routledge & Kegan Paul, 1984.

1987   *Essays Metaphysical and Moral*, Oxford, Basil Blackwell, 1987.

Book edited with introduction

1964   *Problems of Space and Time*, New York, Macmillan, 1964.

Articles and discussion notes (including critical notices but not short book reviews). Items reprinted in *Essays Metaphysical and Moral* indicated by EMM.

1949   'The river of time', *Mind* 58 (1949), pp. 483–94. (A very slightly revised version of this was reprinted in A.G.N. Flew (ed.), *Essays*

in Conceptual Analysis, London, Macmillan, 1956.)
'Whitehead and Russell's theory of types', *Analysis* 10 (1949–50), pp. 93–6.

1950–1   'The theory of types again', *Analysis* 11 (1950–1), pp. 131–3.
'The theory of types, a further note', *Analysis* 12 (1951–2), p. 24.
'Descartes and the wax', *Philosophical Quarterly* 1 (1950), pp. 50–7.
'Reason and conduct', *Philosophy* 25 (1950), pp. 209–24.
'Excogitation and induction', *Australasian Journal of Philosophy* 28 (1950), pp. 191–9.
'Heinrich Hertz and the concept of force', *Australasian Journal of Philosophy* 29 (1951), pp. 36–45.
'Theory construction', *Philosophy and Phenomenological Research* 11 (1951), pp. 457–73. (Reprinted in A. G. N. Flew (ed.), *Logic and Language*, second series, Oxford, Basil Blackwell, 1953.)

1952   'The concept of force', *Australasian Journal of Philosophy* 30 (1952), pp. 124–30.

1953   'A note on categories', *British Journal for the Philosophy of Science* 4 (1953), pp. 227–8.
'A variant of the "heterological" paradox' (*with* J. L. Mackie), *Analysis* 13 (1952–3), pp. 61–5.
'The moving "now"', *Australasian Journal of Philosophy* 31 (1953), pp. 184–7.
'The temporal asymmetry of the world', *Analysis* 14 (1953–4), pp. 79–83.
'A variant of the "heterological" paradox – a further note' (*with* J. L. Mackie), *Analysis* 14 (1953–4), pp. 146–9.

1954   'The relevance of modern analytic philosophy for science', *Australian Journal of Science* 16 (1954), pp. 165–70 and 215–18.
'The humanitarian theory of punishment', *Res Judicatae* 6 (1954), pp. 368–71.

1955   'Contradictories and entailment' (*with* U. T. Place), *Philosophy and Phenomenological Research* 15 (1955), pp. 541–4.
Critical notice of W. V. Quine, *From a Logical Point of View*, *Australasian Journal of Philosophy* 33 (1955), pp. 45–56.
'The existence of God', Antony Flew and Alasdair MacIntyre (eds), *New Essays in Philosophical Theology*, London, S.C.M. Press, 1955, pp. 28–46. (This is a corrected version of a paper which originally appeared in *Church Quarterly Review*, 1955).
'Metaphysics, logic and theology', Antony Flew and Alasdair MacIntyre (eds), *New Essays in Philosophical Theology*, London, S.C.M. Press, 1955, pp. 12–27.
'Mr Mayo on temporal asymmetry', *Australasian Journal of Philosophy* 33 (1955), pp. 124–7.

'Spatialising time', *Mind* 64 (1955), pp. 239–41. (Reprinted in R. M. Gale (ed.), *The Philosophy of Time*, New York, Doubleday, 1967.)

1956   'The reality of theoretical entities', *Australasian Journal of Philosophy* 34 (1956), pp. 1–12.
Critical notice of A. N. Prior's *Formal Logic*, *Australasian Journal of Philosophy* 34 (1956), pp. 118–26.
'Extreme and restricted utilitarianism', *Philosophical Quarterly* 6 (1956), pp. 344–54. (A revised version of this has appeared in Philippa Foot (ed.) *Theories of Ethics*, Oxford, Oxford University Press, 1967, and in other anthologies.) EMM
'Moore's paradox, synonymous expressions and defining' (*with* B. H. Medlin), *Analysis* 17 (1956–7), pp. 125–34.

1957   'Plausible reasoning in philosophy', *Mind* 66 (1957), pp. 75–7.
Critical notice of H. Reichenbach's *The Direction of Time*, *Philosophical Quarterly* 8 (1957), pp. 72–7.

1958   'Philosophy and religion', *Australasian Journal of Philosophy* 26 (1958), pp. 56–8.
'Professor Ziff on robots', *Analysis* 19 (1958–9), pp. 117–18. (Reprinted in A. R. Anderson (ed.), *Minds and Machines*, Englewood Cliffs, N.J., Prentice-Hall, 1964.)

1959   'Sensations and brain processes', *Philosophical Review* 68 (1959), pp. 141–56. (A slightly revised version of this has appeared in V. C. Chappell (ed.), *The Philosophy of Mind*, Englewood Cliffs, N.J., Prentice-Hall, 1962, and in many other anthologies.) EMM
'Man's place in the universe', *Humanist* 74 (1959), pp. 20–2.
'Incompatible colors', *Philosophical Studies* 10 (1959), pp. 39–42.
'Measurement', *Australasian Journal of Philosophy* 27 (1959), pp. 1–22.
'Ryle on mechanism and psychology', *Philosophical Quarterly* 9 (1959), pp. 349–55.
'Can biology be an exact science?', *Synthese* 11 (1959), pp. 359–68.

1960   'Sensations and brain processes: a rejoinder', *Australasian Journal of Philosophy* 38 (1960), pp. 252–4.

1961   'Further remarks on sensations and brain processes', *Philosophical Review* 70 (1961), pp. 406–7.
'Colours', *Philosophy* 36 (1961), pp. 128–42.
'Extreme utilitarianism: a reply to M. A. Kaplan', *Ethics* 71 (1961), pp. 133–4.
'Free-will, praise and blame', *Mind* 70 (1961), pp. 291–306.
'Gödel's theorem, Church's theorem and mechanism', *Synthese* 13 (1961), pp. 105–10.
'Dispositional properties', *Analysis* 22 (1961–2), pp. 44–6.

1962   '"Tensed statements": a comment', *Philosophical Quarterly* 12 (1962), pp. 264–5.

'Brain processes and incorrigibility', *Australasian Journal of Philosophy* 40 (1962), pp. 68–70.

'Sir William Mitchell, KCMG (1861–1962)', *Australasian Journal of Philosophy* 40 (1962), pp. 261–3.

1963   'Is time travel possible?' *Journal of Philosophy* 60 (1963), pp. 237–41.

'Materialism', *Journal of Philosophy* 60 (1963), pp. 651–62. EMM

1964   'Causality and human behaviour', *Aristotelian Society Supplementary Volume* 38 (1964), pp. 143–8.

1965   'The identity thesis – a reply to Professor Garnett', *Australasian Journal of Philosophy* 43 (1965), pp. 82–3.

Critical notice of P. A. Schilpp (ed.), *The Philosophy of Rudolf Carnap*, *Australasian Journal of Philosophy* 43 (1965), pp. 84–96.

'The methods of ethics and the methods of science', *Journal of Philosophy* 62 (1965), pp. 344–9.

'On the compatibility of freewill and determinism', *Common Factor* 3, (autumn 1965), pp. 6–9.

'Conflicting views about explanation', *Boston Studies in the Philosophy of Science* 2 (1965), pp. 157–69.

1966   'Nonsense', W. H. Capitan and D. D. Merrill (eds), *Metaphysics and Explanation*, Pittsburgh, University of Pittsburgh Press, 1966, pp. 20–8.

'Philosophy and scientific plausibility', P. K. Feyerabend and G. Maxwell (eds), *Mind, Matter and Method: Essays in honor of Herbert Feigl*, Minneapolis, University of Minnesota Press, 1966, pp. 377–90. (Serbo-Croat translation in *Pitanja* 10, nos. 7–8, 1978.) EMM

1967   Comments on the papers, C. F. Presley (ed.), *The Identity Theory of Mind*, St. Lucia, University of Queensland Press, 1967, pp. 84–93.

'Religion and science', Paul Edwards (ed.), *The Encyclopedia of Philosophy*, New York, Macmillan, 1967, vol. 7, pp. 158–63.

'Space', Paul Edwards (ed.), *The Encyclopedia of Philosophy*, New York, Macmillan, 1967, vol. 7, pp. 506–11.

'Time', Paul Edwards (ed.), *The Encyclopedia of Philosophy*, New York, Macmillan, 1967, vol. 8, pp. 126–34.

'Utilitarianism', Paul Edwards (ed.), *The Encyclopedia of Philosophy*, New York, Macmillan, 1967, vol. 8, pp. 206–12.

Critical notice of W. V. Quine, *The Ways of Paradox* and *Selected Logic Papers*, *Australasian Journal of Philosophy* 45 (1967), pp. 92–104.

'The unity of space–time: mathematics versus myth making', *Australasian Journal of Philosophy* 45 (1967), pp. 214–17.

1968 'Time', R. Klibansky (ed.), *Contemporary Philosophy, a Survey*, Florence, La Nouvelle Editrice, 1968, pp. 329–37.
'Quine's philosophy of science', *Synthese* 19 (1968–9), pp. 3–13.

1969 'Causal theories of time', *Monist* 53 (1969), pp. 385–95. (Greek translation in *Deucalion* 8 (1980), 383–94.) EMM

1970 Critical notice of D. C. Dennett, *Content and Consciousness*, *Mind* 79 (1970), pp. 616–23.
'Ryle in relation to modern science', Oscar P. Wood and George Pitcher (eds), *Ryle: A Collection of Critical Essays*, New York, Doubleday and Company, Inc., 1970, pp. 283–306. EMM

1971 'Reports of immediate experiences', *Synthese* 22 (1971), pp. 346–59.

1972 'Space–time and individuals', Richard Rudner and Israel Scheffler (eds), *Logic and Art: Essays in Honor of Nelson Goodman*, Indianapolis, Bobbs-Merrill, 1972, pp. 3–20. EMM
'Further thoughts on the identity theory', *Monist* 56 (1972), pp. 149–62. EMM
'Science, history and methodology', *British Journal for the Philosophy of Science* 23 (1972), pp. 266–74.

1973 'Science and religion', *The Australian Rationalist* 3 (November 1973), pp. 3–7.
Critical notice of J. L. Mackie, *Truth, Probability and Paradox*, *Australasian Journal of Philosophy* 51 (1973), pp. 258–64.

1974 'Materialism' and parts of 'Time' in 1974 edition of *Encyclopaedia Britannica*.

1975 'My semantic ascents and descents', Charles J. Bontempo and S. Jack Odell (eds), *The Owl of Minerva: Philosophers on Philosophy*, New York, McGraw-Hill, 1975, pp. 57–72. EMM
'On some criticisms of a physicalist theory of colors'. In Chung-ying Cheng (ed.) *Philosophical Aspects of the Mind-Body Problem*, Honolulu, University Press of Hawaii, 1975, pp. 54–63. EMM

1976 'The philosophical Andersonians', *Quadrant* (January 1976), pp. 6–10.
'The revival of materialism', *Listener* 95 (1976), pp. 535–6. EMM
'Under the form of eternity', The Seventh Walter and Eliza Hall Lecture, The Walter and Eliza Hall Institute of Medical Research *Annual Review*, 5, (1976–7), pp. 36–42. EMM

1977 'Benevolence as an over-riding attitude', *Australasian Journal of Philosophy* 55 (1977), pp. 127–35. EMM

'Cosmic coincidence', *Proceedings of the Russellian Society*, University of Sydney, 2 (1977), pp. 23–30 (mimeographed).
Critical study of James W. Cornman, *Perception, Common Sense and Science*, *Philosophia* 7 (1977), pp. 163–9.

1978   'Hedonistic and ideal utilitarianism', *Midwest Studies in Philosophy* 3 (1978), pp. 240–51.
'Distributive justice and utilitarianism', John Arthur and William H. Shaw (eds), *Justice and Economic Distribution*, Englewood Cliffs, N.J., Prentice-Hall, 1978, pp. 103–15. EMM
'Die Ethik der Wissenschaft', Dietrich Wahl (ed.), *Ethische Probleme der Wissenschaft*, Berlin, Akademie-Verlag, 1978, pp. 122–4.
'Is Occam's razor a physical thing?' *Philosophy* 53 (1978), pp. 382–5.
'Utilitarianism and justice', *Chinese Journal of Philosophy* 5 (1978), pp. 287–9.
'The content of physicalism', *Philosophical Quarterly* 28 (1978), pp. 339–41.
'Cortical localization and the mind-brain identity theory', *The Behavioral and Brain Sciences* 1, part 3, (1978), p. 365.

1979   Critical notice of Robert L. Causey, *Unity of Science*, *Synthese* 41 (1979), pp. 451–9.
Obituary of T. G. H. Strehlow, *Proceedings of the Australian Academy of the Humanities* 5, 1979, pp. 45–6.
'A physicalist account of psychology', *British Journal for the Philosophy of Science* 30 (1979), pp. 403–10.

1980   'Utilitarianism and generalized benevolence', *Pacific Philosophical Quarterly* 61 (1980), pp. 115–21. EMM
'Time and becoming', Peter van Inwagen (ed.), *Time and Cause*, Dordrecht, D. Reidel, 1980, pp. 3–15. EMM
'Computational processes, representations and propositional attitudes', *The Behavioral and Brain Sciences* 3 (1980), p. 97.

1981   'Ethics and science', James Martineau (Samuel Lovell Bequest) Lecture, delivered at the University of Tasmania, 17 April 1980. University of Tasmania Occasional Paper 30, 1981, 20 pp. Reprinted in *Philosophy* 56 (1981), pp. 449–65.
'Utilitarianism and criminal justice', *Bulletin of the Australian Society of Legal Philosophy*, special issue (1981), pp. 1–19.
'Physicalism and emergence', *Neuroscience* 6 (1981), pp. 109–13. EMM
'The reality of the future', *Philosophia* 10 (1981), pp. 141–50. EMM

1982   'Metaphysical realism', *Analysis* 42 (1982), pp. 1–3.

'Why moral language?' *Zeitschrift für philosophische Forschung* 36 (1982), pp. 153–68.

'Sellars on process', *Monist* 65 (1982), pp. 302–14. EMM

'Prior and the basis of ethics', *Synthese* 53 (1982), pp. 3–17.

'Difficulties for realism in the philosophy of science', in L. J. Cohen, J. Łos, H. Pfeiffer and K.-P. Podewski (eds), *Logic, Methodology and Philosophy of Science* VI, Amsterdam, North-Holland, 1982, pp. 363–75. EMM

1983   'Physikalismus und Willensfreiheit', Bernulf Kanitscheider (ed.), *Moderne Naturphilosophie*, Würzburg, Königshausen und Neumann, 1983, pp. 95–106.

1984   'Ockham's razor', James H. Fetzer (ed.), *Principles of Philosophical Reasoning*, Totowa, N.J., Rowman and Allanheld, 1984, pp. 118–28. EMM

1985   'Davidson's minimal materialism', Bruce Vermazen and Merrill B. Hintikka (eds), *Essays on Davidson: Actions and Events*, Oxford, Clarendon Press, 1985, pp. 173–82.

'Laws of nature and cosmic coincidences', *Philosophical Quarterly* 35 (1985), pp. 272–80. EMM

Obituary of S. I. Benn, Academy of the Social Sciences in Australia *Annual Report*, 1985–6, pp. 42–3.

1986   'How to turn the *Tractatus* Wittgenstein into (almost) Donald Davidson', E. LePore (ed.), *Truth and Interpretation*, Oxford, Basil Blackwell, 1986, pp. 92–100.

'Realism v. idealism', *Philosophy* 61 (1986), pp. 295–312. EMM

'Quine on space–time', Lewis E. Hahn and P. A. Schilpp (eds) *The Philosophy of W. V. Quine*, The Library of Living Philosophers, La Salle, Illinois, Open Court, 1986, pp. 495–515.

'Utilitarianism and its applications', Richard M. Fox and Joseph P. DeMarco (eds), *New Directions in Ethics*, London, Routledge and Kegan Paul, 1986, pp. 24–41.

Forthcoming articles

'Space, time and motion', in *An Encyclopaedia of Philosophy*, London, Croom Helm.

'Philosophical problems of cosmology', *Revue internationale de Philosophie*.

'Methodology and ontology', K. Gavroglu, G. Goundarulis and P. Nicolakopoulos (eds), *Criticism and the Growth of Knowledge: Twenty Years After*, Proceedings of conference in Thessaloniki, 1986, Dordrecht, D. Reidel.

'The drift to idealism', C. Wade Savage and Mary Lou Maxwell (eds), *Science, Mind and Psychology: Essays on Grover Maxwell's World View*, Lanham, Maryland, University Press of America.

Book reviews (excluding critical notices and review articles)

1950   of D. G. James, *The Life of Reason*, *Mind* 59, pp. 121–3.
of H. Weyl, *Philosophy of Mathematics and Natural Science*, *Mind* 59, pp. 410–11.
of T. J. Higgins, *Man as Man, The Science and Art of Ethics*, *Philosophy* 25, pp. 368–70.
of Nathan Isaacs, *The Foundations of Common Sense*, *Philosophy* 25, pp. 377–8.

1951   of C. H. Whiteley, *An Introduction to Metaphysics*, *Philosophical Quarterly* 1, pp. 176–7.
of P. W. Bridgman, *Reflections of a Physicist*, *Philosophical Quarterly* 1, p. 181.
of Bernard Bolzano, *Paradoxes of the Infinite*, *Australasian Journal of Philosophy* 29, pp. 55–8.
of Henry Margenau, *The Nature of Physical Reality*, *Philosophical Review* 60, pp. 411–13.
of D. Hilbert and W. Ackermann, *Principles of Mathematical Logic*, *Australasian Journal of Philosophy* 29, pp. 196–7.

1952   of G. Sommerhoff, *Analytical Biology*, *Australasian Journal of Philosophy* 30, pp. 145–50.

1953   of Carl G. Hempel, *Fundamentals of Concept Formation in Natural Science*, *Philosophical Review* 62, pp. 473–5.

1954   of J. H. Woodger, *Biology and Language*, *Australian Journal of Science* 17, p. 79.

1955   of J. R. Kantor, *The Logic of Modern Science*, *Philosophical Review* 64, pp. 129–30.
of Margaret Macdonald (ed.), *Philosophy and Analysis*, *Australasian Journal of Philosophy* 33, pp. 199–200.

1958   of Peter Geach, *Mental Acts*, *Mind* 67, pp. 415–16.
of John C. Begg, *Essays on Thoughts and Worlds*, *Australasian Journal of Philosophy* 36, pp. 237–8.

1959   of Louis O. Katsoff, *Physical Science and Physical Reality*, *Philosophical Review* 68, pp. 406–8.
of Kurt Baier, *The Moral Point of View*, *Meanjin* 76, pp. 120–1.

1960   of *Indian Journal of Philosophy* 1, no. 1, *Australasian Journal of Philosophy* 38, pp. 85–6.

1961   of Henry Margenau, *Open Vistas*, *Philosophical Quarterly* 12, pp. 378–9.

1962   of Ernest Nagel, *The Structure of Science*, *Journal of Philosophy* 59, pp. 216–23.
of Herbert Feigl, and Grover Maxwell (eds), *Current Issues in the Philosophy of Science*, *Australasian Journal of Philosophy* 40, pp. 110–12.
of Richard Schlegel, *Time and the Physical World*, *Australasian Journal of Philosophy* 40, pp. 254–5.

1963   of R. J. Butler (ed.), *Analytical Philosophy*, *Australasian Journal of Philosophy* 41, pp. 424–6.
of David Pole, *Conditions of Rational Inquiry*, *Philosophical Review* 72, pp. 104–6.
of G. J. Whitrow, *The Natural Philosophy of Time*, *Philosophical Review* 72, pp. 405–7.
of Jan Berg, *Bolzano's Logic*, *Journal of Philosophy* 60, pp. 562–4.

1964   of Adolf Grünbaum, *Philosophical Problems of Space and Time*, *Journal of Philosophy* 61, pp. 395–402.

1965   of J. Fodor and J. J. Katz (eds), *The Structure of Language*, *Australasian Journal of Philosophy* 43, pp. 116–18.

1968   of D. H. Monro, *Empiricism and Ethics*, *Philosophical Review* 78, pp. 259–61.

1969   of Richard Swinburne, *Space and Time*, *Philosophical Quarterly* 19, p. 375.
of Wilfrid Sellars, *Science and Metaphysics*, *Australasian Journal of Philosophy* 47, pp. 80–2.
of *Proceedings of the Third International Congress for Logic, Methodology and Philosophy of Science*, Amsterdam, 1967, *Australasian Journal of Philosophy* 47, pp. 402–4.

1970   of R. M. Martin, *Belief, Existence and Meaning*, *Australasian Journal of Philosophy* 48, pp. 400–1.

1973   of J. P. McKinney, *The Structure of Modern Thought*, *The Age*, Melbourne, 7th April 1973.
of D. M. Armstrong, *Belief, Truth and Knowledge*, *The Age*, (Melbourne), 18 August, 1973.
of Ferdinand Gonseth, *Time and Method*, *The Australian Rationalist* 3, no. 2, p. 20.

1974   of David Lewis, *Counterfactuals*, *Australasian Journal of Philosophy* 52, pp. 174–7.
of J. R. Lucas, *A Treatise on Time and Space*, *Philosophia* 4, pp. 355–9.

1975   of Eric P. Polten, *Critique of the Psycho-Physical Identity Theory*, *Philosophy of the Social Sciences* 5, pp. 83–6.

of Anthony Quinton, *Utilitarian Ethics*, *Metaphilosophy* 6, pp. 204–9.

1977   of Robert S. Cohen and Marx Wartofsky (eds), *Methodological and Historical Essays in the Natural and Social Sciences* XIV, *Archives internationales d'Histoire des Sciences* 27, pp. 157–8.

of Helier J. Robinson, *Renascent Rationalism*, *Philosophy of the Social Sciences* 7, pp. 311–22.

of Robert S. Cohen, C. A. Hooker, A. C. Michalos and J. W. Van Evra (eds), *Proceedings of the 1974 Biennial Meeting*, Philosophy of Science Association, *Boston Studies in the Philosophy of Science* XXXII, *Australasian Journal of Philosophy* 55, pp. 213–15.

of Colin Howson (ed.), *Method and Appraisal in the Physical Sciences: The Critical Background to Modern Science, 1800–1905*, *Philosophy of the Social Sciences* 7, pp. 425–6.

1980   of G. F. Macdonald (ed.), *Perception and Identity, Essays Presented to A. J. Ayer with his Replies to Them, Times Literary Supplement*, 11th July 1980, p. 779.

of Paul M. Churchland, *Scientific Realism and the Plasticity of Mind*, *Australasian Journal of Philosophy* 58, pp. 316–18.

of Thomas S. Kuhn, *The Essential Tension: Selected Studies in Scientific Tradition and Change*, *Metaphilosophy* 11, pp. 281–5.

of Alvin I. Goldman and Jaegwon Kim (eds), *Values and Morals: Essays in Honor of William Frankena, Charles Stevenson and Richard Brandt*, *Philosophy* 55, pp. 557–9.

1981   of D. M. Armstrong, *The Nature of Mind and Other Essays*, *Quadrant* 25, no. 4 (April 1981), pp. 48–50.

1983   of Amartya Sen and Bernard Williams (eds), *Utilitarianism and Beyond*, *Philosophy* 58, pp. 413–14.

1985   of Paul M. Churchland, *Matter and Consciousness*, *Mind* 94, pp. 306–7.

1986   of Anthony Manser and Guy Stock (eds), *The Philosophy of F. H. Bradley*, *Idealistic Studies* 16, 283–4.

Index

Index by Keith Seddon